Dayclean

A BAHAMIAN NOVEL

Linda Maria Davis

DAYCLEAN
Copyright © 2023 by Linda Maria Davis
Published 2023

This work has an historical backdrop that is primarily Bahamian. Except for the historical inclusion of some characters, businesses, events, and places that are mentioned factually out of necessity, for the most part, the plot is entirely fictitious. Any similarities to actual personalities or names are coincidental and were created from the author's imagination.

All rights reserved solely by the author. No part of this book may be reproduced or transmitted in any form including photocopying, recording or by any form of information storage and retrieval without written permission of the author except for the use of brief quotations related to critical reviews and certain noncommercial uses permitted by copyright law.

Front cover illustration: Erle Bethel

Back cover design: One Rib

Photograph on back cover: Kimberley M. C. B. Stuart

ISBN 979-8-873660-43-8

Dayclean

A BAHAMIAN NOVEL

Linda Maria Davis

TABLE OF CONTENTS

Dedication 7

Acknowledgement 9

Chapter One 11

Chapter Two 24

Chapter Three 52

Chapter Four..64

Chapter Five...81

Chapter Six 95

Chapter Seven 117

Chapter Eight 146

Chapter Nine 157

Chapter Ten 165

Chapter Eleven 177

Chapter Twelve 182

Chapter Thirteen...201

Chapter Fourteen..213

DEDICATION

This book is written in loving memory of my father Lincoln Davis and dedicated to my mother Carolyn Davis without whom I would not have been able to write this book. I am also eternally grateful for all the brave pioneers of history and those who fought for freedom and justice upon whose shoulders we stand.

ACKNOWLEDGEMENT

I wish to pay homage to the wonderful people of The Bahamas whose ancestry left a legacy that inspired me to write this book.

To my daughter, Kimberley Stuart, I wish to express special thanks to you for your unwavering encouragement, support, for your invaluable assistance in research, and for being my faithful travel partner as I gathered material for this book.

Special thanks to my editor, Sandra Edgecombe for your guidance, commitment and your input which was invaluable in the completion of this work.

Chapter One

Dayclean.....

The familiar streaks of harsh yellow light invaded the dark, tightly closed room the boys called "the barn". There could have been eight or nine of them in that room on any given night. Perhaps even their parents had never really stopped to count them all for there was no need. The chain of command had long since been established and that was all that mattered. Eulease (better known as Sista), the oldest of the Rolle children, mothered and nurtured all the others and everyone else knew his or her place. Every child knew that if an older sibling gave a command and was not obeyed there would be hell to pay because anyone older than oneself could punish the younger individual without remorse or fear of requital. This was the way law and order were kept. Thus, it was that the Rolle family governed itself and was a tightly intertwined, well-oiled unit that was usually impervious and resistant to the pressures of external influences.

Gradually the little room came alive after a few groans, whines, and yawns. Suddenly, there was a shout of outrage.

"Who pee up the bed?" The annoyed voice of Kiah (Hezekiah Jr.) the second oldest brother warned the others of what was to come next. This was an all-boys room. The younger boys slept on a bed of miscellaneous cloths and old clothes strewn on the floor while the two older ones slept on sturdy bunk beds. One child wetting the "bed" meant that his neighbors would invariably be rank and tainted with the distinct smell of old urine. The barn was a small structure built to house the older boys while their sisters and youngest siblings resided within the protected confines of the four-room dwelling with their parents.

"I have a good mind to cut your behind! En' das Josh again. Boy come here!" Kiah was overflowing with righteous indignation. There was a sudden shuffling, then sounds of a struggle and legs and arms escaping to safety. It was no joke. When Hezekiah Rolle Jr. got angry everyone knew it was better to run. But poor Josh, still clouded by a sleepy stupor, had been basking in the cool moisture of the little pool that he slept in and was apparently oblivious to Kiah's initial threats. Then Kiah made contact. Josh yelped and hollered but he could not escape his heavy-handed older brother.

The saga of this well-known wake-up call being over, the smaller boys took up their bedding from the floor. Livingston and Zach (which was short for Isaac) were a little older, so they assisted the still sniffling Josh (Joshua) to clean up his mess, and they managed to get their other siblings organized in bringing some order to the disheveled room as well.

By this time, Tommy (Thomas) was pushing the wooden window open while Leviticus (Levi), who was slightly taller (although younger than the former by about one year), picked the stick up from the floor and leaned it outward supported by the window's sill to enable the window to remain open. At last, someone pushed the door open; quite soon the acrid smell was gone, and the fresh morning air soothed their burning nostrils.

All the male children could be accounted for except for Malachi, the oldest of the siblings, who was probably about twenty-three years old. In contrast, it was only on rare occasions in recent years that Malachi had slept in "the barn" with his brothers. Malachi was a little "off-center" mentally. Some people unapologetically denigrated him by even stating that Malachi was crazy, so generally everyone, including his parents, simply left him alone. Sometimes Malachi wandered off for several days and nights and when he returned to the sleepy settlement of Steventon, Exuma no questions were ever asked of him. For the older ones, there was a sense of relief to see their loved one back home, but for the younger ones there was a deep-rooted fear which accompanied his presence; Malachi often reacted violently and on his worst days, he lashed out at anyone he could get a hold of, especially the younger children. Fortunately, on this morning, like most others, Malachi was nowhere around. It was such a common occurrence that no one gave it a second thought.

The boys slept in a relatively small room that was attached to the barn. The actual barn was used as a storeroom for corn, peas, flour, and other supplies as well as dried conch and fish. Papa had built the adjoining room to provide additional

Chapter One

space to accommodate his growing family. He wanted to ensure that Hezekiah and the older boys could have privacy as well as some place to store their books and personal items as well. It was going to be a tight fit, but Papa had promised that he would build bunk beds for the younger boys at some point during this summer.

The main house stood on a hill overlooking several acres of land owned by the former slave owner Lord Rolle. It now belonged to this second and third generation of Rolles who had been liberated from Lord Rolle's plantation just a century before. This modest four room structure consisted of two small bedrooms, a living room, and a pantry (which usually remained undisturbed). The pantry housed an oil stove, a tall wooden safe with heavy pots and earthenware, as well as a water jug, and a clay pot for hand washing and was a room that was reserved for special guests or extremely inclement weather. Every child knew that this little nook was always to remain immaculate or there would be serious consequences.

In the kitchen, Sista's faded house dress, which boldly displayed the 'OK Flour' brand name on several areas of her frock swished noisily from side to side. She swiftly and efficiently served her brothers their breakfast assisted by her younger sister, Wilhelmina, (or Willie as she was affectionately called). Willie wore one of Sista's 'handmedowns' also made of the same light-brown, coarse flour bag material.

Suddenly Mama's voice demanded everyone's attention. She hailed from the back door of the main house, "Eulease, you and Willie feed dose boys yet? You know if dey don't hurry up, they guh be late fer school, you hear?!"

"Yes ma'am, they soon finish," replied Sista, while deliberately accelerating her pace and trying to catch her breath at the same time. Eulease or Sista as she was respectfully called by her sisters and brothers was the oldest daughter and was second in command to Mama and Papa. She had completed her schooling at the Rokers Point School in the neighboring settlement at least seven years before. Now, basically, her lot in life seemed to be to look after the other members of her family and to assist with meal preparation. Sista never complained and performed her role with an amazing sense of responsibility and acceptance. As she matured, she became even more indispensable to her mother as she assisted in coordinating the smooth operation of taking care of the household. The younger children lived in an exclusive world of eating, sleeping, or being cleaned up, and were constantly being supervised by Mama or their big sister.

As expected, Ishmael and Alpheus had scurried to the kitchen ahead of everyone else to get their breakfast and of course this dynamic duo somehow managed to get the most of everything by hook or by crook. Ishmael and Alpheus were about eleven and ten years old respectively. These two smirked at their tardy siblings while they hurriedly gulped down what probably was their second or third helping of cornbread or guava jam and homemade bread accompanied by their favorite pear leaf tea. The other Rolle siblings, encouraged by the duo, would then proceed in concert to nearby banana, mango, or sapodilla trees where they consumed these ripe fruits with wanton abandon.

By seven o'clock, every child had been fed, was cleaned up, dressed and complete with a chunk of warm banana bread in hand for lunch. Each was ready to begin the two-mile trek to school. The earth felt cool beneath their toes as they gathered to make their journey. The scenery on the hilltop would appear picturesque to a newcomer, but to the Rolle children the scene was of little consequence. Partially canopied by a colossal sapodilla tree, their four-room frosted-white lime coated house overlooked a narrow dirt road, and running parallel to this thoroughfare was a marshy area (the bay) full of many fruit trees including bananas and lanky patches of juicy sugar cane. Beyond this was the sea itself. It was beautifully aquamarine, warm, and so clear that one could peer into the shimmering water and see the mossy, pink-lipped conchs nestled in their shells on the seabed amongst a myriad of multi-hued fish of all sizes darting through the colorful splash of flora and fauna in all their splendor. In low tide, even the smallest child could pick up the conchs of his or her choice.

The cool morning air softly caressed their faces tempering what undoubtedly would be a scorching day. The younger children often ventured over the 'mountain' as they called it just before their departure to school; it was another elevated part of their hilltop property that flanked the rear of their home. Ishmael, Leviticus and Isaac knew that when Mama called them by their full Christian names, she was prepared to give them a whipping if they did not comply with her instructions. Engaging in typical boyish antics, they ignored Mama and Papa's warnings that many lives had been lost after falling into those limestone holes. Some of the children's favorite 'Potcake' pooches had unceremoniously disappeared after having some unexpected misadventure in one of the deep potholes or cavernous blue holes. Once again, just as she had done on previous mornings, Mama warned the children about the dangers of Steventon's deadly abysses. Her children (especially the older ones) did not know their own specific ages or birthdays because at the birth of each child, only the birth date was written on a piece of paper and put in the same special

Chapter One

bottle for future reference. No child, regardless of his or her age, dared to ask Mama or Papa what his or her age specifically was, as this was regarded as grossly disrespectful. Nevertheless, the older ones knew that their roles and responsibilities were to "look out for" their younger siblings.

It was already seven O'clock. After picking the odd Haden or Peach Mango, juicy sapodillas, or mouth-watering sugar apples to augment his or her lunch, each boy and girl was finally filled with the conviction that it was time to depart for school. Their journey to school required a bit of coordination and the subtle supervision of the older siblings. Hezekiah Jr., who was perhaps almost eighteen years old, had gone on ahead of his younger siblings to meet his friend and colleague Tobias Smith so that they could walk together to Roker's Point school where they taught as monitors. So it was that the four older school-age Rolle children held hands in a moderate circle and enclosed the younger children (Josh, Livingston, and Zach) in a formation popularly known as a 'trainer'. After the three youngsters had been ushered into the circle, they all ran to school; this act was designed to ensure that the siblings all kept pace, and it provided protection if other children tried to accost the group. Ishmael and Alphaeus automatically lead the group, while Tommy and Levi formed the rear guard and Willie, who was in her last year of school, joined in somewhere in between. Their cousins, Una, Carlton, and Bertram Gray (who were approximately eleven, twelve, and fourteen years old respectively) would join them about a mile down the road, which provided additional reinforcement. This was done as a precaution because there had been occasions when groups of children took it upon themselves to attack the Steventon children as they made their way to Roker's Point as if they had no right to be passing through this territory. Although the incidents were few and far between, the Rolles knew that they could leave nothing to chance.

Running barefooted was never an issue for the children of the Out Islands, however the Rolle children had their tennis if they chose to wear them. The boys wore stiffly starched dungarees (made and ironed by Sista) and chambris shirts, while the girls wore cute colorful dresses with sashes. Time and experience had taught them to be almost oblivious of the long, arduous journey that would be strenuous for most children; each day, they traveled several miles, traversing the rugged terrain until they arrived at the small schoolhouse in Roker's Point.

Hezekiah had reached the stage where he had completed all classes and requirements of grade school including the Board of Education's School Leaving Certificate which he had obtained at fourteen and had successfully obtained his Cambridge Junior Certificate examinations two years after. He and his friend Tobias had prepared for the exams shortly after the arrival of their mentor. They had thrived under the expert tutelage of Mr. Henry Clarke who had been born and raised in Mount Thompson and was a strict disciplinarian of the highest order. However, while he passionately endeavored to help any students who showed academic promise, Clarkie (as everyone called him, behind his back of course) showed little empathy or patience for those who were intellectually challenged or unfocused. The veteran teacher of thirty plus years, whose towering physique humbled even the most brazen of his students, never hesitated to chastise or rebuke those who fell out of academic pace. Hezekiah had always been such a keen and able student, so it was no surprise that he along with his classmate, Tobias Smith, (who was six months his senior and of similar academic capabilities) were invited to become monitors at the school. It was a privilege and an opportunity of a lifetime because it was quite likely that they could both be invited to train as teachers and join the Board of Education. The boys were understandably overjoyed with their good fortune. Young boys of the 1940s had nothing much to look forward to on the Out Islands or on New Providence, but to be farmers, or to engage in one or more of the building trades. The limited opportunities had lured many men and even some women toward Florida and beyond where they farmed on the 'Project' or 'contract'. Some families who overtly supported the governing United Bahamian Party (UBP) were assured that the adult males in their household would receive temporary jobs working on roads or cleaning certain areas as necessary. However, for the very few and fortunate, there were limited opportunities such as working in the Commissioner's office, the jailhouse or working for the government as a teacher, nurse, on the police force or at the Bahamas Electric Company in Nassau.

As he neared his rendezvous with Tobias, Hezekiah reflected on an exchange he had several months before with his brothers Tommy and Levi. Since they were close in age, they spent a great deal of their spare time together, and on this occasion, they were out fishing for shad and goggle eyes in the nearby creek. Hezekiah always tried to encourage both not to get stuck on the island doing 'piecemeal work for pittance'. Whenever the opportunity arose, he had implored his brothers to acquire some sort of trade skills since neither seemed particularly inclined to academic pursuits while they were in school. Like all children who attended Roker's Point School or any of the other Exumian schools for that matter, they could read and write satisfactorily and possessed basic mathematical and writing skills up to grade six which marked the end of a student's formal education at fourteen.

Chapter One

Tommy explained his position, "Kiah, you know I like workin' with my hands. I don't like books, tests and studying that much. You know I helped Papa build that dogwood dinghy boat and fix up the house after de las' hurricane. I could buil' an' paint anything. I might even go to Nassau and work with someone 'til I could start my own business as a carpenter. How dat sound?"

"Yeah, bro', that's all well an' good, but I still think it's good to have some certificates under yuh belt so people who want to hire you will know what you could do, what you good for," pontificated Kiah.

Levi was determined to defend himself although he was less confident of his future plans. "I was workin' with ole man Smitty down in Farmers Hill when school close las' summer when he was buildin'. You remember his first wife been dead fer years and he decide to get a new wife – You know Gracie from Rolle Town. So he decide to build a new house on the property. He was pleased with my work. He even tell me if I keep on workin' hard I could be a good mason helper!"

"Boy, don't be stupid! You know what a mason helper makes a week? Must be a couple pennies a week. You can't live off that," retorted Kiah. "I told you fellas if you get yer School Leaving Certificate and especially the Cambridge Junior Certificate you could get a job on The Police Force or even to the Electric Company as soon as you turn seventeen or eighteen. I hear that's where Mervin Cooper workin' – to the Electric Company. Levi, you gettin' tall and muscular. You should try takin' extra classes up in Mount Thompson an' try get your School Leaving Certificate. You still have two more years. You could do it if you put your mind to it. They need big fellas like you on de force. I mean dey bringin' in all dose West Indian policemen because we don't have enough locals. Who knows? They might take you an' you could work your way up. Don't mind Tommy. He too short for The Force but he guh make money anyhow. Let me tell you – you better try get some kinda qualification under your belt. Only laziness and following fashion will cause you not to pass some uh dose exams, anyhow. You two better take your schoolwork more seriously unless you intend to knock around this island fishin' and farmin' fer the res' of yer life."

Truthfully, the boys were immature, carefree, and lacked the ambition of their older brother. Thus far, their basic needs were being met, so they had difficulty envisioning what life would be like beyond the world of subsistence farming and fishing that they had been born into.

Rokers Point School consisted of a large one room wooden building, a small out house and one or two almond and pear trees under which the younger children usually sat to receive their lessons. There were two teachers and two monitors to teach children aged six to sixteen (fifteen- and sixteen-year-olds were usually students who had deficiencies and were not automatically promoted or exceptionally bright students who stayed on with the intention of becoming monitors).

Young Hezekiah Rolle enjoyed teaching in the all-age school, but he was not entirely sure if he would make this his career. He was grateful for the ample monthly stipend of twelve pounds and six shillings which few people on the islands could boast of earning at that time; besides, Mama had grown to depend upon this extra income to support the family. The students respected both Toby and him and rarely presented discipline problems as the discipline would be swiftly and unquestionably meted out; a disobedient boy would be laid out on a desk, firmly held by two older boys while the principal gave him a sound caning. Hezekiah concluded that, most of all, this work was certainly better than breaking his back working the fields and "…What else was there to do anyway?" he sometimes thought to himself. He resolved to continue to master his craft and acknowledged the power and respect afforded to him. He grew to expect that if all things remained the same, he would be promoted to assistant teacher the following year since he would have successfully served for four years as a monitor. These thoughts kept his spirits soaring upwards and sustained him despite the uneasiness that sometimes struggled to invade his comfort zone. Nevertheless, he knew that there must be more to life than what Exuma had offered him thus far. He wondered what Nassau was like. He remembered Mr. Clarke had been boasting about the place, "Boy, Nassau is like a whole different world. Didn't your pappy ever tell you about it? Plenty pretty girls and night clubs and people rushing up and down going about their business! Of course, I'm too old for all that carousing and stuff, but like you so – if you take a trip to Nassau town and see all the action and how it built up near downtown, you'll never think 'bout comin' home. Who knows, you might even find a nice lil wife up there."

Hezekiah was never one to rush into things, so he responded reservedly, "I don't know, Mr. Clarke. I'll think about it, though."

Once again, Hezekiah was pondering. It was breaktime, and since he did not see his buddy Toby outside the schoolhouse, he positioned himself on a medium sized stone with his hand under his chin nibbling on some of his lunch.

Chapter One

Thoughts of the 'contract' or "The project" as some called it left an inflammation deep within him. He felt that for him "The Contract" would not have been an option, but he acknowledged that for Papa there was no other choice. Since Hezekiah was about ten years old, his father had been gone intermittently for many years to work on farms in the United States so that he could provide for his family. Yes, the money, packages of special treats and unique clothing had been good, and Papa was a wonderful provider.... but Papa had seemed to pop into their home for very short periods during those years (usually on a couple of weeks furlough) bringing lots of goodies and clothing from Nassau and the States, then he was gone. It bothered Hezekiah more that most of the younger children hardly knew Papa; although he was older, he felt the loss of those critical years with his father as well. He promised himself that no matter what the situation was, if he had a family, he would never leave them for long periods of time like that. What worsened the situation was that poor Mama was often pregnant and had very young children to care for alone most of the time. He was reminded that one of the good aspects of the 'contract' was that even when Papa could only return home once or twice in a year, the money still came to his family automatically according to the terms of the contract and so did the supplies. Hezekiah loved his father but resented his absences in those years more than the other Rolle siblings. He had many questions, but Papa was not a talker and hardly enjoyed indulging in what he called 'idle conversation'.

Hezekiah had grown tired of brooding. He shifted to warmer thoughts acknowledging that he had been one of the lucky ones to sit the prestigious Cambridge Junior examinations and pass them all at the first sitting, even if it was, like his friend Tobias had admitted, only "by the skin of his teeth". There had been an elderly gentleman named Uzziah Cornish who had hailed from Abaco and had been teaching at the school for five years immediately preceding his retirement. The bald headed, 'bushy-moustached' Mr. Cornish had a focused, military approach to teaching that was both awe-inspiring and unnerving. Nevertheless, as the burly educator marched about his classroom in the evenings, he was a lifeline to the young men. He articulated with an extremely British accent and fondly boasted of the superior training he had received in the United Kingdom, wishing the same for his students. His students often joked that Old Cornish referred to the British Royal family with such familiarity that one might assume he was personally acquainted with them. Nevertheless, Hezekiah, Toby and five other protégés looked upon this experience as divine intervention; despite their ridiculous imitations of their revered teacher when he was out of range, they thrived under his prolific tutelage.

Tobias greeted his friend several minutes after the lunch bell rang, this time prancing with excitement. In the background, on the small, rocky playground, they could hear a group of children dancing, chanting, and singing as they played several ring play games. They moved from one chant to the other:

"Peas porridge hot, peas porridge cold
Peas porridge in the pot nine days old..."

"London Bridge is falling down, falling down, falling down
London Bridge is falling down, falling down, falling down
London Bridge is falling down, falling down, falling down
My fair lady..."

The children continued to entertain themselves in the scorching midday sun.

"Alla balla chicken ga la la
Alla balla boosh..." Then, encouraged by their ringleader, a girl of about ten gyrated in front of her partner while the others clapped and chanted, then the dancers increased the tempo.
"...Come show me your motion, tralalalala
Show me your motion, tralalalala
Show me your motion, tralalalala
She looks like a sugar in a plum, PLUM, PLUM!"

Tobias, the son of Sister Cleomie and Reverend Simeon Smith (who was pastor of The First Holiness Union Baptist Church in Roach's Town) had a plan for both Hezekiah and him to get involved in some lighthearted entertainment for the weekend.

"Man, Kiah, let's go down by The Chicken Nest tonight. Aint no harm in dat," suggested Tobias with a mischievous twist to his facial expression.

Kiah, being the more conservative of the two young men, stated soberly, "Toby, you know aint nothin' but trouble in a place like that. Just a bunch a hooligans and big foot, hard-heeled gals hang out in those places. Most of them only tryin' ter set a trap for you. And Toby, you know just how those fellers from Rolleville go."

"Kiah, you know you only sayin' what you hear people say 'bout that place. I know you never been there. I bet Nathan told you that. Right?"

Chapter One

Hezekiah was embarrassed that he was caught in a lie. "Yeah. That's true. Nathan did tell me that," admitted Hezekiah. He continued, "He's always going up there bothering with those women. I don't believe everything he has to say though."

Toby, of course, was determined to placate Kiah's inhibitions with his subtly persuasive techniques. Besides, he had no intention of waiting until he became a middle-aged man before he found a girlfriend even if Kiah planned on doing so. This suggestion was not wasted on his friend who was becoming agitated, "Toby, the only thing you ever have your mind on is woman. That's gonna be your downfall if you don't take your time, man. You have plenty time to do all that!"

"Kiah, aint nothin' gonna happen. Let's go have some fun, man. We just have to be careful. That's all."

It was almost the end of lunchtime and the children had discontinued their provocative dancing. Some had moved to playing hopscotch or another popular handclapping game:

> *"Eenie meanie miney moe*
> *Catch a tiger by his toe*
> *If he holler let him go*
> *Eenie meenie miney moe ..."*

Kiah was not going to give in so easily. "They don't mind you spendin' yer money down there, but when you start foolin' with their girls, they'll beat yer bad!"

"Yeah man, I know what you mean. I remember me and Nathan, had to haul a wil' ass outta Rolleville one Saturday mornin' just two months ago. I was runnin' and beggin' God for one more chance. Papa probably coulda hear me prayin'," mused Toby. "If Edmond McKenzie and his henchmen had caught us, you all woulda been singing 'In the sweet by and by' ter our funeral, man!" Toby's lanky frame collapsed in laughter, while Kiah found himself chuckling then shuddering at the possibility of being chased by those cutlass wielding, foul-mouthed bandits.

"That's what I'm telling you, Toby. It's too dangerous. It aint worth it. Those fellers don't play." Nevertheless, sheer stubbornness would ultimately prevail over common sense.

"Man, I tell you, some of those girls aint too bad, at all. In fact, I have my eyes on one, right now." added Toby confidently.

"Who?" Kiah was beginning to put aside his fears.

"You know Maebell Jolly, right? The lil cute, brown skin one with the fine voice. You know the one with sorta soft long hair. Man, she is somethin' else!"

Kiah could not believe what he was hearing. "Now I know you gotta be crazy Toby. That's a crazy family you know! She gat about eight brothers, all with fire in their eyes. You ever saw her Pa? His eyes could scare a wild boar, too. I sure Mr. Jolly wouldn't have a problem puttin' a bullet in your behind."

"Yeah man, I good and sure that girl is the one for me." Toby nodded as if he was envisioning his own destiny.

Then it was decided and agreed that the two would meet that very evening at the end of the track road flanked by the native tangle of thick, prickly, vegetation just a mile away from Hezekiah's home. The sound of the school bell brought an end to their horsing around.

Hezekiah reflected for a moment on his responsibility to his family, especially the younger ones. He decided to dismiss his guilt about Malachi just this one time, after all he owed it to himself to lighten up a bit. "Despite his issues, Malachi knows how to take care of himself," he reassured himself. Since he had begun teaching Mathematics and Geography, he felt that many of his peers regarded him as being rather stoical. Nevertheless, a part of him yearned just to be young and carefree.

Toby and Kiah parted company temporarily to resume their teaching duties. The latter knew that he would have to devise a little plan to cover himself because he expected to be gone during the night, hopefully until two or three the next morning.

For Hezekiah, the hours seemed to have gone by quickly, perhaps because of all the excitement that the end of the work week usually brought for most young people. He was aware of the risk, but he was inspired by the thrill of this youthful adventure.

Teachers and monitors had put away the frugal resources of the schoolhouse.

Chapter One

The youngest children used an 8" X 11" slate (which often became chipped and cracked with use) with wooden borders and a slate pen to write with. The older students were more fortunate as they wrote on paper and sat at desks; each had a small ink pot housed in a cavity in the desk and students dipped their makeshift pens into the ink before writing on paper. Once slates, pens, and inkpots were secured, students left for home, some armed with empty water jars that would once again be filled with water for school on Monday morning. The gaping holes in the desks now yawned mockingly where ink pots had been housed, while the wind whistled softly through the cracks in the walls of the eerily quiet schoolhouse.

Chapter Two

When Hezekiah and the other siblings arrived home, they met Papa, Uncle Fical (who was their closest neighbor) along with Jake Smith and a lady who called herself a prophetess sitting on the "dryer" (porch) deep in discussion.

Prophetess Evangeline Horton, who linked her lineage with Georgia in the United States, spoke with a strange lilt and drag in her speech. It was rumored by some that she first became acquainted with The Bahamas after having befriended a Bahamian man while he was on "the project" and subsequently marrying him. However, after he suddenly disappeared, she later discovered that he was already a married man in The Bahamas. Despite this revelation, the caramel-complexioned southern belle continued to visit the islands frequently; she had since made the islands her second home, proselytizing Christian principles wherever she went. Some even conjectured that she was still secretly trying to find her bigamist husband. As was often the case with rumors, no one ever came forward to substantiate the story, and she was never directly confronted about her past.

"Brother Zeke, y'all need to do right by your boy, your first born. Haallelujah! Haallelujah! Your boy's been gowne fo' almost one week now and y'all aint even checked to see where he at? In the name of Jesus, y'all should be shame!" Zilpha and Zeke hung their heads low now, and Zilpha began to weep softly while leaning on her husband's shoulder. A few passersby, including school children and others returning from the fields, became curious and slowed their pace to observe.

Hezekiah felt a twinge in the pit of his stomach. The prophetess was talking about his oldest brother, Malachi, who remained an enigma to him. Her

Chapter Two

declaration was an exaggeration, but it was true that Malachi had not been seen for about two days. Hezekiah wanted to say something in defense of his family, but he knew that it was not his place to do so. Even at his age, he would have been severely rebuked if he had tried to intervene.

As the woman proceeded to deliver her warning, Hezekiah's mind was roaming in a different direction so that for several minutes he had become oblivious of the events that were unfolding. It was not that Hezekiah was unconcerned but as he approached adulthood, he found himself thinking less about Malachi and focusing more on his own personal plans and challenges. He admitted to himself that he really did miss those wild, devilish eyes and the twisted smile that his oldest sibling wore constantly. The two brothers had so little in common that he really could not remember their last rational conversation, although Malachi did have moments of profound lucidity.

It angered Hezekiah that people willingly fabricated stories about his brother because of his appearance and aversion to strangers. Malachi had a short, muscular two hundred- and fifty-pounds frame and protruding front teeth that affected his speech. There had never been any reports of Malachi harming anyone although he had a knack for wandering into distant settlements and startling the residents who did not know him. As the years had passed, people claimed that they had seen his dark shadow walking at night with blood dripping from his face, hands, and clothing. It was true that, occasionally, Malachi did go into some kind of trance, at which time he would start foaming at the mouth, chewing his own tongue, and thrashing about uncontrollably. During those times his eyes rolled back in his head as he emitted blood-curdling howls and groans. His family members and neighbors knew that Malachi suffered from an incurable illness called "the fits" (epileptic seizures) during which times he bit his tongue which resulted in a bloody mouth.

The prophetess, who was also a self-proclaimed singing minister, had long suggested that the Rolle family allow her to lay her hands on the unfortunate Malachi. Prophetess Horton repeated her declaration that Malachi was possessed by demons and only she, with The Lord's divine intervention, could free him from his tormentors.

It was Sister Ella Lloyd's turn to give credence to the prophetess' revelation. Sister Lloyd was a prominent member in the Mission Baptist Church in the settlement of Hart's. She was a dark, fat lady with short, sweaty hands who always carried quinine water and homemade potions. Bringing her own share of doom and gloom, she proclaimed confidently, "Yes indeed. I too think somebody fix him when he was a lil boy." As she spoke, she pointed her right hand straight up to the sky as a sign of confirmation.

"I'm telling you, Brother and Sister Rolle, y'all better find that boy before it's too late. Heed mah warning or you'll be sorry. Lord have mercy!" Prophetess Horton was unrelenting as she threw up both hands indignantly.

As Hezekiah reflected on his brother, the prophetess continued her tirade in a voice that was gradually elevating. "I'm telling you, y'all gonna be sorry if something bad ever happen to that boy, yes Jesus!" Then, without warning, her body contorted as some invisible force seemed to take her in a frenzied grip, then jerked and dashed her to the ground. Her eyes lost their focus, then rolled upward and around in her head. Simultaneously, her arms flailed wildly while her legs shook and quivered until 'the spell' had passed over. Then, silently, The Prophetess lay limply sprawled on the ground.

Someone whispered in amazement, "She havin' the spirit." Sister Ella Lloyd rushed forward to correct the woman's posture, so that she was not indecently exposed. Uncle Fical called for someone to get the Prophetess a mug of water from the kitchen, while Jake Smith moved to retrieve her shoe and the elegant hat that had previously adorned the prophetess' pinned up salt and pepper tresses but were now strewn on the ground.

Quite a crowd had gathered to view the spectacle, mostly from a safe distance. They peered and cowered under the big almond tree on the other side of the narrow street. There was enough fear, reverence, and adoration to go around. Mothers now hastened to leave the scene with their children, while several gentlemen responded with either disgust or fascination as they observed the incident.

Prophetess Evangeline regained her composure momentarily. Jake gently helped her to her feet. Then, unceremoniously, she brushed the dust from her elegant gown and repositioned her matching hat on her head like it was a treasured trophy. Apparently unperturbed by what had just transpired, she bade the Rolle family and the spectators "Good afternoon", spun around to face the east, and proceeded to mince down the slope to the road with her bible tightly clutched at her side.

Hezekiah Rolle Sr. did not utter a word, but Mrs. Rolle called out to the woman as a matter of courtesy. "Alright, Prophetess Horton, when Malachi come back

Chapter Two

this time, we'll let you do whatever you need ter do ter help him. God bless you, Sister."

On the woman's departure, Mama seemed to exhale, emitting an almost imperceptible sigh of relief. She herself had become troubled when she overheard some folks muttering among themselves that Malachi was possessed by some sea spirit because he had been born at sea. It had caused her to reflect on the frightening circumstances of Malachi's birth. She and her husband Hezekiah Sr. had gotten married in Florida and had been frequent travelers to the United States before their family had grown and Zilpha had several young children to care for at one time. The Rolles had been trying to get back to Exuma with their supplies from Florida before the birth of their first child. It seemed that a storm was brewing, and Zilpha was about to give birth while the motor vessel was tossed about on the tempestuous seas. Hezekiah Sr. dared not panic but sent up fervent prayers to God that Zilpha would be safely delivered, and his child would survive. Her labor was long and arduous. The baby boy had been a breach birth, and without the experience of a fellow traveler, a woman who claimed to be a midwife, mother and baby would have perished. Tears flowed down Mama Rolle's cheek unchecked as she relived that nightmare; she rocked from side to side as she began to sing softly to herself, "It is well with my soul. It is well. It is well with my soul …"

Thus, after some deliberation, it was decided that if he did not return by nightfall, a search party would be set up to look for the pitiable Malachi during the night since sundown was fast approaching.

The afternoon seemed no different from any other, as each member of the Rolle clan went about engaging in his or her routine chores. Ishmael and Alpheus, always working together as a team, were papa's chief assistants as he occupied himself by making certain renovations and repairs to the main house; they had already practically rebuilt the family's outhouse after it had been demolished by the last hurricane. Ishmael was close to his papa and was a natural protégé who demonstrated remarkable manual dexterity and natural artistic skills that were amazing for a boy of eleven.

Meanwhile Tommy immediately armed himself with one of Papa's cutlasses and headed to their special field area with Zach and Livingston trailing behind carrying a few other essentials for the job at hand. They would assist him in harvesting any vegetables such as cassavas, sweet potatoes, pumpkin, or eddoes that were full. Livingston thought to himself that if they were lucky, they might even find some juicy ears of corn, which was always welcome at dinner time, especially with corned mutton. As he meandered along the track road leading away from the house going eastward, Tommy made a mental note of the top trees which were growing in luscious clusters in the sand where the cocoa plum trees were also blooming.

"Hey Zach and Livingston, on our way back, let's stop by the cocoa plum patch to get some pond top. I know they good and juicy to eat right now," suggested Tommy.

"Maybe we should go there now before it get too dark to see where we going." suggested Zach as he sprinted nimbly down the slope in the opposite direction toward his favorite snack. Zach did not think twice about abandoning their mission temporarily. Of course, his brothers followed. They immediately began to pull the 'heart' out of the top of the trees and munched the crunchy pond top as they called it. It was not long after that they grew tired of this tasty treat and turned to the cocoa plum trees from which they gathered the sweet, fluffy plums to snack on while they walked to the nearby field reserved for them by their parents.

Levi, being the loner, headed off to the deepest part of Anne's Creek, just across from the Rolle's home. He was on a mission to catch a large meal of whatever he could – snappers, grunts, goggle eyes or shad. His sister Eulease always annoyed him by insisting that he take two of his younger brothers (usually Livingston, Zach or even Josh) with him so that they could learn the skills of fishing. However, he found them to be more of a nuisance and whenever he could, he made an excuse to avoid taking them with him or simply sneaked off to the creak before the appeal could be made. Luckily for him, he thought, this afternoon was one of those when the commotion concerning Malachi had distracted Sista and Mama to such an extent that they did not remember to burden him with his playful younger brothers. So, for Levi, it seemed that all was well in the world. He trotted along the main road, navigated his way through the long track road and followed a pot-holed pathway while practicing his newly discovered whistling techniques. He knew that on this particular day, he could not return empty-handed because there was a big family to feed, and their supplies of dry conch and fish were almost depleted.

He was almost there when he saw the blackbirds. He noted only with slight interest the unusual gathering of those ugly hook-beaked blackbirds perched ominously on some avocado pear trees; he glanced around and mused, "They

Chapter Two

seem to be all over the place." The offensive birds made no attempt to fly away even as he walked quite near to them. Momentarily, it registered to Levi that these creatures were usually portents of death. It gave him an eerie feeling. Then, just as quickly, because it made him nervous, his attention again focused on securing the catch of the day.

As he was passing the cane field, Levi became conscious of a faint haze which caused him to pin his mouth shut and cover his nose to ward off the stench. He did not allow this to distract him, but it occurred to him that some large animal must have died north of where he was walking. The cloudless sky was beginning to darken slightly as the various dark grey hues leaked into the blues to mark the onset of evening. Despite that brief distraction, he trotted along the narrow track road humming a tune to himself. Soon after, Levi found a spot where he could fish at the creek and the smell was forgotten.

After about an hour Levi returned home. He came trotting into the kitchen proudly displaying his catch of the day – a handsome cluster of snappers, schoolmasters, and goggle eyes all gutted and ready to be cooked. "You shoulda seen um, Sista. They were just waiting for my line - great big ones!" boasted Levi as he placed them in a large enamel bowl according to his sister's directive.

The kitchen was the most intense hub of activity. There were three large pots on the fire hearth as Eulease put the finishing touches on the day's meal; she had created a gourmet meal from the corned fish which had previously been hanging on the line outside drying. This Friday, the meal consisted of stew fish in thick, savory gravy, pigeon peas and grits along with sweet slices of plantain, which was a family favorite. Mama had already baked the sourdough bread since early afternoon, so its intoxicatingly fresh-baked smell hovered in the atmosphere as a constant reminder. Bread making was relatively easy since a small piece of dough with yeast (which had been left from the previous day of baking) would be kneaded into a new mixture of dough, then shaped into loaves, left to rise, baked in the rock oven, and served to the family. New yeast would only be shaved off from the block of yeast when there was no more sourdough left. Each day, as if baked by a standard recipe, the soft white bread would be melt-in-the mouth delicious.

By six o'clock, the Rolles were all gathered in the detached kitchen. Basically, most of the family sat in a circle with parents sitting together and their children flanking them, each with an enamel plate and a medium-sized spoon. Each member of the family had his or her own enamel plate and individually colored enamel cup; even the youngest of them knew her special cup and used no other. Sometimes the enamel would become chipped and flake off from the tin but it could still be used because the tin was durable and seemed to last forever. The older children were helping the little ones like Livingston, Josh, and Zach to separate the small fish bones from the meat because accidentally swallowing one of those tiny, sharp bones almost always would result in tragedy. Mama had her hands full trying to supervise Ruthie as she gamboled around basically interfering with anyone's plate that she could get a hold of instead of enjoying her own. It was fortunate that each plate had a slight rim around its circumference so that the food could not easily be spilled despite Ruthie's antics. The family were so involved in completing their meal that no one seemed to notice when Hezekiah stealthily retreated with his plate of food.

Seemingly oblivious to all of this, Ishmael and Alphaeus, with their awkward and lanky adolescent legs hanging out of the kitchen door, sat comfortably scraping the last spoonful of peas and grits and the remains of fish gravy from their plates. The family's two Pot Cake dogs who had been patiently waiting for their treat quickly lapped up the scraps almost before they landed on the ground. Then, unceremoniously, the two partners in crime left their siblings and headed off to engage in some mischief. These two were really a handful. On any given day they could tie a firecracker on the tail of the neighbor's cat and scare him into the next settlement, they could replace Grandpa Cephas' sack of peanuts with sheep feces or steal fruits from Miss Ceva's fruit trees because it totally infuriated her (not because they needed them). Much to the chagrin of the adults, these two were apparently unencumbered by the severe punishments that were frequently meted out to them to curtail their pranks. With each passing year, it became more apparent that these two had become immune to 'cut hip'.

Evening was fast advancing into night. Sandflies hummed in everyone's ears while they claimed their territory as they did each night. Those tiny, flying insects of the evening were beginning to attack their victims and no amount of swatting of these creatures could protect anyone from their continuous stinging onslaught. The only remedy was to ignite a small bonfire if anyone wished to sit outside for a while. Nevertheless, Hezekiah had other things on his mind. He needed to think. He was avoiding the family because he was trying to conceal his excitement about his planned adventure. Also, he had to try to figure out how he could go on the search for Malachi and attend the dance at the same time. He had retreated to the "dryer" where a cool sea breeze

Chapter Two

was blowing gently across his face. This made him feel so relaxed that he felt like spreading his bed right outside near the front door and spending the rest of the night there regardless of the insects. "No, not tonight," he corrected himself thoughtfully, "I have another mission – and I'm definitely going to have some fun." After all, he could not let his friend Toby down. Hezekiah convinced himself that Malachi probably was going to show up by morning because he never stayed away longer than a day or two, anyhow. Then he thought, "God, what if we get caught?" Just as quickly as he thought it, he dismissed the unnerving thought.

What could possibly go wrong? There was nothing that he could think of, but he knew he had to be careful. Hezekiah planned to initially go out on the search for Malachi, then, at an opportune time, he would sneak away unnoticed. The younger children needed to horseplay around for a while, then he would settle Josh and the others to bed and carry out his plan. It was Friday evening, and he intended to punctuate his mundane existence with some fun.

"Boy, this is one night I wish I knew how to use that smoothing iron," thought Hezekiah. His sisters or mother did all the washing and ironing for the males in the family. He knew that he would have to load up the iron with coal, but controlling the heat was the biggest issue; definitely, a small disaster would happen because he would have to hold the crude implement near the fire periodically to heat it then iron his clothes. Hezekiah had no intention of destroying his favorite shirt. His last resort would have to be to beg and bribe Willie to iron quickly for him while Mama was still busy with the youngest of her brood. Hezekiah edged his way down the rocky slope toward the back of the house. There he spotted Willie rinsing the last of the dining utensils, while one of the brothers was carrying a pail of water to a makeshift structure that the boys used for bathing. This was his opportunity.

"What you need a nice shirt like this for? For tonight? You can't be wearin' this to get it all tear up goin' through coco plum patch, prickle, and saw bush, eh? You'll tear your shirt, Kiah!" Willie relentlessly questioned him much to his annoyance. Although Willie was younger and slightly built, growing up with mostly male siblings had made her feisty and more aggressive than most girls of her age.

"Look Willie, just do as I ask you and stop askin' so much questions! Why you so nosy, girl? This man's business. You just do the woman's work. Iron the shirt please and I'll pay you a lil somethin' when I get back."

Willie chuckled, "Boy, Kiah, you is somethin' else now. Go get the shirt, but don't get me in no trouble with Mama. Mama ALWAYS say, 'what's done in de dark will come out in de light!'"

Kiah disliked her ominous suggestion and it showed on his face.

"What you gettin' vex for? I aint tell you nothin' bad. I was just sayin'…" Her voice trailed off.

The iron was almost hot now and the lighted coals glowed inside it. Hezekiah could not wait for this inquisition to be over. Willie laid out the shirt and began ironing. "Who tell you I doin' anything in the dark except for lookin' for my brother?"

"I know you, Kiah. Somethin' just ain't right." Willie continued. The girl was so persistent, thought Kiah. He knew he had to exercise restraint. This was one time he could not afford to antagonize his sister.

Hezekiah felt that she would finish the task more quickly if she talked less. "You jus' better hurry up before Mama walk in here and catch you ironing!"

"Mama'll skin you an' me fer sure. I tryin' ter hurry up but dis ole smoothin' iron kinda heavy an' I have ter be careful so I don't burn de shirt."

After ten minutes that seemed like an eternity, Willie smiled. She held the shirt out towards her big brother as her round face beamed with pride. "Finished!"

"Thanks." Hezekiah practically snatched the shirt and darted out of the kitchen door to prepare himself for the evening's adventure. He felt confident that Willie would keep his secret.

"Kiah," She laughed and called out to him although he left before she could finish her sentence, "Watch yerself now, cause remember what's done in the dark…" The screen door slammed behind him.

Someone had already lit a small fire and left it smoldering at a safe distance from "the barn" hoping that the smoke would ward off the bloodsucking sandflies. For a moment, Hezekiah wondered what Toby was doing, and concluded that Toby must be engaged in the same process as he was. Since the younger boys had bathed, Hezekiah was able to do the same and was quickly dressed. He

Chapter Two

nimbly strode up the rocky incline past the big sapodilla tree which hovered over the house and shaded it on the eastern side, then hopped on to the "dryer".

The air was still. Except for a barking dog or the sound of the odd cricket, the homestead was slipping into sleep mode. Since the "dryer" (which was attached to the front of the house) had no roof, Hezekiah inadvertently peered at the darkening sky. Mercifully, there were a few puffs of breeze that refreshed him. He hoped there would be no rain. Now, as he glanced down toward the front of the yard, Hezekiah observed that some individuals were already heading off in the distance. He figured that the men were probably calling Malachi's name periodically since he was known to respond better to calls for him at night. Malachi was a night creature who was likely to be walking as darkness fell. In fact, in recent times, few people had seen him during the daytime; when people tried to approach him during the daytime, he sometimes behaved like a cornered animal who had been startled. Hezekiah watched the remaining flickers of light from the trail of lanterns, knowing that he had to catch up with the search party.

Hezekiah moved carefully off the "dryer" and down to the dirt road below. His tall, athletic frame easily caught up with the last group of men who had headed out. One of the men had a lantern while the others each held five or six "bunkers" (made of dry thatch) in their hands which they planned to light (one by one) to assist them during their journey. This reminded Hezekiah of the times when they would go crabbing for hours during the rainy season and return with sacks of white or black crabs. Sista was the chief crab catcher in her family; it was amazing to see her catch crabs with two bare feet and one hand while leaving one hand free to skillfully manoeuver each crab into her crocus bag without being bitten. When they returned from the hunt, Mama would always be beaming with delight. Tonight, however, the participants were too somber and resolute for one to mistake this event for the popular recreational activity.

As the group moved westward away from Steventon, nightfall had brought little coolness to the air. It was a muggy summer evening especially as Hezekiah had now broken away from the group and headed towards his inland rendezvous. The plan was to meet Toby by the creek. This was perhaps a better alternative to going down the long dirt road which curved around the creek and would take much too long. They would be able to cross over the creek and get to Rolleville in no time. He was relieved that he could no longer hear the haunting voices calling "MALACHI! MALACHI". Could it be that he was being too selfish? A wave of guilt came over Hezekiah. Despite his thoughts, he sincerely hoped that when he returned home, his oldest brother would be home again. He was grateful that his thoughts could not be detected by others. The atmosphere seemed so eerie and unusually still that he was happy when the occasional cricket and lamplighter flew by or landed on him.

"How much further could it be?" wondered Hezekiah. He certainly did not like walking that lonely track road on such a pitch-black night … Suddenly, there was a rustle and the bushes parted.

"Kiah! What take you so long? I almost thought you wasn't comin'." This was a voice Hezekiah was relieved to hear. Toby had sprung out from nowhere.

He was happy but a bit peeved with his friend. "Toby, you almost cause' my heart tuh jump outta my body! What you spring outta the bushes like that for? You tryin' to play ghost or somethin', eh?" They were crossing the shallow water of the creek now with their high-top tennis now draped over their shoulders.

"No man, I jus' glad you made it. Let's hurry up. If we walk fast, we'll get there by ten O'clock. That'll be good time." Toby assured his friend.

"I just hope it don't be high tide when we come back 'cause we'll have to walk all the way around…" pondered Kiah. Nevertheless, he felt better as he walked with his friend. He briefly explained the reasons for his lateness, then, as they left the water behind and paused for their feet to dry, they proceeded to chat about their plans for the night. As they walked, their constant chatter made the trek through some bushy areas and over the uneven terrain seem shorter.

The duo had been walking for some time when they heard the rake and scrape music before they could even see the place. The Chicken Nest Club was in full swing. The club was a makeshift structure which resembled a large, open cabana with a thatched roof. The roof provided shelter for the Outback Boys who played regularly on Friday and Saturday nights. On the other hand, the patrons either danced the night away on the bare ground, sat around the few wooden tables sipping a drink or stood in the shadows engaged in small talk or romantic embraces in the shadows.

The hours passed too quickly. Hezekiah had already danced a couple of numbers, so he was content to stand on the sidelines sipping some kind of sweet drink (minus any alcohol) and observe the interactions of the various individuals who were in attendance. He spotted Toby who had left him for some time. There

Chapter Two

he was with his arms around the waists of two young ladies. Hezekiah could only see their backs since they were turned away from him. He wished that he had even half of Toby's charm. Though he was not particularly good looking and only of average stature, Toby still seemed to have all the girls eating out of his hands. Hezekiah was classically 'tall, dark and handsome'; however, he had difficulty talking to even one girl without his nerves breaking down on him. Of course, if a girl turned down his offer for a dance, he was likely to give up and stand in the shadows for the rest of the night until he and Toby decided to leave. Hezekiah had a rugged attractiveness and commanding stature although he was unaware of it.

Toby exuded confidence and made it clear that he was on a mission. He was now gliding toward the dance area with the shorter of the two girls trailing behind him and tightly clutching the hand of his dance partner. The band was playing a slow dance number and Toby easily fell into step as he held his partner closely to him. Hezekiah, on the other hand, was more comfortable with the traditional dances he had learned like the quadrille, heal and toe polka or knocking the conch style. He always looked forward to Rushin' that was held down at the church hall in Steventon where he and other participants would repeatedly move in a line around the aisles of the hall dancing to the church music. Hezekiah's spirit was lifted when he threw in his penny contribution each time to participate in the dancing and handclapping once again with the other church folk. Unlike Toby, he only felt comfortable slow dancing with a girl that he felt some affection for.

A hint of cool breeze had brushed past him which relaxed him momentarily. Sensing the mood of the patrons, the band continued playing what the patrons called the "slow groove". Hezekiah then became distracted by a moderately tall, medium-built young lady who was standing alone just a few yards away from him. He was surprised at his own ability to make the request, "May I have this dance?" and he was even more surprised when she politely reciprocated. He was proud of his own boldness and smiled while trying to conceal his delight. For about twenty minutes, he was lost in the energetic yet relaxed demeanor of his partner. Although they exchanged only a few words, he learned that she was Gaylene Smith of Nassau, but she was visiting relatives in Alexander. Gaylene had indicated that her relatives were getting ready to leave the dance. Hezekiah found himself holding onto her hand as he whispered to her that he hoped to see her again sometime soon. She smiled but said nothing, then walked away. Hezekiah could not understand the slight fluttering in his chest, but he assured himself that he would see that young lady again.

He reflected on the night and concluded that, so far, he was having a good time even though his friend Toby had left him for quite some time. Now, alone again, for some reason Hezekiah began to experience a strange twinge in the pit of his stomach that he could not explain.

"Where in the world is Toby?" wondered Hezekiah. "It's just like him to disappear without saying a word." He estimated that it had to be after 1:00 a.m. since the sizeable crowd and the excited voices of merrymakers had dwindled to about ten people. In fact, the band had taken its last intermission.

Then just as suddenly as he had left, Toby appeared as if he had popped out of a magician's hat and startled his friend again.

"Kiah, you look bored, man. What happen? You ain't havin' a good time?"

"Man, where you been?" asked Kiah anxiously. "We need to get home. You know what time it is?"

As usual, Toby had an excuse. "Kiah, give me a break, man. I had to walk that girl home. Man, she is something else. Uhm hmmm!" Toby patted the left side of his chest for emphasis. "She right here, right here, Kiah. That's the one for me."

Kiah questioned his friend, "You mean the lil cute one I saw you dancin' with mos' uh the night?"

"You gat that right. That's mine." Toby boasted. They were now walking briskly along the track road which would take them back the way they came.

"How you mean that's yours, Toby?"

"You know! And I think she like me too, but maybe she was a lil drunk too, but dat work to my advantage. Man, I never met a girl like her yet. She jus', you know sweet, sweet, sweet!" Toby was spinning around in the road now and grinning from ear to ear as if he could not contain his excitement.

"Now Toby, I hope you didn't ..."

Toby threw up his arms in exasperation. "Kiah, why you always so serious and worrying about stupid things. We young. Aint no harm in foolin' around a lil bit. Nothin' dat serious happen. We supposed to enjoy life. That's what we came here for, right? Anyway, ain't no time for all this talkin'. Let's jus' try ter get home before dayclean."

Hezekiah agreed hesitantly.

There was no point arguing with Toby anyway, so Kiah shook his head from left to right in submission and kept walking. They had to cross over some elevated terrain and walk through a patch of bushes before they could get to the creek. Although it was early morning, the temperature still seemed uncomfortably warm after they had been walking for a while. The two young men sprinted purposefully over the hill and were headed down the slope on the other side when they heard the dreaded sounds.

"Hey, you! Stop! We wan' say somethin' to you!" The voice was brash and insistent. The two friends glanced simultaneously behind them and fearfully faced their pursuers. They could hear fast approaching footsteps that seemed to be coming toward the bushes on the other side of the road where they were walking. The hint of moonlight was just enough for them to have seen where they were going, so the darkness prevented them from seeing their harassers.

"Oh Jesus, Kiah, those Rolleville fellas comin' ter rob us or somethin'! What we ger do? Man Kiah, I shoulda listen ter you!" Toby was petrified.

"Let's keep on running. See the creek there. If we could get there, they probably'll leave us alone. Come on Toby!" panted Kiah.

"Yeah, man, cause if they catch us, they guh kill us, fer sure!" Toby was running so hard and was so consumed with fear that he seemed to be hyperventilating. They could hear the stomping sound of perhaps a dozen feet as the mob tore through the bushes to catch their prey. Hezekiah and Toby were running faster at this point. He could hear Toby panting and wheezing slightly as he struggled to keep pace with the taller and more agile Hezekiah. They ran through the shallow water of the creek with their attackers close behind them. Hezekiah knew that he had to make it home for more than one reason, and he was resolute in his quest. Their pursuers were hurling rocks and vitriolic threats as the two friends advanced to the water's edge. Some of their adversaries entered the water brandishing cutlasses and pieces of wood.

Suddenly Hezekiah heard a thud, then Toby uttered a groan, stumbled, and fell into the water. He knew right away that his friend Toby had been hit. Something told him to keep on running, but there was no way that he would leave his best friend to face the brutal men alone. Hezekiah threw himself flat into the water and lay still, waiting for a similar fate. There was no more splashing of feet in the water, and within minutes the atmosphere was quiet. For some reason, the men had retreated.

Instinctively, Hezekiah jumped up and turned his friend over, desperately hoping that he had not drowned. As he propped him up, Hezekiah called desperately, "Toby, Toby! Wake up! Stay with me. You gotta stay with me! Don't give up!" Hezekiah felt the blood on the back of Toby's head, and reassured Toby as he dragged him up, "You gonna be all right, buddy. Jus' stay with me. I'm gonna get you home." Toby had swallowed some water, but after coughing for a few seconds, he began to breathe better. Toby was bleeding profusely from the head wound, but Hezekiah could do nothing more at that moment but to try to get him out of the water and onto dry land.

Toby was only semi-conscious. It was a combination of desperation and intestinal fortitude that enabled Hezekiah to get Toby through the water and down the dirt road. Once they were on the dirt road, Hezekiah removed his own shirt and tore off a portion of it so that he could bandage his friend's head to minimize the bleeding. He trudged along as he partially dragged and lifted Toby's limp body. Sometimes he had to stop briefly to rest. Despite the trouble he would be in, this was one time that he wished someone was passing by to help him, but the road remained deserted and quiet.

Hezekiah believed he could hear his own heart beating. He sat down once again, while laying his friend on the ground so that he could rest before struggling to carry him along with him again. Toby's breathing was shallow, and he never spoke a word. Hezekiah had not realized that so much time had passed until he saw that the moon had disappeared although it was still dark. They were both so muddy and sticky with dirt, blood, water, and miscellaneous particles that Hezekiah wondered how he would explain the situation to anyone. Fortunately, he knew that Steventon was just a short distance away. This motivated him to renew his efforts to get his friend lifesaving help and to get himself cleaned up before being discovered.

Hezekiah could see the house ahead. He concentrated his energy for just a few more steps as he lifted his weak friend onto the "dryer" of the Smith's home. He

Chapter Two

prayed that no one would see him. He was thankful that Toby's family did not have any dogs. He eased Toby onto the floor and propped him up against the wall near the front door. Blood was still trickling from the gash on the back of Toby's head into the bandage. Hezekiah checked Toby one more time to ensure that he was still breathing. With his fists, he pounded three or four times on the front door to alert the residents, then ran hastily toward the road again using whatever energy he had left. He was certain that Toby's parents heard the noise and would come and rescue their son.

He looked back at Toby's house once but had to resist the temptation to wait until a relative came outside. Hezekiah saw a few streaks of light far in the horizon to the east of him as he walked through Steventon. "Oh God," Hezekiah thought, "It must be about five or almost six o'clock by now." He could hear one or two roosters crowing nearby. He wondered if Malachi felt like this-uncomfortable, out of place and misunderstood. It was an awful feeling. His house was just ahead of him. He only needed to sneak around the back. Hopefully Mama had not started her morning activities. He had to get cleaned up. "Mama might be praying by now," thought Kiah hopefully.

Then he saw the shadows. As he approached his destination, he was surprised to see what appeared to be a cluster of people on the "dryer". Some were even standing near the seagrape tree in the centre of the front yard. This did not feel right. "What are they doing there so early...?" He asked himself, then almost choked on his own thoughts. Then he remembered. It could only mean that they had found Malachi.

"Thank goodness," He thought to himself. He felt relieved that Malachi was back home. There were faint streaks of light on the horizon and his greatest concern for the moment was to remain hidden. He dodged along the fading shadows of the trees and buildings. His legs felt heavy as he climbed clumsily up the gradual elevation which would enable him to get near the outhouse where he could bathe, but first he needed clean clothes. Hezekiah eased the barn door open and saw, as he predicted, that his young brothers were still asleep. He found his shelf and grabbed whatever clothing he could find, then hastily ran to get some water for a bath.

Now that he was clean and dry, Hezekiah proceeded to join the group on the "dryer". He was tired and could use a cup of fever grass tea but that could wait. Before he got to the front, he heard a voice of one in distress. He wondered why his mother was crying. Zilpha's voice had turned into a wail now. Her voice pierced the quiet of the morning and Hezekiah Sr. (Zeke) was trying to console her.

Hezekiah approached his parents cautiously, not understanding what was going on. He expected to be bombarded with questions, but no one seemed to notice him. Everyone was preoccupied with the night's events. A body was laid out and partially covered in a huge crocus bag. The flies could not contain their excitement as they buzzed disrespectfully. The stench was almost unbearable. Hezekiah's heart began beating fast as he dealt with the shocking reality. He only ventured near enough to see that the bloated corpse was wearing Malachi's blue and black plaid shirt and black pants. It seemed that he was barefooted. Hezekiah could see in the dim light that it was Malachi. Poor Malachi needed to be laid to rest swiftly since exposure to the elements and the summer heat had begun to take its toll on his remains. Hezekiah later learned that his brother's body had been discovered around 1:00 a.m. in a bushy area near a coconut tree about a mile away. Someone had a wagon so with the assistance of several men, they loaded Malachi's body onto it and transported his remains to his parents' home.

"Soon as dayclean, we gatta bury him." Someone said softly.

"Yes, we need to get the poor feller covered up as soon as possible," agreed another gentleman who was dressed in blue overalls and armed with a shovel.

"May the Lord have mercy on his soul." Another person added.

Pastor Simeon Smith was already there. He turned to the parents, "We'll have a service for him right at the graveside just as soon as those fellers finish digging a hole for the body. That's the best we can do fer him."

Hezekiah was overwhelmed by so many emotions that he felt as if his chest was going to burst. His brother was dead, and now his friend was seriously injured. He felt helpless. He wanted all of this to be a dream, but he knew it was not.

Malachi's remains was placed in a crude wooden box that had been hurriedly constructed by Mr. Phalmon Gray who was a 'Jack-of-all-trades' and was especially gifted at carpentry. Eight men carried Malachi to his final resting place in the local graveyard early that Saturday morning. Hezekiah Sr., Zilpha, and Hezekiah Jr. were the only close members of the Rolle family at the interment. As expected, word had filtered to some of the neighbors about Malachi's demise. This resulted in quite a sizeable gathering of people who were mostly dressed in their regular work or yard apparel since there had been no time for funeral preparations. Of course, there were those who had only come for the gossip or due to curiosity but, for once, there was little chatter because most who attended were genuine mourners. Pastor Smith continued to console the bereaved family. Hezekiah found it ironic that the Pastor appeared to be so composed and prepared to conduct the brief service even as his own son needed urgent medical care. Hezekiah wondered how Pastor Smith would react when he discovered that his only son had been so seriously injured. It disturbed him more when he envisioned the Pastor's reaction after discovering that Hezekiah had left Toby on the porch to die. The thought of this caused Hezekiah to shudder. Pastor Smith remained stoic as he conducted an abbreviated service, and the body was committed to the ground. Zilpha was sobbing loudly now; Zeke clung to his wife as he held on to that manly strength that would prevent him from openly weeping for his first born. Malachi had spent only a short time with them, and he left them just as mysteriously as he had lived with them.

"There is no pain that heaven cannot heal, Brother Zeke and Sister Zilpha. Weeping endureth for a night but joy cometh in the morning. May his soul and the souls of the faithful departed rest in peace." The pastor endeavored to provide comfort to the bereaved.

Someone raised another hymn, "When peace like a river attendeth my way …" and the other mourners joined in the singing.

"Ashes to ashes, dust to dust …" The pastor stood over the gaping cavity and completed the last burial rites after Malachi's coffin had been lowered into the grave. Hezekiah could no longer restrain himself. He began to weep as if something had been trapped within him and the lid had just been unscrewed. His grief was so deep as he reflected on the fact that he had not been there to help his own brother, especially as he lay alone, dying in the open air.

The haze of death and decay had disappeared from the earth, and all were relieved. The Rolles never envisioned that it would end like this for Malachi. Although he could not think of a better option, Hezekiah was also mortified by the fact that a human being could be disposed of with so little formality. His parents turned their attention to their distressed son and huddled around him, drawing him to them as they bore their individual and collective grief. Malachi's passing seemed like a catharsis for the Rolle family. The gravediggers continued to toss dirt until the coffin was covered and a slender mound was left at ground level to mark the grave. The family stood watching from under a blooming red Poinciana tree that was nearby.

The gathering of mourners gradually dispersed. After the Rolle family had watched the gravediggers complete their task, Pastor Smith walked with Hezekiah and his parents to the front of the Rolles' property. It was here that Pastor Smith apologized for not being able to stay awhile with them but promised to see the family later. He hurriedly explained that he had received some troubling news from home earlier on, so he needed to get back there urgently to deal with the matter. Hezekiah's grief now turned to panic. He broke away from his parents and ran toward the back of the yard crying out openly as he prayed that Toby would be alright.

The wafts of breakfast filled the air and Hezekiah was reminded of the hunger pangs that were gripping the walls of his stomach. He wondered if he would be able to eat because he felt that food right then might make him sick to his stomach. Exhaustion and anxiety had taken control of every fiber of his being. He wanted to hear some news about Toby; in fact, he wished he could go there. He wondered what Toby would say about the incident. What would people say when they found out that he had left his friend by the door without knowing his condition? Should he have stayed? Surely, he had done the best he could. He passed the well and paused to draw some water because his throat was parched. After this refreshment, he went far to the back of the yard where he leaned his head against an almond tree and was thankful for the rest spot because he could go no further. His mind was in a confused state, and he needed to rest, then he would figure out what he should do. He had lost his brother, Malachi and perhaps his best friend too. Somewhere deep within his consciousness, Hezekiah could not free himself from Willie's words that were really Mama's maxim, "What's done in the dark will surely come to the light."

Pastor Smith had arrived home to find his wife Harriet trying to treat and provide some comfort to Toby while awaiting transportation to take him to Georgetown. He was disturbed by the situation, but he struggled to maintain his composure for the sake of his wife and children. Harriet was the pastor's second wife; the first Mrs. Smith had died several years ago in childbirth leaving the pastor to raise Toby and the newborn baby girl on his own. Toby had still not regained consciousness but was no longer losing blood. Ironically, his twelve-year-old sister was now diligently assisting their stepmom in applying first aid while their two young sisters watched curiously on the sidelines. He had been cleaned up and was lying on a makeshift bed in the living room with a fresh bandage around his head. Toby appeared to be delusional as he uttered indecipherable words to his stepmother. Everything was being done to ensure that he was resting comfortably. Fortunately, Pastor Smith had a bicycle, so a family friend borrowed the bicycle and promised the Smith family that he would ride to the commissioner's office in Georgetown. His son needed urgent help and the commissioner was the only person on the island with a vehicle. Hopefully, if the commissioner could come, he could transport Toby so that he could get much needed treatment. Pastor Smith hoped that Commissioner Hart had not travelled to Long Island for the weekend to visit with his wife's family. The men had been friends since childhood, so he felt confident that Oliver Hart would not let him down if he was on the island.

News usually travelled fast throughout the neighboring settlements, so it was not surprising that word of the brutal attack on Toby had spread like wildfire. By midday Saturday, even people in Georgetown were speculating about what had happened. Some were insisting that Toby had been badly beaten and left to die on the side of the road. There was a rumor that Toby had been to a dance and had left with some friends; some were insisting that he had been seen walking away with a female while others felt certain that they had seen Toby walking with a male friend, but no one could give specific names or times.

Pastor Smith prayed for God's mercy. He had already lost his second oldest son to tetanus shortly after Toby was born. His oldest son had migrated to the United States and gotten married several years ago, and one daughter had gone to live in Nassau with Pastor Smith's sister a year before, hoping to find a job or a husband. Apart from Toby and his twelve-year-old sister from the first marriage, the other two children (by his second wife) were quite young. Toby was the only boy. He reflected on Toby. Of all his children, Toby was the one that he had grown to depend on. Although Toby was mischievous at times, he was developing into a fine young man who had already indicated that he wanted to become a teacher. It was his dream that Toby would take over the ministry when he retired, but Toby had let his father know in no uncertain terms that he had no interest in becoming a clergyman.

Toby's injuries weighed heavily on Hezekiah's psyche. He had been sleeping when they caught him. They had grabbed his arms and legs and Hezekiah struggled helplessly to free himself from his captors. They had hoisted him off his feet and were carrying him. He shouted for help. They were taking him towards a cliff, and, although he could not see their faces, he knew their intent was to throw him over so that he would fall to his death. Then Mama's voice came to him clearly and accusingly, "What's done in the dark will come to the light." The arms tightened their grip and as they took him closer to the cliff's edge, Pastor Smith held out his bible and looked directly at Hezekiah. Then Malachi stepped out from behind the pastor with unseeing eyes and a bloated face that was deformed as in death; Hezekiah could see that Malachi was trying to say something to him but could not understand one word that he was saying. Hezekiah was calling out for help, but there was no one willing to help him… Suddenly, Hezekiah was awakened from his slumber by his siblings.

"What happen to you, Kiah?"

"What you doin' in the back here? We were lookin' all over the place for you. You need to come and get something to eat. Come on, Kiah!"

"You must be having a bad dream," Ishmael suggested while he and Alphaeus were tugging on Hezekiah's arms. Willie, Tommy, and Levi were talking to him all at once as if he had been away for a long time and they were happy to see him.

Hezekiah was still struggling as his brothers and sister sought to find out what was troubling him. Willie, Tommy, Ishmael, Alpheus, and Levi had come looking for him. Hezekiah was thankful to see his young siblings and felt fortunate that he had only been dreaming. Mama and Papa were resting and trying to recover after the tragic events of the day. Hezekiah was hungry and was grateful for the hot plate of food and the limeade that Sista had placed before him. He ate so fast that he hardly remembered what he had eaten, but it was good.

"Hey, Kiah, why you so quiet? What happen? You still thinking 'bout what happen to Malachi? Did you see the body?" asked Thomas.

"That's true he start to swell up an' all the worms was comin' outta his body, Kiah? That's what I hear some people saying. I heard he look bad. I never saw a dead person before," added Levi and waited anxiously for a reply.

"Look, I really don't want to talk about it. You should be glad because that wasn't a nice thing to see. I think that our brother is in a better place now, and we need to stop talking about him like a piece of trash that somebody threw away. He was a human being, and we must always remember that he was one of us." said Hezekiah harshly. Although he realized that his siblings were enquiring out of childish curiosity and teaching had taught him to tolerate this, on this day, he refused to engage in any more flippant banter about the demise of Malachi.

Chapter Two

"Willie come help me with these clothes! You need to stop beatin' up your gum and help me clean up this place. When Mama wake up, you know she guh be vex if she meet these things all over the place like this. Leave those boys alone. Don't let me have tuh call you twice!" That was a warning from Sista that Willie knew she had better not ignore. Not long after, her four brothers also decided that they ought to leave Kiah alone. They wandered off to the Bay to cut some cane to snack on later and to look for some corn to roast down in the field. There was never a dull moment for them because there were so many of them that someone could always think of something interesting to do.

Sista hailed to the youngsters just before they disappeared, "If you all find any jelly coconuts while you wanderin' around, bring couple back so we could have some coconut water." The heat was really trying to get the best of her.

"Lord this some heat, nah. I could do with somethin' to cool muh throat," Sista said to herself as she wiped the sweat from her forehead which was partially covered by a green and white kerchief. They were all feeling the onslaught of an unrelenting 95 degrees of blistering heat, and there was not even a wisp of breeze blowing.

"O.K, Sista!" They shouted in unison. They ran off gleefully, but they knew that if they brought nothing else back, they had to return with some good jelly coconuts. They didn't want to give Sista a reason to use the tamarind switch.

Hezekiah heard their playful banter and chuckled to himself. He knew that Sista could tackle one or two fellows and win the fight too. She was strong and angular in stature. His oldest sister was as stubborn as a mule and could fight, kick and stomp like one. Nevertheless, he knew that her aggressive persona masked a kind, loving spirit that motivated her daily to care for her siblings unselfishly. She could read and write although she had not received much of an education because Mama often needed her to stay home to assist her with the young children. Hezekiah hoped that one day his eldest sister would get married, move to another settlement, and live a happy life, but it seemed like most of the eligible bachelors of her age group shied away from her because of her unladylike, aggressive ways. Hezekiah could still remember one bold and debonair young man who claimed that he had "come to the house to court Eulease". Papa was still away on "the project" so Mama had to be the one to give consent and this she did. The young man seemed to be well-mannered and appeared to come with good intentions. Eulease was in her late teens then. Of course, Mama sat with the couple for a while as was customary. Mama listened to the young man trying to talk to Eulease, but except for a nod or a shake of her head, Eulease refused to utter a word. So, after a while, Mama thought it best to leave the living room for a short while to give them some privacy. Mama had just gone to the kitchen briefly when she heard the commotion; it was apparent that some people were breaking up her house. Mama snatched off her apron. She could hear the distinct voice of a man hollering and pleading for his life. As she entered the living room, Mama spotted the water jug on the ground in fragments. She was horrified to see that Eulease had the young man in a headlock and was punching him to pieces. Eulease was tall and strong, but her demeanor was usually calm and gentle. However, something had angered her. Mama had to grab a slender piece of wood from the windowsill and hit Eulease one or two moderate blows across her back to get her to release the hapless fellow. As soon as Eulease had released her grip, the young suitor fled for his life leaving one foot of his shoes behind. Hezekiah reflected that this was the last suitor to come calling on Sista that he knew of.

He found himself thinking about Mama who had endured so much as she had to contend with raising so many of the children practically on her own. He knew his Mama was a strong woman and he loved her so much. Thank goodness Sista was there to help her, especially with the cooking and cleaning. He knew that Mama was especially fragile now as she had recently lost her older sister due to an undiagnosed illness.

Hezekiah Jr. attended church as usual with his family on Sunday, but on that day his heart was heavy. There was still no news of Toby. Hezekiah walked past the Smith home twice after dinner on Sunday, but he could not muster the nerve to approach Toby's family. No one seemed to have any news, and it was apparent that his name had not yet been linked to Toby's mishap.

Then the news that Hezekiah wanted to hear eventually filtered down to the Rolle homestead on Sunday afternoon. Hezekiah Sr. had informed his wife that by chance he had met Pastor Smith while the latter was on his way home from his church. Mr. Rolle was in the "barn" which had two sections - sleeping quarters for the boys and an adjoining food storage room. Hezekiah Jr. listened just outside the "barn" window as his father explained to his mother what Pastor Smith had told him about Toby. Hezekiah Jr. heard his father telling her how Pastor Smith had explained to him that his son Toby had received a serious head injury. Fortunately, after the commissioner had been contacted by the messenger on the bicycle, Commissioner Hart subsequently sent a message to the flying doctor who had by chance been attending to a patient at the clinic in George Town. As

Chapter Two

soon as Dr. Caruthers, a middle-aged, white English doctor, received news of the injured patient in Steventon, he went as requested by the commissioner to treat and pick up the sick patient. On Saturday evening, the flying doctor's seaplane had landed right in the Smith's yard and within forty-five minutes, Toby had been stabilized and was being taken to Nassau. Pastor Smith explained to Hezekiah Sr. that since Toby had been transported to the hospital in Nassau, he had heard no news, but he was praying that Toby would survive the terrible ordeal.

Hezekiah was overcome by a wave of relief. He found himself resting his head against the wall of the "barn" as he exhaled carefully so that his parents would not hear him outside. He could hear them shuffling around food containers and fixing items on the shelves of this little room in which corn, grits, rice, flour, and other key food items were stored. They probably were checking to see the quantity of supplies that remained. He felt slightly better, and comforted himself that Toby would return home soon.

Another week had passed and once again Hezekiah was tortured by the fact that he was passing the Smith house and he wanted to stop, but he could not. He sensed that both Pastor Smith and his wife were at home, but he knew that he could not face the hurt look on their faces when he gave his explanation. This time, something else prompted him to approach the house. He knew that the longer he took to explain himself, the situation would seem worse. Also, as he passed, he could see Pastor Smith sitting on his porch smoking his pipe and looking out over into the street. He knew that Pastor Smith saw him, but the reverend gentleman only continued staring without acknowledging that he saw him.

Hezekiah approached the steps and ascended the porch cautiously.

The austere Pastor Smith puckered his mouth as he drew on his pipe, then exhaled a light plume of smoke.

"Have a seat my son. I have been waiting for you to come. You and Toby were friends, weren't you?" inquired Pastor Smith. His voice was deeper than usual and pensive.

"Yes, Sir but …" Hezekiah stumbled for words.

"Boy, don't you have something to say to me?"

"Yes – no Sir. What do you mean?" Hezekiah did not expect this line of questioning.

Pastor Smith's voice was laced with a slight hint of anger now although he appeared to be calm. "You understand what I'm asking you, don't you?"

"Yes Sir, but I didn't do anything to Toby, although we were together when it happened." Hezekiah explained.

The Pastor's voice was heavier now and more elevated as he preached, "My boy, you are emerging into adulthood, coming of age, some would say. Your papa would be disappointed in you. Zeke is a strong man who never backs down from anything and I know he would expect you to do the same regardless of the consequences. A man must be a man and admit his mistakes, face his demons no matter what they are. You can't keep running away because it will eat you up inside."

"This is what happened, I swear, Sir." Hezekiah looked directly into Pastor Smith's eyes and was relieved to see only compassion there.

"My son, I do not blame you for what happened to Toby for I know my son. Toby is willful and stubborn, but I don't understand who would do this to him. Did he get into a fight or argument? He almost got killed. I want to know who did this."

"Sir, let me tell you what I know happened." Hezekiah shed his burden as he recounted the events from the time that he met Toby on the road to the moment that he left Toby near the door of his home."

"Son, you saved my boy's life and for that I will always be grateful. Only a friend like you would have risked your life to save Toby. I expected you to come to me sooner, but I understand that you were afraid. I know your Papa and Mama would be disappointed in you if they knew what you did so this incident will remain between you and me."

Hezekiah inquired about Toby's condition. Pastor Smith admitted that he really did not know what was happening with Toby, but he believed that he had been taken to The Bahamas General Hospital in Nassau for treatment and hopefully he was recovering. Pastor then thanked Hezekiah for coming and gave him a reassuring embrace before Hezekiah was on his way back home. Hezekiah was truly grateful that his prayers had been answered.

Several weeks later, the Rolle family, like some other families in the area, found that some of their food and other related supplies had become depleted.

Chapter Two

Hezekiah Sr. hoped that he could restock the storeroom. Mr. Rolle had already indicated that he would send a couple of his older sons on a much-needed trek to Georgetown to get some essential food items for the family. As expected, the patriarch of the family would probably dispatch Hezekiah, Tommy, and Leviticus, if the weather permitted. It was June, which was within the hurricane season, but there had been no bad weather since early May. However, the mailboat had not come to Exuma for weeks perhaps because something had happened, and Hezekiah Sr. did not know of the circumstances; perhaps it had run aground on a treacherous reef, or it had broken down. Papa's usual monthly order from E. L. Sawyer on Bay Street in Nassau was delayed by two weeks so the Rolles had to resort to an alternate plan to get much needed supplies.

Providing for his family was the priority of Hezekiah Sr. who was a skilled carpenter and a natural farmer. His specialty was onion farming. The winter season was harvesting time for local farmers, so Hezekiah Sr. travelled to Nassau frequently with sacks of onions which he sold to Milo Butler & Sons on Blue Hill Rd. In difficult times, Hezekiah Sr. had resorted to doing odd jobs in Nassau to earn a few shillings to take care of his enlarged family. Over the years, he had never been afforded an opportunity to even work on weeding the roadsides in Exuma because he supported the opposing political party, so he sometimes resorted to seeking odd jobs as a handyman or road worker in Nassau. It was on one of these occasions that Hezekiah discovered E. L. Sawyer grocery store. He resorted to ordering groceries from Sawyer's after establishing an account with old man Sawyer, the elderly white Bahamian gentleman who was the owner. Even when Hezekiah Sr. had been on The Project, he wanted to ensure that his family would always have all the necessities that could not be grown on his Steventon property. Most of the accounts maintained by E. L. Sawyer were white clientele, but Mr. Sawyer considered Hezekiah Rolle to be a dependable customer. Hezekiah was one proud black man who would never shirk his responsibilities. If it was his last pound, he always paid his bill at the end of every month without fail. He could never bear the thought of anyone giving his family handouts, or that his family needed anything that he could not get for them.

Hezekiah Sr. was a stern and unrelenting disciplinarian whose word was gospel in the household, but he was cherished by every one of his children and his wife followed his wishes without hesitation. He was well known for masking his emotions on most occasions, but he loved his wife and children and would spare them nothing. In fact, in the 1940s when Hezekiah Sr. was on the "contract", it was customary that as the mailboat came to Steventon, the family could not

49

conceal their excitement because each one knew that there would be lots of treats, fine clothing, unique footwear from "The States" and grocery from E. L. Sawyer sent by Papa. There would be colorful dresses with puffed sleeves for the girls, knickerbockers, shirts and khaki pants for the boys, generous lengths of cloth with accessories for his wife and Eulease to sew dresses along with special kitchenware. Papa never forgot the order of coffee beans which Mama would parch and grind up with a pestle so that she could make a delicious brew which was his favorite.

Since Papa was now a permanent fixture, when the mailboat came in, the older boys were proud to take turns going with their father in his dinghy boat that he himself had built. Therefore, when the mailboat sailed in and dropped anchor, several hundred yards out to sea, the tall, muscular, middle-aged Hezekiah Sr. always selected two of his sons to accompany him and retrieve their supplies from the boat. Papa's final decision on who would accompany him in the dinghy was the only thing that quelled the arguments as the boys jockeyed, cajoled, and argued their way into being selected. Even young Josh would join the melee, but Papa would say gently, "Josh, you will have your time. Let the bigger boys do this job." He exercised patience in placating Josh.

In recent years, since the project ("contract") began to be dismantled as American men returned to work and replaced the contract workers when the war ended, there was less of a need for Bahamian workers. Hezekiah Sr. eventually returned to his family and full-time onion farming. After decades of merciless exposure to the sun, Hezekiah Sr.'s youthful, moderately dark complexion had changed to a parched and somewhat wrinkled deep bronze. All that was left of his jet-black tightly curling hair were a few patches of salt and pepper hair growing in a curve behind a profoundly receding hairline and a bald spot in the middle of his head that he kept covered with a cap. With a quiet resolve, he strived to make up for the time he had lost because he had been away from his family while working on the contract.

School was about to close for another summer holiday and Hezekiah Jr. felt a pressing desire to leave this quaint island that he had called home for almost eighteen years. The long-awaited summer break was fast approaching, and he looked forward to going to summer school for teachers and monitors in Nassau. He felt strange because he and Toby had planned to attend these training sessions together, but everything had changed. Nevertheless, he looked forward to mingling with experienced teachers and meeting other monitors. He felt bored now and unfulfilled. Toby was like an alter ego; Hezekiah missed his friend's exuberance and novelty. There was a need for Hezekiah to jumpstart his social life, and he longed to extricate himself from the sheltering wings of his parents, although he loved them dearly. At his age, he felt that he was soon becoming a man and longed to shake off their overbearing influences. Sometimes, he felt profound sadness. He began to wonder if this was how Malachi had felt - out of place and misunderstood. He derived some comfort in thinking that God was leading him in a different direction. He even speculated that perhaps by crossing the waters, as some people liked to say, he may change his luck.

Chapter Three

Hezekiah literally strutted as he walked down Bay Street to begin his summer sojourn. This 'boy' from the 'Out Island' had already endured the turbulent seven-hour journey by mailboat and finally he had arrived at the place that others had convinced him to be the 'promised land'. Now that his feet were on dry land, he hardly felt the weight of the loaded cardboard box on his shoulder, which contained dry conch, miscellaneous fruits, and vegetables, while in his right hand he held his brown suitcase. A few people looked at him inquisitively, but he did not mind at all. This was a golden opportunity and Hezekiah Rolle Jr. intended to make good use of it. The boat on which he had travelled to Nassau rocked slightly as he left it behind by the dock which was near the market slip on Bay Street. He walked past a noisy place and mumbled to himself that he had never seen so many fish in one place, and for sale, because on "the island", people didn't buy fish. He had always assumed that people simply went to the sea and caught fish as they wanted them. It was strange to see men and women desperately hustling and arguing over prices and portions of fish as if their lives depended on it. He later learned that this place was called the Buttman.

He stood momentarily in front of the Royal Bank of Canada and made a mental note to himself that he should try to open a bank account. Although he never actually articulated his concern, he later discovered with a pious acceptance the fact that the only black employees of this bank were the doorman and the messenger. This was simply the status quo. Hezekiah turned to the south. He walked up the gradual incline and stared in awe at the Royal Victoria Hotel which stood majestically on the corner of East Street and Shirley Street. He paused briefly before crossing over as a horse and carriage passed him while being guided by a single driver with a whip. He adjusted the load he was carrying and

Chapter Three

crossed over then turned right onto East Street. He could feel the unrelenting scorch of the midday sun on his back and was relieved to know that he was wearing a light shirt and a wide-brimmed floppy straw hat that Sista had plaited for him since the previous summer. He peeped through the sturdy fence and could see the ballroom as he walked past. Hezekiah wondered what it would be like inside that hotel, but he accepted the fact that unless he worked there, he would never have the experience of dining or dancing in this hotel because only white patrons were allowed inside. Most of the guests were seasonal visitors who came every year to enjoy the simple way of life and the hospitality that Bahamians were renowned for. In subsequent years, each summer that he came to Nassau, he found himself standing, studying in awe the many symbols and representations of colonialism and the British Empire that occupied the capital.

Hezekiah began his ascent up East Street Hill. He observed the site of the original hospital (The Bahamas General Hospital) from a distance which was being rebuilt at the time. The temporary location was in Prospect Ridge on what he had been told was a magnificent structure on the R. A. F. Base. He was quite fascinated by the relative modernity of Nassau in contrast to the quaint island of Exuma, so he made up his mind that these weeks that he would be spending in Nassau while attending summer school were going to be purposeful and worthwhile. He had a lot to learn about city life and was prepared to do so. He walked past the popular Rusty's Guest House which was the preferred choice of many natives who were visiting from the Out Islands. Hezekiah wiped away the beads of perspiration which had begun to stream down his face, and he longed for some cool coconut water or some limeade because his throat was parched. Then he spotted it – Mortimer Candy Kitchen. Despite the heavy load that he was carrying, he practically ran to the shop on the hill and quickly purchased the largest strawberry snow cone that they had. After placing the items that he had been carrying on the floor nearby, Hezekiah took his slow time eating the snow cone, secretly hoping that it would last forever. As he stepped out of Mortimer's, he looked across the street on his right and saw the Hillside Theatre which was one of the popular movie theatres frequented by residents of the Bain Town and nearby areas. He knew that he had almost arrived at his destination and felt relieved.

Hezekiah could not wait to see his uncle's eager and joyous expression when they greeted each other. Although he had not seen his uncle in five years, he knew that his uncle was expecting him. In previous years he had stayed with an aunt who lived on Market Street, but Aunt Ida had moved far away into Fox Hill at her husband's insistence. His mind quickly shifted to the present when he spotted his Uncle Cardy's ramshackle house; he noted that it had deteriorated considerably since the last time he had seen it (perhaps due to the hurricane of the previous year). Hezekiah could see that the thin, faded curtains were drawn tightly. After knocking at the door of the rickety wooden structure, which was anchored on four stilts, he tried the front door but found that it was locked. Hezekiah put down the load that he was carrying and sat on the top step that led to the verandah and porch. He realized that he might have to wait for several hours for the residents to come home so he decided to make himself comfortable.

Around 5:00 p.m., Cardinal arrived. He seemed a bit surprised to see his nephew, but this was soon replaced by his interest in what Hezekiah had brought in the packages.

"Hey boy, what you gat dere?"

"Uncle, I aint see you in so long. How you doin', man?"

"Everything Okay, although tings kinda rough right now but I tryin' to make it, you know. I wasn't expecting you til next week. Ida told me you wasn't coming til next week…."

"Sorry about that, Uncle Cardy." This was an awkward moment.

"Kiah, let's go inside, then." Once inside, Cardy did not wait for an invitation, but he immediately began to remove and sample everything that Hezekiah had brought in the box.

Cardy reassured his guest, "Well son, look like we guh have some conch stew dis evening. Dis dry conch look like it ready for de pot. I guh fix dis before Rosie reach home." Hezekiah smiled warmly as his uncle shuffled about preparing the food. Cardinal Clarke had not changed a bit.

The next week had passed by quickly. Sunset of Friday evening had sneaked up and begun to cast its dusky blanket. As usual, 'over the hill' (which included the area that spread out just beyond Collins Wall and came close to Chippingham) was beginning to morph and assume its coarse and decadent demeanor. McCullough Corner was no different. The summer heat forced people out of their tiny one and two room wooden houses into whatever yard space there was available to be shared by residents of the homes within a particular yard.

Chapter Three

There were many smells that were pleasant and some that were virtually unbearable. The familiar smells of oil lamps and one and two burner oil stoves contrasted with the smell of frying fish, crab fat and dough or guava duff. Yet, one could never escape the foul-smelling odor emanating from the essential structure that served as an outside toilet within each yard. Forming the backdrop to all of this was the heady smell of raw, cheap liquor which could be nauseating to one who was a newcomer to this environment.

Lovers could be seen walking along the narrow street caught up in their own private euphoria. The occasional burst of a woman's garish squawk followed by her guttural laughter, or the echo of a man's menacing voice could be heard as he cursed drunkenly or threatened his wife with his ultimatum. Then there was the tic tac of a Raleigh bike with the large chain guard as someone passed by. These sounds could be both captivating and disturbing.

As usual, an assortment of male personalities had gathered outside of Cardy's two room house (which he shared with his girlfriend) and they were fully engaged in a game of pokeno. "Hey Kiah, you sure you don't want join in. Ain't no sin tuh gamble on a Friday night after yer work hard all week. Come in at least fer one round," said Cardy suggestively. The men sat on makeshift seats and illuminated the area with one oil lamp as they played the card game and gambled.

Although he needed to relax after a week of summer school, Kiah had no interest in gambling, and, even if he considered having a drink, his stomach was still half empty after his mini meal of an extra thin slice of pork chop and white rice, so drinking moonshine would certainly make him feel queasy. "No thanks, Unk Cardy. I'll watch. I'm still tryin' to learn the game."

Cardinal persisted with his line of argument, "O.K. Kiah, but remember, this aint der island. Tings different over here. Yer work hard through de week, so when der weekend come yer gatta have some fun."

Kenny, who was in his early twenties had just begun nurse training at the hospital in Prospect Ridge, he dedicated some of his spare time towards acclimatizing Hezekiah to the sights and sounds of Nassau.

Kenny had taken Hezekiah under his wings. He encouraged his new friend, "Kiah, I don't blame you. If you know what's good for you, you wouldn't start drinking. Don't pick up any of these bad habits you see these fellas carryin' on with around here." Even the more forlorn of the associates nodded in agreement with Kenny.

Then Kenny in his usual style decided to put a different slant on the conversation, "Let me tell you all something. People in Nassau could never be as wicked as people on the island. Out island life aint all paradise."

Cardy interjected, "Man I spend all my life on the island. I from Rolle Town. I never been hungry a day in my life in Exuma. We used to have it so good, hey Kiah. We used to give half the food to the pigs to eat. Look here, the crawfish you all does be killing yourself trying to get in Nassau, man we use that for fish bait, and watermelon – we does feed that to the hogs.

"You serious, man?" asked a fellow named Eddie.

Cardy reassured his audience, "I tell you we always have meat and fish - dry conch, fresh fish, mutton, pork, salt beef, and chicken. You name it, we have it. For relish we had every kind of vegetable - cassava, sweet potato, yam, eddy. I wouldn't talk 'bout roast corn."

Hezekiah was now motivated to join in. He boasted, "Now Uncle Cardy, you know on Sunday morning we'll have potato bread or sweet spongy corn bread, or homemade bread with cane tea. I tell you nobody could bake bread better than my mama. Then Sista used to take a delight in cookin' crab soup with black crabs…"

"Yeah man. Cause the black crabs aint as rank as the white crabs and taste better in soup," chimed Cardy.

"Tell me 'bout the cane tea. How you all make tea from cane?" inquired Bulla Lloyd who lived in the yard next to Cardinal and constantly sucked on his pipe.

"Easy. You grind the cane in the cane mill after you cut it from the field. Then you peel it, cut it in pieces and boil it 'til the juice come out in a pail. After that, take the juice outta the pail, scald it 'til it start to froth, skim it off, strain it in a strainer and you got your cane juice." Kiah boasted confidently.

Eddie asked, "What's a strainer?"

Kiah willingly explained, "Oh, that's a sea fan or sea fanner. You have to use that

Chapter Three

to strain the cane 'til you're left with clear cane juice. Man, when we sit down to eat, everybody gets a big enamel cup of that juice and their own personal plate – each of us had a special blue plate. Then you eat 'til you can't move, man!"

"That's true," agreed Cardy. "If it wasn't for that Greek grocery store out there on East Street or the lil petty shops through these different corners, we'll hardly have anything to eat, right? You know, island people does look out for one another and they aint mean with their neighbors…"

Kenny decided to bring some balance to this one-sided perspective, "Listen here. That's all well and good but you can't tell me anything 'bout those island people. I have personal experience. You see me here? I am a living testimony that some of those people does deal in darkness and wickedness."

"What you mean by that, man?" quizzed Spy who had positioned himself on a large stone near Kenny so that he could hear every word.

"I don't really understand it myself, but you listen to my story, and you could decide. I remember I was small, probably 'bout six or maybe seven years old when this happened."

"Where this happen, my brother?" Spy (who had lost one eye in an accident) was more than curious as he dived into the remains of the tafia that he had been drinking. He was sitting so close to Kenny now that he was almost under his arm. Others began to gather also like the annoying insects that were attracted to the flickering lamp light. The surrounding darkness formed an ominous backdrop behind the sapodilla tree that they sat under.

"We were still living in Mangrove Cay, then. And just like typical lil children, I remember just being happy and runnin' all over the place jus' enjoyin' everything, playin' and havin' fun. It was summertime on the island, you know, so life was perfect, and everybody was relaxed."

Herbie stopped chewing tobacco for just a minute, spat on the ground and urged, "Get on with the story, man. You want us grow beard before you finish, eh?"

"I getting' to it. I getting' to it, man. But, you have to understand that even after all these years, I still have a hard time talkin' 'bout this. Before I start, let me tell y'all, as God is my witness, this is what happened." Kenny was leaving no room for doubt. All eyes and ears were attentive to him.

"This was a Sunday afternoon and just after me and the other children had dinner, I went outside to see if I could find any of the neighborhood children to play with. I didn't see anybody nearby, so I decided to pass by the playground. It so happen that the playground was near the Catholic church and Father Elias Cruikshank, who was from England lived right next door. He was new to the parish and middle-aged. Sometimes, the people used to complain that he was tryin' to make too many changes and he was too old-fashioned. You know Out Island people could be stubborn and like to follow their old traditions. Still, most people liked him.

I had just spotted a couple of my friends playin' in a neighbor's yard when Father called to me and ask me to bring one of the hymnals from the church for him. He told me I could go through the side door he always used to get in the church easily from his house. He stood on his porch just a few yards away waiting for me to come back.

I just went skipping along. There was a lot of grass. Then I remember running through something that looked like pieces of hard tear-up paper that was in the grass near the church door. That area was a bit moist. I jus' playfully kicked some of the pieces outta my way and went inside as Father told me.

Within seconds, I was in and out of the church and gave Father Cruikshank the hymnal. The sun was blazing down. Suddenly, I felt tired and thirsty, so I decided not to play anymore, and turned back to go home. By the time I got home, although it was quite nearby, I felt feverish and drained. I turned the doorknob and by then I hardly could walk. I told my Mama I wanted to lie down because I didn't feel so good.

I was tired but I couldn't get any rest. My legs started hurtin'. I had bad, bad pain. Mama was strugglin' all by herself to raise me, my sister and two brothers, so you know we didn't have much. I remember that hand-me-down pants I was wearin'. The legs was cut off couple inches below the knee. As I hang my feet off the bed, I remember screaming when I saw my legs. My sister came runnin' and Mama heard me too. My legs were purple and so swollen that the veins looked as if they would pop outta my skin. Mama had to tear my pants' legs open to help my circulation. I hollered in pain and terror when I saw that even my feet were smooth and tautly swollen to almost twice their normal size." Kenneth was unveiling the graphic image of his affliction when he was interrupted by a latecomer.

Chapter Three

Montie, another one of the regulars, had not caught the beginning of the story, but he had heard enough that his eyes were riveted on the narrator as he asked, "Kenny, how you manage, man?"

"Believe me, that wasn't the worse part. When I tried to stand up, it was a good thing Mama and my big Sis was there holding me 'cause I woulda fall to the ground. I couldn't walk." Kenny had an expression on his face which indicated that he could not believe it himself.

"You know how long I was like that? Six years! I couldn't walk, go to school, play with my friends, and you know this was a difficult time for my mama." Kenny continued to tell his tale.

"For years I had to stay home either lying in bed or sittin' up in a chair on the porch. Father Cruikshank came to see me and prayed with me whenever he got a chance. He went back to England a few months after I got sick though. Although the swelling had disappeared, I was cripple. Since I couldn't go to school, the Catholic nuns used to take turns teaching me my lessons so that I could keep up with the other children. People in the neighborhood thought I had polio and did whatever they could to help my mother. When the flying doctors came to our settlement, one of them who came by to see me said it was not polio, but he couldn't understand what was wrong with me. The nurse used to check on me at least once a week but for all those years there wasn't any improvement.

Then, one day, a family friend of ours came by askin' 'bout me. I almost forgot about him because he been in Nassau for a couple of years and did not come back. He was a Haitian man. I never knew his real name, but I remember that he was only slightly taller than I was and we used to call him Shorty. Shorty was humble, soft-spoken, and willing to do any kind of work to earn a living.

One day, Shorty surprised us and appeared out of nowhere. He greeted my mother like he used to see us every day. 'Mammy, where your boy, Kenny? That's my lil fwend. I don't see him outside. Where he is?'

As I sat inside, I could hear her talking to Shorty. My mother answered with tears runnin' down her face, 'He right in there, Shorty. Go look at him. He can't walk.' For years, I hardly left the yard, and when I did, my brothers, sister or mother had to lift me, and sometimes the neighbors used to help.

Shorty peeped in the room, then when he stepped inside our tiny front room he stopped suddenly and started holdin' his hand over his nose like he was warding off a bad smell. I couldn't understand this 'cause I didn't smell anything. He walked up to me, looked at me closely and said to my mother, 'Mammy, I sorry, so sorry Mammy. This bad things, bad people. One something in de boy is poison, but I see if I could help do something. Do exactly what I say, OK, Mammy?' Shorty was trembling as he spoke to Mama. 'I come back soon, soon to help you, Mammy, OK?' After this, we didn't see Shorty for a couple of days, and I almost forgot what he promised.

Our friend came back that next weekend before midday. Shorty was holding a medium-sized glass bottle filled to the brim with a thick, black, gooey mixture. He was talking to Mama, telling her what to do. At first, Mama looked scared because she was shaking her head, but eventually she decided to do what Shorty suggested.

Shorty reminded my mother, 'Mammy do jus' what I say, every, every 'ting, alright?' Shorty glanced back at me once, then he was gone.

My mother calmly told me, 'Ken, drink this now, all of it. Swallow every drop.' I swallowed and wanted to vomit. The taste was horrible, I tell you. Because it was so thick, it was like I was swallowing slime and sludge. Mama had to hold my mouth open and beg me to keep it down. I shuddered and shivered just to make it stay down. Then I went to bed and tried to go to sleep.

I woke up in a cold sweat around midnight. The twisting pressure in my stomach caused me to wake up. It feel like something was ringing my stomach and forcing something that was too big through my body. My belly was hurting so bad that I was groaning and doubled up in pain. My mother, brothers and sister came running to help me. 'I need to go to the toilet, Mama. Take me to the toilet!' I begged.

Mama let them lift me and instead made me sit on a white slop bucket to relieve myself. She stayed with me but told the other children to leave. I couldn't understand what was happening to me, but I felt a bearing down pressure and a gush of something that I can't describe. All I know is that there was a swoosh as it forced its way out of me along with everything else.

A couple of minutes later, it was all over. Mama lift me off the bucket, clean me up and put me on the chair nearby. I could see it. In the middle of all that had come out of me was a small octopus-looking creature. Yes, a black, slimy,

Chapter Three

nasty-looking octopus. It was trying to get out of the bucket, but the bucket was too deep and Mama covered it, anyway.

By this time, the other children were there too. My oldest brother, Sam strained to lift the bucket outside with my mother close behind him. I could not believe that all of that stuff had come out of me.

Mama urged, 'Be careful, Sam. Don't let none waste. I have something to pour over that, then we gotta burn everything.' This is exactly what she did. It was the middle of the night, but Mama used kerosene oil and some other stuff to make a bonfire outside. She quickly burned the whole mess until there was only a burned-out patch by our front door. Now that I think about it, grass or nothin' ever grow in that spot maybe even to this day."

Kenny continued his story, "For a couple of minutes, my family had forgotten about me because of the excitement of the fire. Then they turned around. Everybody's hand went to their mouth. I was standing up in the doorway. Before they could say anything, I began walking toward them. After six years, I was walking. I felt well again." Kenny ended his story triumphantly as he wiped the beads of perspiration from his brow. Those who were gathered in the yard breathed a unified sigh of relief. The men seemed to exhale for the first time since he started this tale.

"I bet Shorty was happy when he came back and see you walking, hey?" asked Montie excitedly, and some in the group nodded in support.

Kenny completed his story. "Oh, I almost forgot. This is the curious part. Next day, me and Mama went to look for Shorty where he said he used to live just a mile or so away. We asked about Shorty but, you know, those people told us they didn't know anybody named Shorty. Now you know, on the island everybody knows everybody, right? Well, even after we described him, everywhere we went trying to find him, no one on the cay or on the mainland had seen or heard of any such person. We never knew where Shorty went and never saw him again."

Kenny ended his story by saying, "I believe Mama understood what really happened, but from that day we never talked about Shorty or the awful things that I had gone through. It was only years afterwards that I figured it out. You see, somebody must be put down something for Father Cruikskank. Remember him? They were tryin' to 'fix' him. But what happen was I walked on the shredded pieces that somebody put down for Father to walk on. That was supposed to kill him, I guess, but instead I got it. Although I suffered a lot, the only reason that didn't kill me was because it wasn't meant for me. I think even Father Cruikshank understood the evil around him and that's why he went back home. And Shorty – He was my good angel who saved me from a life of misery." The group was enthralled by the mesmerizing tale and for the rest of the night, the conversation kept circling around the subject of obeah.

At first, the summer days in Nassau seemed to pass by slowly. Hezekiah was feeling worn and beaten up by his living situation. Despite being paid twelve pounds and six shillings per month for three years as a monitor, he had little control of his finances. Sometimes he struggled with the fact that Mama had insisted that he send most of his summer school wages back home to her; Hezekiah knew that those funds enabled the family to subsist, especially since Papa had come home from the Contract. Through the week, Cardy and his girlfriend did not eat proper meals or cook, so Hezekiah was left to fend for himself. On most days, he felt that he did not have enough to eat, and his abode was discouraging. One Sunday afternoon, shortly after he had arrived from Exuma, Hezekiah was feeling particularly discouraged. When he found himself alone with a sober Uncle Cardy, he jokingly confronted him, "Uncle Cardy, you ever think about getting' outta dis mess, dis muck and dis mire over de hill and going back home or moving someplace else?"

"Who me? What I guh do on the Out Island, anyhow? Aint no jobs there and I aint guh be no farmer or fisherman! Das why I never gone on the Contract!" retorted Cardinal.

Hezekiah grumbled, "Sometimes, I miss Steventon so much, I just feel like packin' up and going back home or another island 'cause things really tough here in Nassau."

"Kiah, you know what your problem is? You need to be makin' yer own money. You can't keep takin' care of your Mama dem for the rest of yer life. You need to make a life fer yourself, you know," Cardinal stated candidly. "Your Mama dem need to understand that," he added.

"Now Uncle Cardy, you know that's easier said than done. I just don't know what to do," replied Hezekiah in frustration. "You know Mama and Papa had all of us, struggle to take care of us, and now we supposed to help them."

Chapter Three

Hezekiah began to accept the fact that his Uncle Cardy was not about to change his lifestyle and probably could never understand his nephew's dilemma.

Cardy had learned to cope with his problems years ago. He drank alcohol more than he ate food. Being the naturally gregarious person that he was, as often as they came, Cardy welcomed the motley crew of ne'er-do-wells, hangers-on, and philosophers into his yard. Hezekiah was even more disturbed by the fact that there was never a shortage of alcohol to imbibe, while nourishing food was often a scarce commodity. Cardy's girlfriend Rosie, a plump lady from Cat Island who was at least ten years younger than Cardy, usually sat on the porch quietly watching the fellows while they gambled. When Cardy was clearly too intoxicated to be aware of whether he was winning or losing, Rosie would coax him to leave while struggling to get his lanky body inside the house.

Chapter Four

With one foot slightly elevated, he posed on the other. The majestic, rust-colored rooster penetrated the early morning air with his well-known rendition which awakened the tightly knit 'over-the-hill' community.

Gradually, doors creaked open and wooden windows yawned outward to welcome the new day. As the neighborhood slowly awoke, Jenny stepped onto the narrow porch as she often did to cherish the morning air that carried the blended aromatic scents of various flowering plants which grew wild and provided a contrast in the otherwise desolate yard. As she escaped the confines of the two-room wooden abode, she realized that it must have rained sometime during the night.

Jenny stepped lightly off the porch, and her slippers sank softly into the loose, moist dirt and debris which covered the ground. She carefully tipped along the pathway behind her home as she made her way to the small wooden outhouse which the three families who lived in the yard shared communally. She ignored the ever-present malodorous haze which emanated from the structure and noted casually that the latch on the door of the rickety toilet seemed as if it could fall off at any moment. Jenny gingerly stepped inside. The two crudely utilitarian holes were vacant, awaiting the next patron who would sit there. She deftly used a short stick to secure the door from the inside by hooking it inside a piece of rope which she tightly wound and knotted around a nail near the door. She had to protect her privacy.

As she returned to the porch to position herself on the stool, Jenny was deep in thought. She hoped that today would be different. She needed an opportunity

Chapter Four

– any opportunity – although she knew that they were few and far between. Her thoughts were briefly punctuated by the animated departure of her Uncle Maurice; his tall frame in overalls easily leaped off the porch as he departed for work at the shipyard. As he had brushed past her, he grunted something that was probably not too pleasant, and she cringed ever so slightly. She watched her uncle, who was her grandmother's son, walk until he disappeared down East Street and she felt relieved. She guessed that it was probably just about 6:30 a.m. The mild hint of a cool breeze caressed her face and comforted her.

Jenny acknowledged that for as long as she could remember, poverty and lack of opportunity had gripped the bowels of men who could just barely feed their families scraps and provide meager supplies for their children. She was also acutely aware that the plight of many single mothers was even more devastating because women could only find a few odd jobs washing and cleaning or baby-sitting for the white folks on the Eastern part of the island. Jenny had not been able to finish school due to personal circumstances, but she knew that she wanted more for herself than to become a charwoman in someone's house; she refused to accept this as her lot in life.

Life had trained Jenny to be tough. Nevertheless, she shuddered as she reflected on the hand that had been dealt to her in her short life and felt disgruntled. Just a decade before, Jenny's father, who was a khaki-colored man with dark-brown, curly hair in his mid thirties had been a carpenter by trade. He had been working for the Baxters in Orange Hill for many years as a handyman doing odd jobs for them each day (and sometimes on weekends). She remembered that each day her papa used to set out at dawn and walk to and from work 'out west'. Theophilus and Alsaida (Saidie) Thompson (Jenny's parents) had very little in terms of worldly possessions, but they had done their best to provide the necessities for their two young daughters. Their mother sacrificed to ensure that the girls participated in the Girls Lydia Club which was a club for young girls to teach them social skills and graces along with sewing and other activities which appealed to girls; Jenny and her sister Leah loved it. The girls wore cute little dresses with matching accessories and shoes whenever they were going out, especially to church. Jenny, the fairer of the two sisters, was nick-named "Shamba" (meaning "red girl") which Jenny hated, and some even referred to her as having "good hair" because her hair was ginger-colored and moderately soft in texture. While Jenny was robust and rather athletic in physique, Leah was dark and slight in stature with shoulder length, coarse hair like her mother.

Jenny's mind meandered down the corridors of her memory, and she smiled subconsciously. She cherished those playful school yard memories of spinning top, shooting marbles, playing hopscotch, and especially playing 'porking' (She knew she had been able to throw a ball with precision at her intended target resulting in agonizing pain). Jenny was always fiercely protective of her sister. Of course, if any boy or girl meddled with her or antagonized her sister Leah, there would be a mean fight in which she would always be the victor.

She smiled as she reflected on all the rote learning, the rhymes, recitations, songs and hymns that had become a part of the school routine. Her memories of attending Western Junior School on Hospital Lane were indelible. There were so many things that the teachers had inculcated in her and all the other children that she knew she could never forget them for the rest of her life. As a young girl, she remembered being fascinated by stories about a place far away that had a king who ruled over British colonies like The Bahamas. Jennifer recalled how she and all the children sang patriotic songs in school such as "We'll never let the old flag fall, for we love it best of all. We don't want to fight to show our might, but when we start, we'll fight, fight, fight…." After all, it was what their parents had also been taught to appreciate. Quite naturally, it was instilled in Jennifer and her peers that they were to revere Britain and the Union Jack. Jennifer recollected Empire Day, which was celebrated annually on May 24, as the capstone of the people's allegiance. On that day, Bahamian school children throughout the archipelago gathered for this public celebration and affirmation of the people's pride in being a part of the British empire. This event was duplicated throughout the islands of the Bahamas. In Nassau, school children, smartly dressed in their school uniforms, stood in the sweltering heat on Clifford Park waving small British flags and shouting "Rule Britannia" as British government officials and dignitaries drove by. This was worthwhile for the children who were given a bag of treats for their participation. It was a spectacular affair that glorified British rule.

Jennifer recalled how, with their usual excitement, she and her sister would scurry to get dressed and make their mama proud as they held hands and skipped to school. Duncombe All-Age School was a one-room building located not far away on Lewis Street. Her mind suddenly shifted to the day of the Burma Road Riot and with good reason. On this fateful day, June 1st, 1942, everything seemed to be moving in slow motion. At that moment, she and the other school children had been on the playground frolicking. As usual, even as they played sometimes with separate groups of children, Jenny was keeping a careful watch over her more vulnerable sister who was eleven although she

Chapter Four

herself was two years younger. Suddenly, their play was punctuated by one of their teachers, Miss Wildgoose, who was shouting to the children to get back into the building immediately. Almost simultaneously, the school bell rang, so the children returned without hesitation.

Once they were inside, the head teacher, Mrs. Roker, belted out her instructions, "You all must go home now, quickly. There's trouble and fighting on the streets. You have to go now. Go straight home, you hear?" Jenny saw the look of fear and confusion on Mrs. Roker's face and Jenny, like the other children, did as she was instructed. Leah latched onto her sister's left hand and, like one unified ball of energy, Leah and Jenny stopped for no one until they got to their corner. Their school mates did likewise as they scattered into the various alleyways and streets west of Collins Wall near the East Street and Market Street area.

It was late morning, and it never occurred to the siblings that their Mama, Saidie, probably was not at home. To augment her husband's meagre income, Saidie used to wash clothes and iron for several families in the neighborhood such as Miss Thomas through McCullough Corner and Mrs. Bastian who had a shop several corners away on Taylor Street. Saidie was a dark, slightly built woman who had been complaining of chest pains for several months, yet she never hesitated to take a job if the opportunity arose. Jenny and Leah both uttered a yelp of delight and held out their arms as they turned into Hay Street and saw their Mama's yellow kerchief tied around her medium length, plaited ponytail. Saidie was smiling and holding out her arms to receive her children. (A tear now trailed down Jenny's face as she reflected and yearned for that tender touch that she held onto only in precious memories.) The girls knew at that moment that they would be safe despite what was going on around them. After Mama had gotten word of the Burma Road riot and the violence on Bay Street, she had abandoned Miss Thomas' wooden washboard and tin tub and apologized to her employer stating that she had to get home and ensure that her children would be safe. Mama smelled like the octagon soap that she had been scrubbing clothes with, and the girls joyfully buried themselves in her dress. That night Papa had come home exhausted and a bit battered. He limped into the house and slumped onto the nearest chair complaining that he had been gun-butted and had to run for his life while he was coming from work.

Mr. Thompson explained to his family, "It look like war going on out there. People stabbing and killing up one another. I didn't know what was goin' on 'til I tried to go on Bay Street to buy something for you all to eat but it look like all hell was breakin' loose out there. Mind you, I saw people rushin' about, but I didn't pay it no mind. Then when I reach Bay Street, I never see nothin' like that in my life! Men was breakin' open shop windows and plenty looting was goin' on. Seemed like the people dem gone crazy. Then I see the officers comin'. I tried to get away but one of them catch me right here." Mr. Thompson pointed to his forehead where the trickle of blood had partially dried on his forehead. He continued, "I ran away as quick as I could. That's how I get here in one piece." His wife quickly brought a damp cloth and began treating the cut. Despite the misadventure, the family was relieved that nothing worse had happened to him.

For the Thompson children and other young children, the Burma Road Riot was a surreal event that they did not understand so it terrified them. Additionally, the Bahamas was a British colony, and it was World War II. A major problem was created because Bahamian workers and American workers had been hired to build British military bases at a rate of eight shillings per. day. Tensions arose when Bahamian workers discovered that local colonial officials had convinced the company to pay the Bahamian workers four shillings while the white American workers were being paid twice the amount. The Bahamas Federation of Labor attempted to intervene on behalf of the Bahamian workers to no avail. As a result, the Bahamian workers on this project took to the streets from the over-the-hill area where they lived and converged on Bay Street. After they demonstrated in front of the government offices on Bay Street, the men realized that their concerns would not be addressed, so their protests became a riot. There were arrests, serious injuries, and several Bahamian workers lost their lives.

The Thompsons were a very close-knit and loving family despite their financial challenges. Jenny remembered that her Papa had one major weakness at that time which was alcohol. Theophilus Thompson usually remained sober throughout the week (perhaps because he had no money then), however, on a payday Friday he would arrive home quite late smelling of whisky, 'thirty-days' or whatever cheap liquor he could procure, along with nearly empty pockets. Mr. Thompson earned twelve shillings per week, so after he had squandered several shillings away on alcohol and paid the rent man, Saidie was left to juggle the few remaining shillings and pennies to ensure that some food was on the table. The look of chagrin and disappointment would be etched on Saidie's face. Jenny never understood why her Mama never confronted her husband about his irresponsible behavior. Saidie was a gentle, even-tempered woman; Jenny could never recall her parents arguing. Nevertheless, whenever her father brought home a bag of beans or a quart of pigeon peas and some

Chapter Four

rice for the week with no meat except perhaps some pigtails or chicken feet, Mama's face would hold a sadness that reflected a broken heart. Jenny had grown accustomed to seeing her Mama's face fall in despair, and she gradually began to understand why Mama, who was about thirty years old, looked like a much older woman.

Inevitably, Saidie continued to work even while her health declined. Jenny was reminded of the rasping cough that her mother had developed which had become more persistent as the months passed. To make matters worse, after Mama revealed that she was pregnant, Papa was sometimes elated while on other occasions he seemed troubled. The sisters became more fearful and concerned about their mother as she continued to fade from them with each month that passed.

Jenny remembered, how one day when they were playing Doll House under the guinep tree in their backyard, Leah chuckled and remarked to her sister, "We already have to sleep to the foot of the bed now. So the baby must be guh sleep on the roof, eh?"

"Must be chile, cause I ain't know," Jenny agreed absent-mindedly as she attempted to thread a makeshift needle made of a large fish bone that Papa had found and given to her. They laughed together, not truly realizing the seriousness of the family's plight. Naively, they accepted this development in much the same way that they had grown accustomed to being bitten on their toes or fingers almost every night by ravenous rodents. Jenny could never forget how they trembled at night when they heard the rats squeaking and scurrying over the wooden floor doing damage to the little that her family had. Jenny preferred not to think about the times when she and Leah had tried to sneak their rank, urine-soaked bed things onto the clothesline to dry. Although Leah was the older of the two, she had taken much longer to stop wetting their bed cloths which had several layers. The sisters were loyal to each other so on occasions when Mama was tired of this and inquired about who had wet the 'bed', she would have to whip both girls because none would reveal who the unfortunate culprit was.

Now Jenny shuddered as if cold fingers had touched her in the center of her back and she jumped slightly, subconsciously trying to avoid its effect. A slow stream of tears flowed down her light-brown cheeks as she remembered that fateful day. She had no specific date and could not remember the day of the week, but she knew that this was the day when her entire life changed. Not long after the Riot, on a typical school day, Papa had already left for work. For some strange reason, Mama seemed not to be able to get out of bed. The girls could hear their Mama groan in agony at times.

"Mama, you alright?" inquired Jenny as she felt Mama's forehead which felt quite warm and moist.

Mama responded, "I just feeling a lil tired, but I going ter be alright. Just the baby pressin' down on me hard and I having trouble breathing. But don't worry 'bout me. You all get ready for school. This bad feeling soon pass over, okay." Mama reassured her girls as best she could and softly squeezed their hands in hers.

The girls were proud to show their mother that they could bathe and dress themselves without her assistance and they eagerly returned to her. By this time, however, their Mama seemed more distressed and appeared to be doing her best not to disorient her daughters. She whispered anxiously between deep breaths and groans, "Jenny, Leah, I think the baby comin'. Go call Miss Deveaux!"

The sisters were panic-stricken. They had never seen their mother in such a state, so they sprinted to their nearest neighbor whose house was located just a few yards from theirs in the same yard.

They called out desperately while knocking briskly on the door, "Miss Deveaux, Mama sick! Mama sick! She say the baby comin'. You could help us, please, ma'am? Mama say for you to come there." insisted Jenny.

Miss Deveaux came to the door, with dripping wet hands and still dressed in her night clothes. Leah tearfully explained, "Mama say she feel like the baby comin'. We don't know what to do, and Papa gone to work. Mama ask for you to come, please!"

"Lord Jesus, what is this? An' I gat my chirrun ter get ready fer school, too. Tell yer Mama I comin' soon directly. You all girls go back ter yer Mama til I come. I ger let dese set put on dey clothes, den I comin', you hear?" said Miss Deveaux who was trying to navigate through the confusion of this situation. Miss Deveaux was a buxom lady in her early forties, was a single parent of five children, however, the oldest was a fifteen-year-old girl who was able to help her younger siblings to prepare for school.

Chapter Four

Jenny tried hard to recollect the rest of the events that took place that day, but even after all those years, much of what had occurred that day came to her in disjointed blurs. She brooded over the fact that, despite her protests, she and Leah were forced to go to school that day. She remembered that their walk to school was labored; they cried and clutched hands more tightly because they could feel that something was terribly wrong. Silently, each prayed that their Papa would miraculously return and do something to help their mother.

Immediately after school, the girls practically flew home only to find that Hay Street was strangely still and quiet. The large sapodilla tree loomed ominously as they entered the front of the yard. Jenny and Leah looked for their mama, but, instead, they spotted Miss Deveaux's ample body draped over the stool on the porch. She was wearing a strange, vacant expression on her face that they could not understand. The girls stepped cautiously into their yard.

"Where Mama, Miss Deveaux?" Jenny and Leah echoed each other.

"I so sorry. O Lord, I so sorry!" Miss Deveaux groaned, and the girls became confused. Her voice was breaking as she released the dreadful news,

"Leah, Jenny, your Mama gone – she didn't make it."

"What you mean she ain't make it?" asked Jenny incredulously.

"Your Mama was real sick and she had a hard time when the baby was coming. Saidie was too weak. Girls, she dead!"

The girls screamed wretchedly and fell into her lap as Miss Deveaux continued talking, almost robotically, "When Mother Nettie, the midwife, reach the house, she couldn't hardly do nothin' to help your Mama. But she save the baby though. You all have a baby brother…" Miss Deveaux's voice trailed off. She shrugged her shoulders and cried softly.

A few curious passersby and neighbors paused to extend their sympathies and then went on their way. The girls heard some neighbors saying that a Catholic priest had come to pray for their mother and read the last rites for her before she expired. Despite Miss Deveaux's efforts to console the sisters as they buried themselves in the woman's ample chest, they felt no comfort or relief.

Jenny remembered sadly that those weeks after Mama's passing went by in a whirl of confusion and uncertainty. Papa had named the baby Justin. At first, Theophilus (Papa) was inconsolable over the loss of his wife. He sank into a depression that could only be slightly relieved by his excessive indulgence in alcohol. Jenny wondered if Papa hated the baby since he never spoke about him. Their father seemed oblivious to their material, physical or emotional needs. Since their mother's death, Jenny and her sister had found themselves being constantly shuffled from one house to another. They were often sheltered and fed by family and people in the community whom they hardly knew. As for their brother Justin, Jenny and Leah had only seen the infant a few times when a kind neighbor or well-wisher had taken them to see him. The sisters never discovered how and when it happened, but they learned that their baby brother was being cared for by a woman named Rachel. Their visits to see Justin were rare because their mother's cousin Rachel who was in her late thirties lived in Coconut Grove which was quite a distance away. Rachel had no children, and it was apparent that she welcomed the opportunity to have a child of her own. Jenny vaguely remembered that he was medium brown-skinned and had a beige-colored birthmark which looked like a small walnut just below his left knee. As the months and years passed by, no one mentioned baby Justin anymore and so it was that memories of him faded as if he had never existed. In her reflections, Jenny noted curiously that Rachel's name was mentioned at her papa's funeral; Jenny had overheard someone saying that Rachel had died while another person contradicted this by saying that Rachel had gotten married to a policeman and moved to one of the Out Islands.

Later, as she grew older, Jenny was tormented by the fact that she had no idea where her little brother was, and no one else seemed to care or was willing to let her know. She was also mortified that she had only been to Marshall View Cemetery on the day when her mother was buried. Whenever she had asked her father to take Leah and her to their mother's gravesite, her father kept promising to do so. As time went on, he became so infuriated by this suggestion that he threatened that he would beat her for being disrespectful. She knew this was no idle threat. In later years, her mother's burial place also became a distant, sad memory.

After months of mourning Saidie's passing, Papa began to spend less time at home, often leaving the two girls to fend for themselves for days. This, unfortunately, was not the worst part. The girls assumed that Papa's pain at the loss of his wife became so unbearable that, subconsciously, he responded in kind to them. Their papa who had previously hardly wanted his little girls'

Chapter Four

feet to touch the ground because he thought that they were so precious began to mete out severe cruelty upon them and impose unreasonable, merciless tasks for them to complete. Jenny cringed as she relived the countless times that they had been severely punished by their father.

Leah, who had previously been a carefree and 'happy-go-lucky' child had grown into a pensive and desperate soul. She sought to stay away from home for as long as she could each day as she dreaded Papa and his relentless wrath. She soon found a way out. By the time that Leah had reached the age of twelve, she had begun to work doing odd cleaning jobs for a few of the neighbors. Thus, she was spared much of Papa's animosity because she was away from the house on most days and usually was given something to eat by her benevolent employers along with a few pennies for her efforts. School soon became a distant memory for her, and Papa never once questioned her or expressed concern that Leah had dropped out of school.

Jenny, on the other hand, had endured much more than her sister. She had to clean the house before going to school. She had to seal a leaky tin tub with Lifebuoy soap each morning, then she would tote water in a bucket from the faucet which was several hundred yards away by Miss Mackey's yard. Quite often, the water would continuously leak out, so she could find herself making up to eight trips in one morning before she could fill the tub. Whenever Papa came home and met the tub empty or there was insufficient water for his bath, Jenny could expect a whipping.

School was another place which filled Jenny with dread. Almost every school morning, she was late for school because she could not complete her household chores on time. As she stepped up to the gate of Western Senior School on Blue Hill rd., she would hear the school bell ringing. The headmaster would be standing there with his cane outstretched waiting for the latecomers. He asked no questions as he towered over Jenny's terrified and exhausted frame. "Hold out your hand girl and stop wasting my time!" he would bellow. He hit his target several times with precision due to years of experience and waved his weapon for her to go to class. Tears came to her eyes as she watched the swelling of her reddened hands and she prayed for the hours to pass so that this pain would subside. As soon as school ended, she looked around for nothing or anyone as she ran home with robust strides to face whatever awaited her. Papa expected Jenny to prepare something for him to eat, however, he often left no provision for this so Jenny would just sit and wait. Sometimes, in the evening, Leah would bring home a few scraps of meat or a piece of sweet bread if she could sneak it away from her workplace and Jenny gratefully received it. After saving her pennies, (if Papa did not find it first) Leah would sometimes purchase little necessities for her sister and herself.

Jenny remembered that the situation worsened with each year. Papa brought less and less money home and she relied even more upon the benevolence of people in the community for subsistence. There were people like Mrs. Pinder who, despite having a family of her own, would always provide Jenny, her sister and other children who stopped at her door with a hot slice of bread covered with Oleo margarine to fill their stomachs after school; Mrs. Pinder and her rock oven were a life saver. About a year after her mother's passing, Jenny's Papa began to spend most of his spare time hanging around a West Indian woman named Miss Sophia Cummings who spoke with a strange snappy accent. She made her disdain for the girls quite apparent as her only utterances towards them were threats and insults. Jenny visualized the time when her school shoes had developed holes. The shoes had become so worn that they refused to stay on her feet, so she waited to appeal to her father for a new pair when he came home. Just before dark, she desperately searched for her father at his sweetheart's house only to be told by Miss Sophie, "You better get from round here, you lil red heifer! If you wan' pretty up in new shoes, you better get up off your lazy ass and go work! You ain't learnin' nuttin' in school no how." What Jenny found most hurtful was that her father never uttered a word in her defense. She missed many days of school because she had no shoes and no school uniform. Her head throbbed as she recollected angrily how her father had asked Miss Sophie to make a school uniform for her. Instead of sewing a pinafore dress and a blouse, the hateful woman had sewn the pinafore and added sleeves and a collar so that it was an over-sized one-piece dress rather than what was required. Her father's threats to punish her if she refused to wear the ill-fitting uniform mostly annoyed Jenny. Jenny was more concerned about attending school as often as possible, so she swallowed her pride and withstood the cruel teasing of some insensitive students.

As the years passed, Jenny had learned to look forward to weekends, holidays, and the long summer breaks. It was during those times that she spent many hours at Mrs. Eunice Allen's house; she had gradually taken Jenny under her wings soon after she had lost her mother. At every opportunity, the girl would find herself at Mrs. Allen's side. Mrs. Allen was a popular seamstress who took a special interest in her protégée. Mrs. Allen lived in a two-story house that was tastefully furnished and filled with lovely flowing curtains that she had made to accompany the many decorative pieces and souvenirs which fascinated Jenny

Chapter Four

and took her into a different world. Mrs. Allen was impressed by the girl's manual dexterity and keenness to learn. It was under this lady's supervision that Jenny began to acquire exceptional sewing and cooking skills. Despite her personal circumstances, she was becoming a refined and polished young lady. Although Mrs. Allen had six children of her own and a husband, her compassion and concern for Jenny inspired her to treat Jenny as one of her own. Jenny was helpful, cooperative, and appreciative of Mrs. Allen and never did anything to disappoint her. She was leaving her teen years and emerging into womanhood gracefully despite the hardships that she had faced. For years, Mrs. Allen had fed her daily whenever she came by, and she offered her clothes from time to time. On some special occasions, this genteel lady would dress Jenny in a lovely dress and afford her the opportunity to attend St. Agnes Anglican church with the Allen family. Mrs. Allen's children treated her like their sibling.

Fortunately for Jenny, there were several other artisans who had established their businesses in East Street and nearby areas. One of the neighbors, Ms. Claudia Brown, was an enterprising lady who knew of her situation and had reached out to Jenny. She had introduced Jenny to some simple ways of earning money. For example, Ms. Brown and her family used to distribute small decorative shells by the quart. People in the neighborhood like Jenny used to collect these shells from Ms. Brown and arrange them on strings to make necklaces then return batches of these strings of necklaces to Ms. Brown who would pay them for the items. Jenny engaged in this activity on a weekly basis which helped her to earn a shilling or two per week when the shells were available. As Jenny entered her late teen years, she became even more adept at using a sewing needle. The Pennerman family who lived through Mason's Addition had set up a business where they used to plait bags, fans, and hats from silver and white top trees. Jenny often worked along with these people sewing linings into plaited bags or sewing shells and raffia onto these bags. The finished products were always extremely beautiful and in high demand by those who could afford them. These bags would then be sold at places like J P Sands store, which was near the Bank Slit behind Royal Bank, at the local Straw Market and at other stores on Bay Street. By these means, Jenny was able to take care of her basic needs.

Jenny's reflections soon returned to the matter at hand that had consumed her thoughts since she had awakened. She desperately needed a steady job. Since her father had passed away two years before, she found herself living with her paternal grandmother (Maude Smith) along with her uncle who treated her as if she was a disease that he wished he did not have and needed to be rid of. Uncle Maurice (better known as Mo) often exhibited his meanest behavior during his frequent tirades when he would insist that Jenny pack up her things and leave the house. Jenny's grandmother tolerated her, but she was an extra mouth to feed. In more recent times, Jenny was further pressured by her Uncle Maurice who had indicated that she would have to contribute toward the rent very soon, and this was a matter that troubled her because her earnings were inconsistent. Most of the time when Uncle Mo brought something home to cook, it would barely be enough to be shared between Mo and his mother, so Jenny's needs were often overlooked. She was thankful for her mentor Mrs. Allen who continued to advise her and provide for her in any way that she could. However, since all of Mrs. Allen's children had completed school, she had begun to travel to the United States, and sometimes spent several weeks there visiting her children, one of whom was married and had recently given birth to a child. Regrettably, it was on many of these occasions that Uncle Mo would choose to forcibly eject Jennifer from the house at night.

"You better find somewhere to go girl 'cause we can't keep takin' care uh you," Mo would snap at her. Nevertheless, she would remain on the porch and cry into her lap because she had nowhere to go.

Then later in the night, Mo would check to see if the girl had left and, as always, she would still be there and he would retort, "You can't understand, eh? We don't have nowhere fer you to stay. We can't feed you and you aint servin' no purpose here anyhow. Take yer georgy bundle an' leave!" Sometimes the humiliation and harassment went on until early the next morning.

Jenny's grandmother would usually wait until her wretched son fell asleep, then she would peep outside and whisper to Jenny, "Come chile, come lie down and rest yourself 'cause I know you tired. Don't mind Mo. He don't mean nothin' by it. Go sleep. It soon mornin'." Then the elderly woman would sigh and return to her bed. It was the best that she could do.

One morning, Jenny was particularly apprehensive because Mrs. Allen had asked her to come to her house. She wanted to discuss a particular matter with her. Mrs. Allen was all that Jenny had except for her sister Leah who had been working as a live-in maid for several years which provided her with food, shelter, and a small income. For about a year, Leah had been working with a family on Eastern Rd. who were formerly from Abaco. Leah exuded a carefree spirit which appealed to her employers because she always seemed to be enthusiastic. In fact, the Alburys sometimes asked her to accompany them to care for their young children when they travelled abroad. Coincidentally,

Chapter Four

on the same morning that Jennifer had the appointment with Mrs. Allen, Leah presented herself to Jennifer with her bags packed and her heart-shaped face glowing with joy. Her black hair was pulled back in a short ponytail, and she wore a pink hat tied with a ribbon that matched her dress. Before Jennifer could tell Leah how nice she looked, Leah gushed out the words excitedly, "Jen I have a job in the States! I'm leaving today. I'm going to work for some white people minding their children. Miss you. Love you! I will come back an' see you soon as I can, okay." Leah and Jenny hugged each other tearfully then Leah hopped into the waiting car and was gone. Jenny missed her sister dearly, but she learned to accept this situation just as she had grown to accept other circumstances that she had to endure.

After Jenny ensured that she was properly dressed, she waved and said, "I gone Grumma. I'm comin' back later, okay?" Jenny's heart was beating fast as she wondered if she had done something to offend Mrs. Allen. She loved Mrs. Allen dearly and knew that the latter would be devastated if anything ever happened to affect this relationship.

Jenny was comforted when Mrs. Allen greeted her warmly at the door and welcomed her inside. She offered Jenny a sweetened cup of hot pear leaf and ginger tea with a chunk of warm Johnny cake and butter which she gladly accepted. As they sat in the well-ventilated living room, the sunlight peaked in through the space separating the curtains which swayed lightly as the breeze blew from the east.

Mrs. Allen asked Jenny how she was doing and inquired about her grandmother as well to which Jenny responded that all was well.

"Well Jenny, I was wondering if you've been thinking about what you are going to do with yourself. I would like to see you do much better. Do you have any plans?" asked Mrs. Allen gently.

"No ma'am. I mean yes, I've been thinking. I want to get a job so I could take care of myself," replied Jenny nervously.

"What kind of job do you think you could do, Jen? You like sewing or cooking maybe?" asked Mrs. Allen.

Jen looked shyly at Mrs. Allen and sighed, "Well, I wish …."

"Jen, I know you are a smart girl. I want to help you. If I pay for some typing classes for you, you think you might like office work?"

"Yes ma'am!" shrieked Jenny. Her face was flushed with excitement. She jumped out of the chair and rushed over to her benefactor to hug her. "O Mrs. Allen, I will not disappoint you. Thank you so much!" The tears streamed down her eyes. She could not believe what she was hearing.

"I could send you to Flowers Typing School on Market Street. At least you could get a start there. That might help you to get a job and you'll be able to go from there. I've tried to put a little money aside for you. I wish I could've done more for you but there was only so much I could do because of my own family …." Mrs. Allen's voice tapered off. "This is the best I could do to help you although I wish I could do more." explained Mrs. Allen as she patted Jenny on her shoulder.

"Yes ma'am. I understand." Jenny responded in acknowledgement.

"I will take you to Miss Flowers myself so you could get started on your classes right away. I'm going away for a month or two soon so I'll pay for your classes in advance, and you wouldn't have to worry about that."

Jenny felt like she was walking on clouds as she went to and from classes several times each week. She was a keen learner, and her instructor was impressed by the level of proficiency that Jenny was demonstrating after just a few weeks. Although her living situation had not changed, Jenny began to look at herself differently. For the first time in her life, she had looked closely into her own face and liked what she saw. Jenny was moderately slim, yet most would regard her as being physically well-built. Interacting with Mrs. Allen and her family had taught her to be graceful and genteel in her demeanor. Even with limited resources at her disposal, Jenny began taking a little more time fixing her hair. She even built up the courage to make her hair more manageable by straightening it with a hot comb which enabled her stretched-out brown tresses to rest neatly on her shoulders. When she looked in the mirror, she smiled and was always thankful that her once gingerish-brown hair had matured into a more tolerable brown color. Although her clothes were modest, Jenny always used her ingenuity to ensure that whatever she wore complemented her physique. For the first time in many years, she felt alive.

By another amazing stroke of luck, one afternoon, Mrs. Flowers presented a proposition to Jenny when the other students had left. "Jenny, I am really

Chapter Four

impressed at how fast you learned to type. You are just a natural. Have you started looking for a job, yet?"

"No ma'am. I still have plenty to learn. I am going to wait 'til classes finish, then I'm going to look for a job," explained Jenny.

Mrs. Flowers was a settled African American lady with medium length salt and pepper hair which she kept pulled back in a tight bun and wore little round spectacles. Her husband had worked at the R. A. F. base and Jenny got the impression that he had served in the U.S. army. Mrs. Flowers indicated that Mrs. Allen had befriended her from the early years when she had first come to The Bahamas.

"Well, you are truly my star pupil, Jenny. Mrs. Allen has been my friend since we were young women, and she always speaks very highly of you like you were one of her children." She paused momentarily then revealed her thoughts. "I think I know where I could get you a little job, but it is only for two weeks while the person is on vacation. That'll give you a start."

Jenny beamed with delight as light tears welled up in her eyes and moistened her face, "Mrs. Flowers, I don't know how to thank you!"

"Now, don't thank me yet 'cause I have to talk to the Commissioner first to make sure, O.K.?" added Mrs. Flowers. "I'll let you know when you come back tomorrow, Jenny," she assured the excited young lady. Then she quickly checked, "You eighteen, right?"

"Umm yes ma'am. I turned eighteen last month!" The words seemed to gush out of Jenny's mouth while she was running out of the door and trying to catch her breath at the same time.

Jenny started work at the Chief Out Island Commissioner's office on the following Monday. The small office was nestled upstairs over Mr. Willie Weeks' Bicycle Shop in his building on Bay Street. Commissioner Bowe was personable and patient. He referred to Jenny as "Miss Thompson" and treated her with the utmost respect. The office consisted of three rooms which included the commissioner's office, the main office where Jenny sat behind a desk with a typewriter, and a bathroom with a flush toilet. This was Jenny's first encounter with such a modern convenience, so she approached it with caution and appreciation and inquired about its function before using it. For two weeks she assumed the responsibilities of the gentleman who normally performed such clerical duties as stamping and delivering letters, conveying information to and from various government departments, along with some light typing. Mr. Bowe had given her some concise yet helpful instructions about her duties and she carried these out with precision. Jenny treasured this opportunity and worked like her life depended on it.

There were not many visitors to the office, and these were usually related to official business. On the Monday of her second week there, at about 10:00 a.m. there was a brief knock at the door made of jalousie panes, so Jenny could tell that someone was trying to peer inside. "Come in," She said calmly.

The young man entered and greeted her politely. He wore a quizzical expression as he asked, "Is Mr. Whylly here? I came to collect my check."

"He isn't here right now but I will try to help you. What's your name please?" She responded using her best professional voice.

"My name is Hezekiah Eugene Rolle." He smiled at Jenny broadly as he spoke.

"I'll be right back," she assured the visitor, then walked lightly towards the commissioner's office, knocked and went inside.

After a moment, Jenny returned and told the visitor that the commissioner wished to speak with him. Hezekiah thanked her and went inside the commissioner's office.

Three minutes later, Hezekiah exited Commissioner Bowe's office with a small envelope in hand and spoke to Jenny, "Thanks a lot. I really appreciate it." He walked toward the door, looked back at her momentarily then appeared to change his mind, but he said pleasantly, "Have a nice day."

"You too, Mr. Rolle," she replied and reciprocated with a smile.

Chapter Five

Summer was basically over. Hezekiah had some decisions to make. He had been a monitor for several years and was ready to take the next step and begin his teaching career. He had grown accustomed to life in the city. For several years he had been coming to summer school in Nassau for training and with each passing day, he felt less inclined to return to his old routine in Exuma. Even with the challenges, at twenty, he had experienced relative independence in Nassau and could not quite wrap his mind around the thought of being dictated to by his parents anymore.

Hezekiah had gradually adapted to living with his Uncle Cardinal (who was his father's younger brother) during the last two summers. Uncle Cardie was as different from Papa as day was from night. Truthfully, Papa had worked hard all his life, but he certainly never could look as 'war-torn'. Although he was probably in his early forties, the scars on Cardinal's face and arms reflected that he had been in more than a few bar room scuffles and street fights during the fifteen years that he had been living in Nassau. In previous years, Hezekiah used to pack up his dirty clothes and send them back on the mailboat to his mother to be cleaned while she would send a suitcase full of clean and ironed clothes in return. However, this year, he only sent his clothes back twice for cleaning while he attended summer school. His friend Kenny had patiently taught him how to care for his laundry. In a few weeks, he had become quite proficient at the task of washing and ironing his own clothes although he enjoyed neither. Mama, on the other hand, was extremely disturbed by her son's strange behavior and she vowed to come to Nassau soon to discover the reason for this turn of events.

Kenny had been a good tour guide for Hezekiah when he could find the time and had taught him well. After having spent two summers in Nassau, Hezekiah could now navigate his way around the 'over the hill' area quite impressively and he felt almost comfortable. His favorite places were all within walking distance. The Hillside Theatre was located just outside Mason's Addition and another favorite hangout of moviegoers was the Cinema Theatre which was also a stone's throw away on the corner of Lewis Street and East Street. Kenny did advise Hezekiah that if you really wanted to impress a girl, you ought to take her to see a movie at the Capital Theatre on Market Street because it was more sophisticated than the other two. There were also numerous petty stores and eateries sprinkled throughout the Bain Town and Grants Town area. Once a week (usually on a Friday), when he decided to treat himself to fish, he could buy a snack comprised of a grunt and one or two rolls which was delicious from Storr's Store on Eneas Jumper Corner, although it was above the means of most people. Another delicacy for Hezekiah was mutton and peas in the can which he sometimes purchased from Storr's as well to prepare at home. Then, of course, there were the incomparable, world-famous, mouth-watering meals and deserts that were sold at the Palm Tree Restaurant on Market Street until the early morning hours.

One habit that Cardie had which was worse than his addiction to alcohol was gambling. He was such a serious gambler that he hardly went anywhere without his dream book; he was devoted to it. There was not a single day that he did not place a bet or play numbers once he had money. Cardie accepted that he and his nephew had very little in common, but he decided to invite him to go along with him anyway to see his friend Maurice. It was a Friday afternoon, so if Maurice was at home, the three of them would hustle a ride to Hobby Horse Hall in the west. He figured that, hopefully, Hezekiah would be willing to lend his uncle a little money so that he could bet on the horses.

Hezekiah was rather surprised at the invitation. He was a bit hesitant at first, but he had nothing to do right then so he decided to accompany his uncle. Coincidentally, he had just received a fiery letter from his Mama that had come on the mailboat along with a box of fruits, vegetables, and corned fish. In her scathing ultimatum to her son, Mama stated that she expected Hezekiah to be on the next boat to Exuma "… or else." Hezekiah welcomed the opportunity to do something that would take his mind off his troubles for a while.

An unexpected rain shower had cooled the atmosphere considerably. A few people were still walking with umbrellas, but the weather was quite manageable.

Chapter Five

Cardie and Hezekiah turned from East Street onto Toote Shop Corner where Maurice lived. As they walked, he was soon able to see the yard where his friend lived and hoped that he was at home. The men could just make out the form of a young, brown-skinned lady examining clothes on a clothesline as they approached. As she turned to climb the steps to the porch and headed toward the door, she did not see them. Hezekiah immediately paused and whispered to Cardie, "I know her! I mean I saw her before."

"Where you know her from?" inquired Cardie. "That's Mo niece," he added.

"I'll tell you later," said Hezekiah with a sly smile.

"Good day! Jenny, you know if Mo home?" called Cardie to the young woman who was about to disappear into the house.

It was quite apparent that he had startled her because she turned around quickly and answered, "Mo aint home yet."

Then she locked eyes with Hezekiah and said, "You came to the office this week. Uhmm, Mr. Hezekiah Rolle, right?" She checked to ensure that her dress was buttoned properly and felt slightly embarrassed about her worn yard clothes.

"Yes. But you can call me Hezekiah," he added quickly.

Jenny could not conceal her nervousness and embarrassment, but she flashed him a friendly smile anyway. She turned her attention to the older of the two men. "I believe my uncle and his girlfriend might come home soon. You all could wait if you want or I could give him a message," suggested Jenny.

"No, no. That's okay. I'll catch him another time," explained Cardie. He indicated to Hezekiah that he was ready to leave.

"Uncle Cardie, I'll catch up with you in a lil bit. I want to talk to Jenny about something. We could go to the race track another day, okay?" suggested Hezekiah.

Cardie glanced quizzically at his nephew then at the young lady who seemed equally surprised then he walked away.

"I hope I'm not bothering you, but can I talk to you a moment, Jenny?" asked Hezekiah hopefully.

"Okay. What do you want to talk about?" asked Jenny.

"Are you busy right now?"

"Not really. I just came from work though. I didn't expect you to come here – you know, to see me like this…I wish I knew you were coming." Jenny hung her head slightly.

He understood what she was suggesting. "That doesn't bother me Jenny. I like you for who you are."

Jenny looked startled. "But you don't even know me, and you don't know anything about me, Hezekiah.

Hezekiah said gently, "Please call me Kiah. All my friends call me Kiah. I would like to get to know you better if you would let me."

Jenny nodded but kept looking down at her feet. She didn't know what to make of his advances.

"I have so many things to ask you if you don't mind," Kiah said hopefully as he stared more directly into her medium brown eyes. He continued his inquiry, "Is Jenny short for Jennifer?"

She responded in the affirmative and continued to look at her feet. Her mind was racing. What should she do in a situation like this? She had no idea who this young man was and why he could possibly be interested in her. Her legs were suggesting to her that she should sit down for awhile.

For a moment, Jenny began to think that what he was suggesting was probably not such a good idea. She stood up from her chair on the porch and was about to reject his request. "But I really don't know you," she stated.

"Do you mind if I call you Jenny?" Kiah asked.

"No, I don't mind. My name is Jennifer Thompson. You can call me Jenny if you want," she said with a cautious smile.

Chapter Five

"Do you like ice cream, Jenny?" Kiah had been leaning on the verandah, but he stood erect near the steps after Jenny stood up. He waited expectantly for a positive response.

"Yes. I like ice cream."

"Do you want to get some ice cream this afternoon? We could go to Blacks Candy Kitchen and get some if you want. They have all kinds of flavors." Kiah could not hide the excitement in his voice.

"I don't mind, but you need to give me a chance to change," suggested Jenny.

"I'll come back for you in an hour, O.K.? I hope that's enough time for you to get ready."

"That's fine. I'll be ready."

Jenny did not know what to make of this new development. This was a novel experience for her, and she was more than a little flustered.

Hezekiah returned for Jenny exactly an hour later as he had promised. The two engaged in a light-hearted tête-à-tête as they walked towards Bay Street. Once they got onto Bay Street, they turned westward and walked towards West Bay Street where they indulged in some ice cream delicacies sold at Blacks Candy Kitchen. The two were so caught up in each other that they both dismissed the fact that it was customary for black patrons to go to the back window of this establishment and stand on the outside to be served while their white counterparts were allowed to make their purchases inside. Despite its blatant discriminatory practices, this ice cream parlor was a popular spot which attracted people from near and far. They spent at least twenty-five minutes waiting in line for the tasty delights that awaited them, and it was worth it. They walked further westward to the waterfront. The pair was relieved to find a quiet area on the Western Esplanade to sit near a large seagrape tree, and they chatted for an hour or two. Later that evening, as they parted company back at Jenny's home, Hezekiah and Jenny felt as if they had known each other for years. It was not surprising that Hezekiah asked Jenny if he could see her again the following day, then he invited her to see a movie with him that same afternoon.

On that next day, Jenny's Uncle Mo was in a foul mood that his niece was quite familiar with, and he had been drinking a bit that afternoon. She was not surprised when he barked at her, "I see you gettin' dress up to go out again. Who dis man is you goin' out with? He can't jus' come here and take you out without my permission. You aint my child but I's der man of dis house and I'm responsible for you. You better don't bring no problem to dis house." He was pointing his index finger at her now and frowning.

"Uncle Mo, I'm going out with your friend's nephew."

"Who friend?"

"I mean your friend Cardinal."

"O Cardinal nephew," he grunted.

"Yes uncle. He seems nice….."

"Let me tell you somethin', Jenny," interrupted Mo, "These fellers only lookin' to get one thing."

"But Uncle Mo…" pleaded Jenny.

"I don't care who he is. Don't be no fool, girl. These fellers like to chase gown tail. And once dey get what dey want – bush crack an' man gone! Then dey leave you heavy down ter deal wit' yer burden on yer own. You already don't have nothin'. That's all I have to say 'bout that," warned Mo. He had seated himself at a small dining table with two chairs which was located near a southern window so that he could preach to his niece.

The wrangling was so intense that neither one of them noticed when Hezekiah walked up to the front door. The door was open slightly as was customary due to the heat, so Hezekiah knocked gently and waited for a response.

"Remember what I tell you, Jenny," stated Mo as he looked toward the door.

Jenny secretly hoped that Hezekiah had not heard any part of the previous discourse. Tears were welling up in her eyes now and she felt defenseless. She wiped her eyes and stepped to the door while feigning a smile as she greeted her guest.

Chapter Five

"Hello Jenny," said Hezekiah warmly. "Anybody else home?" he continued.

"Uhmm yes. My Uncle Mo is here. Let me introduce you to him."

"Uncle Mo, this is Hezekiah Rolle. Hezekiah, this is my uncle Maurice Smith," explained Jenny.

Hezekiah extended his hand to Mo and responded, "Pleased to meet you, Sir."

"Glad to meet you too," said Mo politely as he rose from the chair to extend his hand also in a handshake.

"Well, good evening Mr. Smith. Jenny and I are going to see a movie. I won't keep her out late," assured Hezekiah.

"Alright, Hezekiah," responded Mo, then he turned and went back inside the house.

"Are you alright, Jenny? You are not wearing your usual happy face," chuckled Hezekiah. Hezekiah sensed that Jenny was concerned about something. He reached for her hand, and Jenny felt comforted.

"I'm okay, Kiah." Jenny held his hand firmly as they set out. After just two days, Hezekiah instinctively understood when Jenny needed quiet and preferred not to talk. Hezekiah was pleased that he was able to pinch off enough funds to take Jenny to see a movie at the Capitol Theatre and, just as he hoped, she was impressed. Quite naturally, afterwards, Hezekiah invited Jenny to have something to eat from the Palm Tree Restaurant (which was just south of the Capitol Theatre). They each decided to enjoy a pork chop sandwich and a cool drink of coconut water. After their tasty snack, Hezekiah and Jennifer took a slow walk to Jenny's abode. Once again, the couple had enjoyed a perfect evening.

Later that night, Hezekiah tossed and turned as he struggled to fall asleep. He was tormented by his personal situation, and he was trying to evaluate the growing feelings of attraction that he felt for Jenny. He was at a crossroad in his life, and he did not know whether to go left, right, or straight ahead. His annual summer stint in Nassau had come to an end. He had very little money left, especially since he had been less frugal than in previous years. He had been a monitor for about six years and had religiously given most of his earnings to his parents except for a little survival money that he kept for personal needs. The original plan was for Hezekiah to return to Exuma and resume his duties as a monitor or teacher. In June, Mr. Taylor, the head teacher at Rokers Point School, had explained to Hezekiah that he was prepared to recommend him to be an assistant teacher upon his return. Hezekiah would be replacing Mr. Darville, an elderly gentleman from Long Island, who had retired at the end of the previous school year. Hezekiah's parents certainly would be happy because this would mean a secure job for him and greater financial security for the Rolle family.

On the other hand, there was Jenny. They had been out together on several occasions, and he was beginning to feel like he had known her all his life. He could not explain or rationalize why he felt so drawn to her. After weighing out his options, he knew that he could not remain in Nassau because he had no job or income. Jenny, on the other hand, had confided in him about her personal challenges. Her future was uncertain due to her living situation. Since her employment had only been temporary, her last day of work had been the previous Friday. He could sense that Jenny was extremely fond of him, and he was determined to ensure that she would be a part of his future if she would have him. He knew that his best option would be to resume his duties at whatever school the Board of Education sent him to. He could not come to terms with the idea of returning home to Steventon without Jenny, yet he wondered what his mother would say.

Hezekiah was not sure of the shift that Kenny was working on Sunday, but he desperately needed someone whom he could trust and confide in. He pondered until he became weary. Then, finally, in the quiet of the early morning, he concluded that the decisions he was about to make would very likely affect his entire future. He made up his mind that he would go in search of Kenny who lived just down the road in a single room unit on Burial Ground Corner. Hezekiah knew that Kenny usually went to the earliest church service at St. Barnabas Church when he could. He decided to wait until late morning to set out. Also, he knew that if he could not find Kenny there, he would probably be passing away the time with his cousins on Odle Corner by playing dominoes or discussing politics in the yard. Kenny had recently broken up with his girlfriend of two years whom he had lost to a policeman who apparently was a more persistent and appealing suitor. Initially, Kenny was shocked and hurt over the situation, however, soon after, he triumphantly stated that he had moved on and would use it as a learning experience.

Kenny had landed a job two years ago in the psychiatric hospital (known as "The Crazy Hill") of the Bahamas General Hospital. "The Crazy Hill" was located on a hill and could be viewed by climbing up the Queen's Staircase (the Sixty-Six Steps). Sadly, passersby could sometimes see the deranged residents of the female ward immodestly dangling from windows while their male counterparts were making their share of hideous, blood-curdling sounds in their ward; it was an unforgettable sight for most. It was not necessarily Kenny's first choice, but he was certainly grateful for the job and the opportunity to work; although he had obtained several subjects in the Cambridge Junior Certificate examinations, the only vacancies at that time were for attendants (males) and auxiliaries (females) in the psychiatric area. Overtime, Kenny made the adjustments and performed his duties as if it was his calling. Many young people shunned the type of work he did. Kenny's responsibilities as a hospital attendant included sluicing out patients' rooms. He often could be seen wearing high rubber boots and using a long length of hose while he worked "knee deep" washing away fecal matter, etc. down a trough with a rough, long-handled square brush. He had a rich singing voice and bellowed out many tunes to offset his state of subservience. Like other attendants and auxiliaries, he also had to bathe patients, clean their rooms, and feed them as well. Worst of all, he constantly smelled of carbolic, alcohol and other hospital supplies, so as soon as his shift ended, Kenny would head home to cleanse himself, and restore some degree of normalcy to his life again. Kenny was a dark, slightly built fellow whose mustached smile presented a modest open gate. He was an optimist at heart. After completing school, he had applied to join the Royal Bahamas Police Force along with several of his classmates, but his application was rejected because he was three inches shorter than the 5'8" requirement. He had even begun taking evening classes as he aspired to obtain some Cambridge Senior Certificate passes and improve his lot in life.

Around eleven on Sunday morning, Hezekiah set out to find Kenny. Kenny was not at home, so Hezekiah headed towards Odle Corner. The sky was cloudy, and the temperature was bearable. In less than fifteen minutes, he located Kenny standing under a leafy mango tree whose branches hung over the verandah of the sturdy blue and white clapboard house. Kenny was still in his "Sunday-go-to-meeting" church clothes. He was engaged in a heated debate with several young men, all of whom appeared to be enjoying their breakfast of sardines and grits as well. They were sitting on some wooden crates and other makeshift seats.

"Hey Kiah, you want some sardines and grits? I believe we have some left." Kenny greeted his buddy eagerly as soon as he spotted him. Kiah was grateful and responded in the affirmative.

"Auntie Glo, anymore sardine and grits left? O.K., let me have one more plate please," requested Kenny whose aunt obliged by passing him an enamel plate with food along with a mug of sweetened bush tea.

"So what's up Bro.?" asked Kenny curiously. Kenny noted his friend's pensive mood.

"Fellers, I guh talk to you all a little later. Give me a couple minutes," said Kenny as he excused himself from his cousins for a while.

Kenny beckoned Kiah to move around to the southeastern corner of the house where they could talk privately.

"Man Kenny, I'm trying to figure out what to do. You know I'm supposed to go back home soon, right?" stated Kiah.

"Yeah, to Exuma," responded Kenny flatly.

"Well, the problem is I don't want to go back."

"Why not?"

"I started seeing this girl and I like her. I really like her a lot, Kenny. I don't think I could go back home to Steventon and just forget about her.

Kenny started laughing as he teased, "What happen man? Your love break down on you, eh Kiah?"

"You know – I have feelings for her. I can't live without her man," Kiah admitted shyly.

"Kiah, look like you let the lovebug bite you, man," said Kenny who was openly laughing at him now. Kenny had seen Hezekiah with Jennifer, and he could see that they were like two peas in one pod.

"Look here Kenny. This is serious. I believe my girl Jenny feels the same way about me, too," explained Kiah.

"Your girl? You sure? You might be thinking she's yours, but she might have another man. Soon as you leave …"

Chapter Five

"No Kenny," interrupted Kiah, "Jenny is not like that. She doesn't have anyone to help her. She doesn't have a job, and if I don't go back, I won't have a job either. I don't know what to do. Give me some advice man."

"Well, you could look for a job here, but they're hard to find," responded Kenny. "Meanwhile, you all ger need something to live off. That's a big problem," continued Kenny, 'cause a woman like her aint gonna wait on you forever. She nice and she nice-lookin'. These fellers 'round here just like sharks. Bush crack, and yuh woman gone. I talkin' from experience."

"Yeah, man. I know," said Kiah slowly. He was thinking deeply.

"When you talk about taking responsibility for a woman you gotta have some money. You plannin' to marry her, Kiah?" Kenny inquired.

"I am thinking about it, but I aint ready yet. I don't have a house or anything," explained Kiah dejectedly.

"I wish I could help you, but I only have enough to look after myself. I mean, you could bunk in with me but that's only one room," explained Kenny.

Kiah responded, "Thanks man. That's okay, I understand Kenny,"

"And you know, when you take a wife, you gotta have somewhere to put her. Women get discouraged quick, too. They always looking for more than you have, man," advised Kenny.

"I tell you, Jenny isn't like that," retorted Kiah.

"So you going to go or stay?" asked Kenny finally.

"I guess I'll probably have to go back. I definitely can't help her or do anything else if I don't have a job…" mused Kiah who was looking deeply into the ground as if it would have an answer for him.

Kenny admitted, "My friend, you might have to take that chance,"

"See Kenny, her uncle is so disgusting. Her uncle could put her outside or make her move at any moment. I don't know what I would do if I lost her!" Kiah was becoming emotional now. A slow flow of perspiration had begun to trickle down both sides of his hairline.

Kenny advised, "You better do something quick then."

"Kenny, she is a beautiful girl, inside and out. I liked her from the first time I saw her," admitted Kiah.

"So Kiah, you know what you have to do then," guided Kenny.

"I have to go back and keep my job. I will talk to her. I know it's not going to be easy, but I will explain to Jen that I will come back for her when I get things sorted out for us in Exuma," explained Kiah decisively.

"What about your mother? You know she aint guh like that. She guh carry on real bad," said Kenny who started jumping around as he imitated Mrs. Rolle's likely response to Kiah's decision. "Boy she guh beat you bad when you tell her that," continued Kenny who was grinning now.

Kiah was pensive as he bade his friend goodbye. "Kenny, I guh see you later in the week. Thanks man. Appreciate it. Oh, thanks for the breakfast. Tell Miss Glo thanks for the breakfast, too." Kiah walked away knowing what he had to do.

He found Jenny at home around 3:00 p.m. that afternoon. He knocked on the front door which was closed and was happy when he heard her voice asking, "Who is it?"

"It's me," he replied. He felt fortunate when he discovered that her Uncle Mo and his girlfriend had gone out for the afternoon.

Jenny invited him to join her on the porch. Kiah helped her by lifting the two chairs outside. Although the sun was still high in the sky, there was a breeze which tempered the heat a bit. Kiah got to the point quickly, "Jen, I need to talk to you about something."

"What is it, Kiah?" Jen asked with a hint of concern in her voice.

"Remember, I told you that since summer school is over, I have to go back to Exuma. Well, I know we just met and everything, but I have to leave you and go back to work," explained Kiah.

Chapter Five

Jenny shivered slightly as if someone had poured cool water down her back, "So I guess that's it then. You have to go. I understand," said Jenny resolutely.

"No Jen. I don't mean it like that. I must leave in order to keep my job. I will come back for you though, as soon as I get some business sorted out," interjected Kiah who for some reason was becoming tongue-tied.

Kiah was holding both her hands in his and looking directly into her eyes as he spoke, "Jen, I really care about you. I love you and I hope that you love me too."

Jen responded tearfully, "I do love you Kiah, but I'm afraid that when you go back to your island, you will forget all about me." She was unable to hide her dejection.

"You are on my mind all the time, Jen. I hardly slept last night thinking about you and trying to decide what to do," explained Kiah. He continued, "I love you, Jen." He reached out to Jen and kissed her softly on her forehead.

Something was rising up inside of him emboldening him. He appealed to her, "Jen, I don't have a ring or anything for you, but I have to know." He dropped on his knees before her and asked, "Jen will you marry me and come to live on Exuma with me?"

"But, but how? ... Yes, I will marry you, Kiah!" said Jen exuberantly. Her face was glowing as she jumped up. Without giving it a thought, Kiah kissed her eagerly on the lips as he cupped her face gently in his hands.

He hugged her close to him and reassured her, "I love you, Jen. I promise you I will not disappoint you. I must leave on the boat early tomorrow morning, but I will come back for you very soon. I will write to you to let you know what I am doing. Promise me that you will wait for me, my love."

"Promise me that you won't forget about me, either," pleaded Jen.

The two lovers had been so caught up in each other that they did not notice several passersby who stared at them momentarily as they went on their way. Kiah was unaware of how long he had been talking on the porch with Jen. He guessed that it was almost six in the afternoon, so he said, "I have to go now Jen." He felt awful because he had no money to leave with her. They hugged each other briefly and shared one last kiss before Kiah departed.

Although Kiah's heart was heavy as he left Jen, he was comforted by the fact that he knew Jen loved him also, and, regardless of the circumstances, he would see her again soon.

Chapter Six

Jenny began the week feeling dejected. Her best friend had gone, and she was jobless again. Early Monday morning, she set out to find a job. By midday, she had convinced herself that she would be willing to accept almost any job with one exception. She knew that the Chinese were always willing to hire black women. She also observed that when you went into a Chinese restaurant or food store, every black woman would be pregnant, and she had heard that many of them had been impregnated by these Asians. She decided that she would be willing to die of starvation first before she succumbed to that kind of degradation.

For several days Jennifer avoided direct dialogue with her uncle, and she was thankful that for at least two days he appeared oblivious of her circumstances. She kept out of his way and subsisted on beans and plain flour pancakes that her grandmother had given her permission to use when there was insufficient food to be shared. She was appreciative because most of the time whatever Mo brought home was only enough for his mother and him to eat, anyway.

Early one afternoon, she could tell that Uncle Mo was experiencing one of his salty moods. She had just overheard him explaining to his mother that they might be laying off some workers at the shipyard where he was working as a stevedore because, as he explained, "things slow". He was thankful that he was still holding onto some of his winnings after he had been gambling at Percy's the other day. He was of course sucking on a bottle of some foul-smelling liquor that Jenny hoped would soon cause him to fall asleep for a while.

Jenny had hoped that she could complete the chore that her grandmother had given her then disappear from her uncle's view. She flinched when she heard her name being called.

"Jenny, I aint been seeing that feller coming around here lately. What you say his name is? Hezzekiel? Hezekiah? O yeah. Hezekiah."

Jenny looked in his direction so that he would not accuse her of ignoring him.

"What happen? Cat got yer tongue, girl?" chided Mo. "I asked you a question and I expect an answer."

"Uncle, he isn't here. He went back home but he …" Jenny started to explain but was interrupted by Uncle Mo.

"Ooooh I see," He slowed his voice to a drag. "Jenny, aint I tell you, soon as that feller get what he want, he was guh be gone. Now what you guh do?" gloated Uncle Mo confidently.

Jennifer had no answer.

"Well, I could tell you one thing. You aint bringin' no bastard baby in this house," Mo glared at his niece as he spoke.

"No Uncle. I'm not pregnant," explained Jenny cautiously.

"Well, I expect you to say that," retorted Mo. He called to his mother, "Mama, you better watch out fer this one!"

He again turned to Jenny to continue his diatribe. "Right now, you 'big up' and think you guh be our responsibility, but I could tell you girl, you have another thing coming," stated Mo indignantly. He pointed at the door to affirm his position.

Jennifer tried to explain, "Hezekiah promised to come back for me. He had to leave because he had to go back to his job."

"Don't be stupid, girl. He probably gat another woman or a wife over there, and you'll probably never see him again," suggested Mo.

Chapter Six

"I'm looking for a job anyway just in case," explained Jenny.

"You better if you know what's good fer you. You better find one soon. You need to make life fer yourself. We can't keep takin' care of you. And you already let that feller make a fool of you."

It was apparent that Mo was finished with his vitriol because he picked up his fedora, placed it on his head and walked outside. Jenny breathed a deep sigh of relief although his tirade had succeeded in dampening her spirit a little.

The next morning, Jenny prepared herself again to go on a hunt for a job. There were not many private offices within walking distance and most of them were owned by whites who were usually inclined to hire family members or close friends of their families. Jenny had hoped to get a clerical or sales job, but she knew that it was highly unlikely. She had combed Bay Street in search of work. Two of her earliest searches had been at the Ironmongery and Maura's where she had hoped for a positive response.

Eventually, she relented and returned to the Stop-N-Shop on Bay Street where she had inquired several weeks before because this store had fascinated her since she was a child. In fact, as one entered the double doors of the large variety store, one was greeted by an overwhelming array of many jars full of candies displayed all along the eastern side of the store. The store was stocked from the floor to the ceiling with all types of household goods, toys and many other miscellaneous items which attracted a constant flow of customers all day. She could remember her mother taking Leah and her there for an ice cream cone or candy treats on Saturdays.

Jenny had also spoken to a middle-aged 'conchy-joe' lady who seemed to be a supervisor at the Tiny Shop (which was also on Bay Street) about giving her a job there. Mrs. Knowles had indicated that she might need an additional person if business increased, so Jenny decided that she ought to check on that prospect first. Jenny had tried to hide her desperation as she explained to the lady that she knew a bit about items used in sewing and that she could do a little sewing as well. This shop was a modified version of a haberdashery store which predominantly sold a lot of cloth, thread, needles, decorative trimmings, buttons and sewing implements along with numerous small articles of clothing such as neckties, scarves, handkerchiefs, underwear, stockings, and socks. When she arrived there, Mrs. Knowles advised her that the only position available was as a shop hand. If she wanted the job, Jenny would have to assist customers in finding items, restock the shelves, clean up as necessary and mop the floor once daily before the store opened. Jenny accepted the position without hesitation and arrived at work every morning at 8:30 a.m. The work was rigorous, so she was happy for her lunch break. She was appreciative that she was actually employed, although the pay was meager. Within weeks, Jenny had grown accustomed to her daily routine and did not complain when she was asked to work half days on some Saturdays when the store became busy.

Jenny had received only one letter from Hezekiah that he must have sent on the mailboat which was scheduled to return to Nassau again just after he had arrived in Steventon. His letter overflowed with his love and affection for her along with his promise that he would return for her. It was already October, and she had received no further word or message from Hezekiah. She reflected on the fact that her uncle had taunted her saying that "a promise is a comfort to a fool". Every time she was tempted to think like that, she chided herself for losing hope. She could picture Hezekiah's smiling face and this was the only thing that kept her going.

Life for Jenny was beginning to improve. She was now able to contribute towards the rent at her grandmother's home and her relationship with Uncle Mo was manageable. Occasionally, an interesting customer would walk through the doors of the Tiny Shop. Although most patrons were women, a few men sometimes entered the store with their girlfriend, wife, mother, or friend. She noted with interest that the male patrons appeared to be lost in the store and needed the most assistance. She had been propositioned and invited out several times by young and older men, but she never accepted any of these invitations. There was, however, one gentleman who had become a frequent patron of the establishment several times in the last two weeks to make small purchases, and on each occasion, he positioned himself so that Jenny would be obliged to attend to him. Her co-workers noticed this unsolicited attention that she was getting and began teasing her about it. He was debonair, always smartly dressed and spoke with a strange, polished accent that was unfamiliar to her. His hat always complemented his elegant suit, and he was in the habit of tipping his hat as he began speaking to her.

On a particularly dreary day, the good gentleman appeared once again but this time he announced to Jenny, "Jefferson Hollingsworth of Hollingsworth & Co." He tipped his hat as usual, but this time he asked that she give her name to him.

Chapter Six

Jenny was nervous and felt that everyone in the store was watching her. She responded politely, "My name is Jenny. Can I help you with something Sir?"

"May I see a few of those neckties just behind you please," he responded smoothly. Jenny could feel his eyes on her, but she did her best to maintain her composure as she reached for several ties.

She handed various samples to her suave customer who then held onto her hand gently while saying, "I would be so grateful if you would allow me to take you out for dinner. Would you agree to that?"

"Sir, I don't know. I can't …Do you like any of these ties or can I show you some others?" Jenny was feeling trapped and uncomfortable now, but she continued to be respectful to this man who seemed to be several years senior to her. Also, she did not want to be accused of being rude to a customer.

He stated, "I see the one that I like but she does not want to give me the time of day. Give me a chance and I will show you that a lovely girl like you does not need to be working in a store like this. I will take the blue one, okay?" The stranger paid for his purchase and walked away without waiting for his change.

He turned around momentarily while fixing his hat and said to her with assurance, "I will be back later when you are not so busy. Okay Jenny?" Before Jenny could utter another word, Mr. Jefferson Hollingsworth had donned his hat and was gone. When Jenny realized that the change that he had left with her was more than her week's wages, she held onto the counter to compose herself because she felt faint. Even though she was initially dumbfounded, she soon became so absorbed in her duties that she eventually forgot about her persistent suitor.

Jenny was happy to see the end of her workday. She was physically and mentally drained. It was still drizzling outside so she felt happy that she had brought her umbrella. As she turned westward on Bay Street to head toward East Street, she heard a car horn to her right and looked directly into the eyes of the charming Mr. Jefferson Hollingsworth. He was beaming as he beckoned to Jenny. She admitted to him that she was surprised to see him there. "What are you doing here, Mr. Hollingsworth?" asked Jenny sheepishly.

Jefferson hopped out of his fashionable two-door convertible red car and opened the door for her saying "Get in Jenny. It is raining and you really don't need to get wet. I will take you wherever you want to go."

Jenny felt uncomfortable with this suggestion and said as calmly as she could that she would be okay and that she did not have a long way to go (which was untrue of course).

"Jenny, if you are going home, I promise that I will take you to where you live and that is all. You must trust me. That is all that I ask." Mr. Hollingsworth was pleading with her now. "I only want to talk to you for a few minutes." It was raining harder by this time so that even with her umbrella, her clothes were getting wet.

"Jenny, this is ridiculous. It is raining. Let me give you a lift to where you are going, okay?" He was smiling with her boyishly under his neat moustache. She acknowledged that he even appeared to be handsome (at least for a man of his age). She found herself laughing at her thoughts as she said, "Okay, but I don't live very far away. Make sure to take me home." He moved quickly to her side, opened the car door for her and let her step inside. Then he adjusted the car's convertible roof top and they drove off.

As soon as she got into the car, Jefferson wasted no time. "Look Jenny, I am a lawyer. I have my own firm. I'm originally from Trinidad, but I've been here for a long time. I don't mean to be fresh but I liked you from the first time I saw you. There is just something about you that is irresistible. You can come and work for me if you wish or we …"

"Mr. Hollingsworth – I mean Jefferson – you seem to be a nice person, but I just can't … I have a friend," she explained.

"A friend?" Jefferson mused and frowned slightly. "You don't seem so sure Jenny? Anyway, he probably can't give you what I can give you. You won't have to work if you don't want to. I will take care of you." The gentleman admitted that he was a widower with two adult children, then he added a few more details about himself to gain her approval, but Jennifer remained inflexible.

"You don't understand. He really loves me. I know he does. Thank you for the ride. I really appreciate it." Jenny had arrived at her destination, and she was relieved. It made her nauseous to think that this man could be her father and was trying to pursue her.

Chapter Six

"Are you engaged? Jenny, if he loved you so much, you would have a ring on your finger. Jefferson reached over and attempted to kiss Jenny, but she pushed him away saying, "No I can't. It wouldn't be right."

"Jenny, you have made me sad. I want you to think about what I have said. I can give you a happy life if you give me a chance. I would like to see you again but only if you want to." Jefferson gave her the location of his law office and told her to come and see him if she changed her mind. He walked around to the passenger's side of the car and opened the door for her. Jenny stepped out with his assistance, thanked him and he drove away without looking back.

Jenny exhaled when she realized that her zealous tormentor was not at home and was pleased to be greeted by her grandmother who had obviously watched the whole spectacle in front of her yard. Jenny was also aware that some curious neighbors had been peeping as well.

"Jenny who was that who dropped you home just now?"

"Oh, it was just someone who gave me a ride because it was raining, that's all."

"I see. Well he was talkin' ter you pretty long. What was all that he had to say so?"

"It was nothing Grumma. He was just talking. You know how men like to talk every time they see a woman." Jenny was smiling at this point and changing from her work clothes into something more comfortable.

"He look rich Jenny. That look like a spankin' brand new car too what he was drivin'. Chile if I was lil younger … A man like that just had to look at me hard and I woulda been gone with him." Miss Maude Smith patted the sides of her hips and grinned as she reflected on her glory days.

Jenny quickly tried to change the subject to avoid her grandmother's mischievousness. "Grumma, we have anything to cook today?"

"I just finish pluckin' the feathers off one chicken what Miss Woods give me this mornin'. I tell her I aint had nothin' to cook. She cut off the head and tell me if I want it, I could have it, but I had to clean it m'self. Chile I was too glad. Thank God for neighbors. So we probably could have chicken souse tonight."

"I'll go by Miss Stella shop for some sour limes, pepper, and if she bake any Johnny cake or rolls I'll get some of them too. O.K. Ma'am?" suggested Jenny enthusiastically as she practically flew out of the door and made her way down the street before her grandmother could respond affirmatively.

When Jenny returned, Grumma had already cut up the chicken into small portions including the feet and had submerged the whole bird into the pot minus the head. The aroma of onions, spice leaves and lime juice which blended with the poultry and potatoes soon emitted an aroma that lingered in the air and teased the nostrils of all who were in the vicinity of Ms. Maude's kitchen. Mo had left some money with his mother to purchase some ice, so when the Milo Butler truck pulled through her corner, Miss Smith was prepared to purchase a half block of ice which was covered in a layer of saw dust to prevent it from melting. This ice could last for about a day and was useful for keeping such perishables as butter. Jenny used the extra limes and some sugar to make a small jug of switcher for the three of them.

Grumma chuckled and said, "I know Mo guh eat his belly full when he get home tonight."

"Yeah he will. Oh Grumma, please do me a favor. Please don't mention anything to Uncle Mo about me catching a ride with that man 'cause you know how he does carry on," Jenny advised.

Jenny fell asleep that night after tossing and turning for what seemed like hours. Her Uncle Mo had been drinking '30 days' as usual that evening. Consequently, when he staggered home, he fell into a drunken stupor shortly after, so the house was deathly quiet, and the neighborhood was still. The night took her on an amazing journey that terrified her. She found herself strolling in a lovely garden with a water fountain and lots of flowering plants. Watching Hezekiah walk towards her with a lovely bouquet of flowers brought a smile to her face. There was a twinkle in his eyes as he approached her smartly dressed in a navy-blue suit, but he could not seem to quite get to her despite the fact that she could see him walking towards her. Jenny had her hands outstretched towards him, yet Hezekiah was not getting any closer. As she studied his face trying to determine what was happening, Jenny realized that she was no longer looking into Hezekiah's face because the face had changed. She was now staring into the face of Jefferson Hollingsworth. Hollingsworth's face seemed disfigured, and his eyes had become hollow glowing holes that stared at her angrily. The flowers had disappeared, and Hollingsworth began pointing at

Chapter Six

Jenny accusingly. Someone began laughing behind her derisively and Jenny instinctively spun around. The figure of a rather tall, dark woman shrouded in black cloth stood very close to her and continued to laugh menacingly at her while reaching out to grab her. Jenny could not see the woman's face but she could see that both the woman and she were standing in a dark bushy area. Jenny became light-headed. She felt herself falling and falling as if she had gone off a cliff and she uttered a blood-curdling scream as she felt her life coming to an end.

"Jenny! Jenny! What happen girl? You screamin' like somebody killin' you! Wake up before your heart jump right outta your body," yelled Jenny's grandmother anxiously as she hastened to awaken her petrified granddaughter.

Jenny was gasping for breath, but she was relieved to find herself in the arms of her grandmother instead of the abyss in her nightmare. Her dream confounded her but, in her usual way, Jenny quickly dismissed it and was grateful to be safe. Her grandmother encouraged her to drink some leftover pear leaf tea which helped to relax her. Jenny slept peacefully for the rest of the night.

Next morning, Jenny was filled with extra energy and zeal to clean the wooden floor of the tiny house in which she lived. She had dismissed her dream and did not spend any more time thinking about it. In fact, she had already collected some soap bush from Miss Mabel's yard just a few houses away from her grandmother's house. In the cool of the morning, she planned to scrub the floors of the two-room house with the soap bush, then go to The Buttman on Bay Street to buy some groceries (as well as octagon soap) that she needed to wash her clothes. Since she did not have to work this weekend, she intended to complete her chores early then relax for the rest of the day. Jenny wiped, scrubbed, and cleaned until the little house was immaculate.

After she had finished, Jenny decided to sit on the porch for a short time and rest. Soon some worrisome thoughts began to filter and meander through the crevices of her mind. She had not seen or heard from her beloved sister Leah for several months. Jenny knew that Leah had travelled all the way to a place called North Carolina with a white Bahamian family whom she had been working for on the Eastern Road since she was in her mid-teens. More recently, some friends of Mrs. Allen had communicated to her that Leah had moved to some part of Florida and was working for an American family as a live-in maid and caregiver for three children. They had also heard that the family may have relocated, but they were unsure of where they were living or if Leah was with them. Mrs. Allen

103

had equivocated about relaying this bit of news to Jenny because she knew this would only add to Jenny's worries. The tears welled up in Jenny's eyes now as she wondered what life was like for her sister and whether she was lonely in such a big country where she knew no one. Jenny literally shuddered momentarily, then in her usual way, she chided herself for opting to succumb to her own negative thoughts.

To add to her woes, Jenny had grown tired of going to the mailboat and being told "Aint no letter for you today." One of the crew members who lived a few streets south of hers began to feel sorry for her and even promised to let her know when any mail came for her.

Jenny also reflected on the chat that she recently had with her 'conchy Joe' co-worker Dorcas Knowles one lunch time as they sat eating bologna sandwiches. Dorcas, who was the niece of the supervisor, had befriended Jenny from her first day on the job and did not treat her differently despite their color differences.

"Girl look how you frettin' over that feller. It soon December. When last you hear from him anyway?" There was a soothing cool breeze blowing as they sat on the busy waterfront chatting. Jenny shook her head in denial and looked away pretending that something had caught her attention.

"You think I should get a bike like that – a three speed? I always wanted one like that," interrupted Jenny who appeared not to hear Dorcas' question. She was pleased that the opportunity arose to change the talk to one that was more neutral.

The brown freckles now stood out on Dorcas' flushed face as she looked in dismay at her friend. Dorcas stood up with her left hand on the side of her waist to emphasize her point. "Right now, he mussee done gone 'bout his business to one next gal. If I was you, I woulda take dat next feller up on his offer. You know the one with the nice car who came to you in the shop the other day. Yeah he kindisha old. Even if you don't love him now, you could learn to love him, especially how he gat money. Jenny you gatta plan fer yer future, yer know. And you's a nice-lookin' girl too. Even if you was ugly, you don't deserve that kinda treatment…"

"Dorcas, I appreciate what you sayin' but I just can't give myself to someone who I don't have any feelings for."

Chapter Six

"So you think you love this Kiah feller then. But you sure he love you?" Dorcas raised her eyebrows curiously.

"I believe so…at least that's what he said," answered Jenny, who was beginning to feel a bit uncertain now as she responded to her friend's probing questions.

"I hope you aint give up yourself ter him, 'cause you know that's all these man want, then they does move on 'cause aint nuttin to wait for any more." Dorcas was persistent as she conveyed her opinion to Jenny. "Just after I leave Long Island, I make that mistake and I will always regret it. I even almost get married couple years ago, but my friend gone out to sea (He was a fisherman, yer know.) and they say he fall overboard and get drown somewhere near Cay Sal Bank. They aint never find his body. Jen don't give up on yerself. See me – I guh be thirty this month and all I have is two chirren to take care of. I don't want see that happen to you.

"No, no Dorcas. He never put that kinda pressure on me. Kiah always respected me, and he always acted as if he cared for me. It's hard to believe he would do that to me."

"You a smart girl too, Jenny. Why you don't try get a job to the Hospital or in somebody office or something? Aint you say you could type?"

Jenny was grateful when that lunchtime came to an end. She had begun to develop a slight headache and did not feel like talking anymore. "Dorcas, you think I should try get a job to the Hospital?" Jenny sought advice from her friend as she attempted to change the subject.

"Girl if I was you, I woulda try anyhow," Dorcas tried to reassure her friend.

Jenny was so deep in her thoughts as she walked toward her home that she did not notice the figure sitting on the porch until the individual sprang up and immediately began to move towards her.

"Kiah what you doin' here? Why didn't you write? I thought something happened." Jenny's words were gushing from her lips uncontrollably as her pent-up feelings forced their way out of her.

Hezekiah grasped her and held her so tightly that she became breathless until he relaxed his grip.

105

"O Jen I felt like I was dying slowly each day that I did not hear from you." Hezekiah began talking faster now as if time was running away from him. "Jen, I was getting worried after I didn't hear from you. How come you didn't write me back? I sent you a couple letters. I gave them to Sista to take to the mailboat after I had to go so far to Rolleville School every day."

Jennifer could only shake her head negatively.

"I guess she didn't send them, since you never got them." He looked disturbed and stared briefly into the distance.

"Kiah, I kept going to the boat, but I stopped going after a while. I didn't get any letters," explained Jenny sadly.

"Jen honey, I am very sorry that I left you so long. Sorry about the letters. My oldest sister is kinda jealous and I guess possessive too. I had some problems since I went back home too. I had to come back to see you and make sure you're okay since I didn't hear from you." Hezekiah was hugging Jenny closely again and admonishing her to believe in him. He continued, "I started teaching to the Rolleville School, but they want me to go to another island. The head teacher there is going to retire next year, and they want me to go and work under him and train so that I could take over from him. I had problems too because Mama doesn't want me to go and she aint happy that I want to get married either. She's upset. But Jenny I am not going without you if you will have me. Do you understand what I am saying?" asked Hezekiah.

"Sort of. So what are you going to do?" Jenny inquired. Jenny felt the cool breeze and shivered slightly as it softly touched her face and arms. She found herself looking deeply into Hezekiah's excited eyes trying to search his heart to determine if he was being truthful. She felt overwhelmed and bewildered.

"Jen, I want you to come with me. I don't intend to leave you behind. I know other fellers must be out there trying to talk to you I'm sure, but I want you to know that I love you with all my heart. Hezekiah was looking deeply into her eyes now as he held her two hands gently and said, "Jenny, I want you to be my wife. I don't have much, but I will do my best to take care of you. Will you marry me, Jen?"

"Yes, I will, Kiah," she gushed. "You know I love you. I never lost faith in you."

Chapter Six

Hezekiah continued excitedly, "I have to talk to your uncle. I don't think he's home yet. I hope he will agree. I have a letter…" Hezekiah was so excited yet a little nervous; it seemed that he was even a little short of breath. "I want to buy your ring, but I have to get your uncle's permission first. I will take you to get it on Saturday. We can go to The Nassau Shop."

Jenny had been so absorbed in her own affairs that she had forgotten about her grandmother. She was jolted to reality when she began to inhale the aroma of the spicy, lemony smell of her grandmother's signature dish – smothered fish. It smelled good and she longed to partake of the pungent seafood dish.

She got up from the bench and poked her head through the door, "Sorry Grumma. I was so busy talking, I forgot to say good afternoon. You doin' alright, ma'am?" She inquired bashfully.

"I see you have company. That's alright," replied Miss Smith as she winked playfully. "I could see you all have a lot to talk about."

"Grumma, you know if Uncle Mo soon come home?" asked Jenny.

"Chile, you know how he go. He could come home anytime. I aint sure. And how they say storm might be coming, he mighta had to work late on the boat, you know," she explained.

"Good afternoon Ms. Smith. How you doin'?" inquired Hezekiah hopefully.

"I'm alright sonny. Haven't seen you for a while. Everything alright?"

"Yes ma'am. Things are okay. I wanted to talk to Mr. Smith about something really important. Maybe I should come back tomorrow. I don't want to disturb you all," explained Hezekiah. There was a hint of disappointment in his voice although he tried to measure his words carefully.

"Now you know Jen's Uncle Mo like to take his lil sip after work so I don't know what kinda mood he'll be in when he does get home, but you could try," explained Ms. Smith.

The wind was growing a bit stronger. There was a possibility that a storm was coming. The older of the two women shivered and inched closer to her front door. "Well, I wouldn't want to upset Mr. Smith especially when he's tired from a hard day at work," hinted Hezekiah uncertainly. With that, Hezekiah politely excused himself by bidding Ms. Smith good evening. The wind seemed to search mischievously through her thin house dress until she finally gave in and retreated inside. The couple chatted for a little while then Hezekiah left reluctantly, after promising Jenny that he would see her the following day during her lunch break.

Jenny did not sleep well. The wind had been howling around their clapboard house for several hours. Claps of thunder and zig-zagged streaks of lightning punctuated the disgruntled sky. Parts of the roof usually leaked particularly when there was a strong 'westerly wind' as Grumma often said, and this occasion was no different. Throughout the night, they had to plug several areas of the house to slow the invasion of the rain as it attempted to beat into the house. While her grandmother slept soundly, Jenny heard her uncle struggling to escape the gale force wind as he tried to open the door. She could smell the whiskey and whatever else he had been drinking. He hurled profanities as the door slammed behind him, flinging him inside. Mo hastened to the tiny kitchen where he changed out of his wet clothes and was soon consumed by sleep. Tropical storms were always unwelcome visitors but fortunately this one did not stay long.

It was a new day, but it would not be business as usual. The rain and wind had fought tempestuously all night and left their trail of destruction. Po Betty superseded Miss Pearl's rooster as she 'tweet-tweeted' her mournful greeting while safely perched in a nearby sapodilla tree. Each time a storm or hurricane came, the people in the over-the-hill community feared that their homes could be damaged or destroyed. Such a phenomenon would be devastating for most families. At the first signs of daylight, people could be seen opening windows and doors to check their homes and yards. Jenny peeped through the front window hopefully because the wind seemed to have subsided a bit and was accompanied by intermittent squalls. She stood in awe as she spotted a neighbor's tin tub sitting upside down in the middle of the road, while debris and other miscellaneous items swirled aimlessly in the rainwater that had settled overnight. Jenny believed that streets in the more low-lying areas were probably flooded. She figured that some of the streets may be impassable because of fallen branches, pieces of wood and other items that had become detached from buildings or had become dislodged from their secure places. Uncle Maurice had already left for work and his niece was relieved. Just before he left, he gave Jenny instructions to hang out his wet overalls to dry on the clothesline if the rain held up or to drape them on the verandah where they could dry throughout the day. She had watched her uncle walk with controlled

Chapter Six

steps as he waded through the water which had subsided to about six inches in the surrounding area.

There was a wonderful breeze still blowing. Jenny found herself musing again about her planned meeting with Hezekiah and felt disappointed that she was trapped in the house; Jenny wondered whether her workplace would even be open. It was about ten in the morning, and she accepted that she would have to miss this one day of work because of the storm. She had considered getting dressed for work and venturing forth in the water with her shoes in hand but when she acknowledged the possibility of walking barefooted on a broken bottle, a crudely opened can or a sharp object, she decided against it. After sharing a simple breakfast of bread and tea with her grandmother, Jenny busied herself tidying up. She grabbed the wet items that were in various parts of the house and hung them on the clothesline after scrubbing them with a bar of Octagon soap. She even decided to boil some dirty clothes to whiten them since she had the whole day ahead of her.

The water had virtually dried up by the early afternoon. Miss Pearl and her children who lived across the street from Jenny were circling their fallen soursop tree which had been struck by lightning during the storm. The slender tree was still laden with several succulent green fruits. The soursop tree was a stark reminder of the day when Miss Pearl discovered that she had lost her husband (Mr. Jenkins) to typhoid fever while he was on the "Project". The tree now lay across the backyard with its fragile roots exposed while the onlookers were overcome with grief as if they had lost a loved one. Miss Pearl had used some of the money that Mr. Jenkins had earned from The Project to purchase a small piece of property and move their house from The Grove to Bain Town. She planted the tree soon after. The children were particularly inconsolable. That tree was their prized possession and now it was gone. All they could do was remove the full fruit and retreat inside.

Jenny was inside considering whether she should check the clothesline to see if anything on the line was dry when she heard the familiar knock on the door. Grumma had gone out to visit a neighbor. Hezekiah stood there smiling as he reached to hold Jennifer's hand. "Jen, how you doing today? The weather didn't bother you too much, did it?" Hezekiah asked.

"I'm okay thanks." She replied pleasantly. "Nothing to worry about."

"How are you?" inquired Jenny.

"I feel good now that I see you're fine. Jen, let's go and look for your ring before the shop close. Can you get ready real quick? Then we can go by The Nassau Shop so you can pick a ring. Would you like to do that Jen?" Hezekiah was holding her gently by the shoulders, hopefully awaiting a positive response. Jenny promised to be ready in a couple of minutes.

Hezekiah sat in a chair on the verandah as he waited for his beloved to join him. He was not disappointed. Jenny hastened to pick in the clothes first and secure them safely in the house. Exactly twenty-two minutes later, Jenny glowed like a ray of sunshine as she hopped nimbly out of the door and the couple headed downtown. They had to walk carefully to avoid some debris, settled water and other items that were still strewn about on East Street. They stopped on the hill at Mortimer Candy Kitchen to purchase some candy and a refreshing snow cone while they were on their way to Bay Street. After about forty-five minutes, they entered the jewelry section of The Nassau Shop. This was Jenny's first visit to this store, and she was mesmerized by the wide array of superior items that were displayed everywhere. Hezekiah was beaming with delight as he wooed his bride-to-be with the many choices of beautiful gold engagement rings and wedding bands. Jenny selected two gold rings that were a perfect fit for her. Hezekiah purchased the engagement ring, but he and Jenny agreed that they should get her family's permission and blessing before she officially accepted the ring. They agreed to catch a matinee movie at The Cinema theatre on the corner of Lewis Street and East Street to pass the time away. Both hoped that after the movie, Maurice would be home from work so they would all be able to deal with the serious matter at hand. They masked their apprehension with their unified excitement and the time passed quickly.

As they turned the corner and headed towards the house, Jenny felt safe as Hezekiah held her arm closely while they walked and chatted about their future together. Some sugar cane and a sack of coconuts were on the verandah, so Jenny felt certain that Uncle Mo was home. As they approached the step, Hezekiah walked ahead, stepped onto the porch, and extended his hand for Jenny to step onto the porch. He continued to hold her hand as he knocked gently on the door. Jenny's grandmother peeped out at the door, smiled at the couple curiously and said, "Well come inside young man. Jenny, you sure have a big smile on your face."

"Good evening Ms. Smith. How are you doing? I would like to talk to you and Mr. Smith for a few minutes if you don't mind, ma'am. Is Mr. Smith home?"

Chapter Six

Ms. Smith responded, "Yes, he home. He just get here but he prob'ly goin' out soon so you better catch him quick 'cause you know he don' stay round here long. Le' me see what he doin'. Hol' on a minute. Have a seat."

Ms. Smith called to her son who appeared momentarily from the small adjoining room. Jenny took one look at him and was relieved to see that Uncle Mo seemed sober. She secretly thanked God for their good fortune.

"Mama, you called me?" asked Maurice. As he spoke, he noticed Hezekiah and Jenny and figured out that they were there to see him.

"Good evening Mr. Smith. May I speak to you for a few minutes please?" asked Hezekiah hopefully.

"What's this about?"

"Mr. Smith and Ms. Smith, Jenny and I are in love, and we want to have a life together. I would like to ask your permission to marry Jenny. I do love her. I promise to take care of her and to cherish her for the rest of our lives." Hezekiah then handed Maurice the letter requesting his permission to marry Jennifer.

Maurice responded facetiously, "You serious 'bout this or you just sayin' this for now, then when trouble come … cause we don't want no trouble; uhmm what you say your name is again? Oh yeah, Hezekiah."

"Hezekiah Rolle from Steventon, Exuma. I am a schoolteacher working with the Board of Education," explained Hezekiah firmly as he struggled to be respectful.

"So you sayin' you takin' her wit' you ter Exuma then."

"Yes Sir. I want to do that if you allow me too."

"Well once you sure das what you want do, I aint have no problem wit' dat. Jenny only have us to help her, you know. She don't have no parents. Just make sure know, once you all married, she's yours and she can't come back here. She'll be your responsibility…" Uncle Mo tried to smile and make it sound like a joke, but they all knew he was serious.

111

Feigning a smile, he shrugged his shoulders and added, "Anyway that's a good thing 'cause we was planning on movin' soon too. I takin' Mama to live with me and my girlfriend soon as we find another place."

"Sir, I am very certain about what I want to do. Do you give us permission? I have the ring and I am ready to propose to Jenny right now."

"Go right ahead then. It's up to you." Maurice quipped. "I goin' out. Good luck."

That evening, Hezekiah proposed to Jenny, and they were officially engaged. Jenny was unbelievably happy, and Hezekiah knew that his dream had come true. Grumma watched in awe as Hezekiah put the engagement ring on Jenny's finger. She was ecstatic and could not stop hugging her granddaughter for her good fortune. That evening, the betrothed couple walked to the Palm Tree restaurant as if they were floating on a cloud. They sat in the popular eatery oblivious to other patrons as they planned their future together.

There was so little time. The mailboat was returning to Exuma next morning which meant that Jenny and Hezekiah would be apart again for several weeks until school closed in December for the Christmas holidays. It was almost midnight, and Hezekiah knew that he had to leave. The couple clung to each other as if their lives depended on it. The boat was leaving in a few hours, and Hezekiah would have to do the same. He would miss one day at work which was not acceptable, but he would have to give a reasonable excuse and ensure that it did not happen again. He walked Jennifer home, and again they were reluctant to part company. By eleven O'clock, Hezekiah was walking briskly back to the guest house to collect his suitcase and head to the mailboat. He noted the stillness of the night which was occasionally punctuated by someone passing on a three-speed bike or a few lovers caught up in their own world as he passed by. Hezekiah reminisced as he was reminded that a few hours before, he was also caught up in a romantic bubble that made him oblivious to the entire world. He already felt lonely, but he knew that he had to get back to Exuma and resume working as the future depended on how well he handled the current situation.

On a cool Sunday morning in mid-December, Hezekiah Rolle and Jennifer Thompson were joined in holy matrimony in a brief, simple ceremony. It was held immediately after the 8:00 a.m. mass at St. Barnabas Church on Wulff Rd. Jenny had gotten her hair straightened and hot-curled by a lady on Martin Street on the evening before. Jenny wore an elegant, white ankle-length dress made of Taffeta which had long sleeves of lace and 'drop-heeled' white shoes

Chapter Six

while Hezekiah looked dashing in his black suit and bow tie. Jenny's mentor, Mrs. Allen had not only 'gifted' her with the material and trimmings for the dress but also sewed it. The only attendees at the wedding were Mrs. Allen, Kenny and Jenny's grandmother. Father Calnan performed the ceremony. They were a lovely couple.

Mr. and Mrs. Hezekiah Rolle had booked a room for a week in Rusty's Guest House on East Street. Although the accommodation was modest, the location was convenient as it was very close to Bay Street which enabled them to get all their business done easily and efficiently. Mrs. Allen had lovingly 'gifted' the couple with some essential items like a cast iron frying pan and a heavy cooking pot from the Ironmongery on Bay Street along with several other items to get them started. Mrs. Allen even came to see them again just before they were leaving for Andros just to ensure that everything was in order.

"Jenny, you are like a daughter to me. I have been saving a little something for you. Mrs. Allen's youthful vigor contrasted with her pinned up salt and pepper hair as she sprang forward to hug her grateful mentee before she slipped some money into her bosom. I pray that you have a wonderful and happy life, Jenny." She then glanced at Hezekiah and said, "Now young man, I want you to promise me that you will always treat my daughter like she's a part of your heart."

"Mrs. Allen don't worry. Jen is a part of me now and I will do my best to provide for her and make her happy," said Hezekiah as he confidently smacked a playful kiss on Jenny's lips. "Thanks for everything Mrs. Allen. I will not disappoint you, ma'am."

With just a few days left, Hezekiah and Jenny scrambled to get many things done to prepare to take up residence in Andros. Hezekiah had been transferred from Exuma to the Staniard Creek All Age School because there was an urgent need for an additional teacher. Mr. and Mrs. Rolle had no idea what to expect but they knew that if they prepared well, life would be easier for them. Firstly, they opened a joint bank account at the Royal Bank of Canada on Bay Street, then they walked down to E. L. Sawyer grocery store where they arranged to order their groceries monthly and have them shipped on the mailboat. They spent an entire day shopping for personal items along with some remaining household supplies to set up their home. Fortunately, their cottage was on the mainland in Fresh Creek, Andros.

One afternoon, Kenny paid a visit to see Hezekiah just before the couple were scheduled to depart. "Kiah, how everything goin'? You all alright? You know I had to come and check on y'all.'

"Man, everything okay. We just rushin' up and down trying to get last minute things done. You know how that is," responded Hezekiah joyfully. "Just came from that shop on Shirley Street. You know the one." Hezekiah snapped his fingers trying to remember the name. "The Snappy Hat Shop. Jen wanted a hat. We just got back."

"I understand. Just make sure you have everything when you go because you can't find most of the things you can get in Nassau on the Out Islands," warned Kenny.

Jennifer's back was turned away from the door as she focused on packing.

"Jenny, how you doin'? You ready for Out Island life?" asked Kenny jokingly.

"I believe so," answered Jenny pleasantly. She was busy packing some items into boxes.

"Well anyway you just watch out fer them Andros gals. This a handsome feller you gat here and them women don't mind tryin' ter tief yer man. I hear they'll be lookin' right at you and writin' lil love notes in the sand with their toes to yer husband. Especially those older ones. They don't play, so be careful you hear?" warned Kenny.

Jenny frowned slightly then forced a smile.

"Man, Kenny what you talkin' about? Aint nobody can get between me and my wife." Kiah gently squeezed Jenny's hand and she felt comforted. He continued, "Jen, I am going out front to talk to Kenny for a couple minutes. I'm coming right back."

"Okay Jenny. Don't mind me. I was only joking." Kenny waved goodbye to Jennifer and stepped outside to chat with his friend.

The two buddies walked to the front of the guest house and stood at the right side of the building under the shelter of a flaming red Poinciana tree. It was a bit breezy outside.

Chapter Six

"Why you trying to upset Jenny with all that stuff about women. I don't like that, man!" chided Hezekiah who was visibly annoyed.

"I didn't mean anything by it, my friend. Sorry about that but I just want you all to be careful," explained Kenny. "I will miss you. Tell me something Kiah. What your mother them sayin' about this whole thing with you gettin' married?"

"Oh. Well. When I went back home before we got married, I told Mama and Papa I was getting married. I told them I wanted them to come to Nassau to attend the wedding, but Mama didn't seem to want to come here. You know Mama and Papa like two peas in one pod; one don't go against the other. She was not happy about me getting married, believe me. Sista said she would come instead but you know I told you Sista sometimes acts like her head aint no good. I really didn't want her to come up here and cause any confusion. I didn't want Sista or Mama them to say anything contrary to Jenny either. Mama was so distressed that she kept crying all the time. Jen has been through enough already. God had it so that Sista couldn't come on the boat 'cause the weather was bad. Right now, Mama aint even speakin' to me. I am basically on my own. I don't feel good about that, but I know that Jen and I belong together, and I can't let anyone or anything come between us."

"You're a lucky man Kiah. Take care of that lady of yours. Anyway, you just take your time and be careful. I will be praying for you all." Kenny was turning to leave when he remembered something. "O Kiah, I almost forgot to tell you. The Matron says she's going to recommend me for nurse training.'

"You can do it you know Kenny. Well, it goes to show that hard work does pay off. You like working in the hospital, right?" asked Hezekiah reassuringly.

"Yeah man. It's alright. I have to go in training soon so you might not hear from me for a while if all goes well. It's a girl I see who workin' there too in the office area that I like, but she don't look like she even notice me. Well, they soon finish building the new hospital so, until then, I'll have to live down to the Prospect Hospital out west. They have a place for people in training to live in there too. That'll be about three years before I finish. I hear that they give you your own room with your own shower and you get three meals a day, Kiah!" Kenny was prancing around in anticipation as he explained, "I should be finished by 1954."

"Man, Kenny that sounds good. You wouldn't even feel that time. I know you can do it but you gatta stay focused. Get your training and if she's for you, you will get a chance."

"That's true, you know Kiah. Pray for me 'cause I know it aint guh be easy." The two friends gave each other reassuring hugs and pats on the back while promising to stay in touch with each other.

It was a lovely day. The seagulls were in their element as they swooped and dived to retrieve scrumptious scraps from the water near the Woodes Rogers Wharf. Even at that early hour, several men and women had already begun setting up their stalls and preparing to hawk their wares to their eager patrons. Quite soon there was going to be a mixture of enticing smells and sights such as an array of native fruits and vegetables, fish, conch, and a myriad of handcrafted items. By late morning, vendors would have their stalls outfitted with such tasty treats as conch fritters, guava duff or coconut pastries. Hezekiah and Jenny had made two trips to the mailboat to secure most of their belongings on the evening before. This made it less stressful for them as they went aboard the mailboat with the other passengers.

Chapter Seven

The young man had just gotten the news that he had been waiting for after what seemed like an eternity. Anthony had been informed that he had been accepted to begin training to become a police officer. It had been his dream since he was a small boy. Of all the adults in the communities that he had lived in, he always had a special admiration for policemen. He was particularly fascinated by their smart, immaculate appearance as they directed traffic on Bay Street, and he was especially motivated by their firm posture and resolute demeanor. The fact that they were highly respected in every community meant a lot to him because they exemplified everything that he wanted to be. He smiled to himself recalling his childhood days when he played 'Cowboys and Indians', but his favorite game had always been 'Cops and Robbers'. He recalled with slight embarrassment how he had always insisted on being the 'good guy' and adamantly refused to be a crook whether he was playing with schoolmates, siblings, or children in the neighborhood.

It was no coincidence that Anthony had been drawn to this career. His stepfather Winston Nairn had moved up the ranks of the police force after having served with distinction for more than two decades between New Providence, Inagua, Cat Island and Andros. He had apparently fathered three other children in two previous relationships, but one had joined the U.S. Army while the other two (who were girls) were married and lived in Cat Island with their families. Officer Nairn and his first wife had been residing on Inagua when she died after a fatal asthma attack which left him with a young son and daughter to care for. Anthony's mother, Blossom, was originally from Nassau. Not long after the demise of his first wife, the widower met Blossom while he was doing some business in Nassau. He proposed to her after a brief courtship, then they married and eventually settled down in Mastic Point, Andros. Anthony was a baby at the time and had no recollection of these events. Mr. Nairn had built a comfortable home and the family had engaged in subsistence farming which augmented their modest income. Mrs. Nairn operated the family's petty shop with such frugality that it gradually became a thriving enterprise after years of consistent effort. Several years later, they were able to build a separate structure on their property to expand the shop.

Life was good for the couple and their three children. The Nairn family unit was strong and thrived in Andros. They were able to withstand all hardships and make the best of the simplicity that Out Island life afforded. Winston was an excellent provider for his family although he had been known to indulge in the 'sins of the flesh' occasionally with some of the local women before he got saved. Of course, his wife fumed and smoldered in anger whenever this happened, but she was always faithful and endured the indiscretions as best she could. Her repentant husband would always say, "Blossie you know how these women go. I didn't mean to… I won't do it again. Plus, you know I love you. I don't love them. Believe me."

Winston Nairn was a strict disciplinarian who treated his three children equally while he cherished the support of his loving wife. Anthony bore no resemblance to his siblings Sarah and Willard because he was medium brown-skinned while they were dark like their father and were tall and slender like him. Nevertheless, the siblings were so close that even if people were curious, they never dared to ask any questions. Because of the remoteness of the settlements, most residents were unaware of the biological differences and could not put all the pieces together about the family even if they were curious.

Since his retirement, Sgt. Nairn and his wife had launched themselves fully into expanding their shop into a mini food store. Around the same time, they engaged the services of a Haitian gentleman named Charlie Jean and his wife Mersous to assist them in growing local produce on their sizable property. The couple in turn were permitted to build a wooden house on a portion of the Nairn's property, and they raised their five children there.

Anthony commenced and completed police training at the top of his class, then entered the government service as a constable in The Bahamas Police Force in 1961. Fortunately for Anthony and the other new officers, living accommodations in New Providence were provided for them and other single officers in the Oakes Field Barracks which was previously used as the R.A.F.

Chapter Seven

Quarters. The work was rigorous, demanding and sometimes dangerous but PC Nairn and his fellow officers felt motivated to rise to each occasion confidently. Generally, there was a strong bond between them which enabled them to overcome most of the crises that they encountered. PC Daniel Woodside and Anthony had been best friends since their school days in Andros while his other close friend was PC Royston Coleby who was a native of Nassau. The constables worked eight hour shifts mainly on foot patrol and directing traffic, but on occasions when large crowds gathered for meetings, rallies, and events like Junkanoo, they were on the front lines and had to be prepared for anything that might happen.

Anthony's brother Willard had gotten married three years before and resided on Market Street with his wife and their baby. Willard had been lucky enough to find a three-room house on Market Street in Coconut Grove which provided adequate space for the young family. On their days off, Anthony spent a lot of time at his brother's home on Market Street where they often chatted and reminisced about the good old days in Andros. They sometimes were joined by either Daniel or Royston depending on their work schedules.

It was certainly an interesting time for PC Anthony Nairn. Anthony could remember his childhood visits to Nassau with his parents. Nassau had changed from the quiet, easy-going town where a modest amount of commerce took place on Bay Street to a bustling hub of ideas and the epicenter of political posturing. He and his fellow officers used to say jokingly to each other that although New Providence was very small as compared to the other islands like Grand Bahama and Andros, there was never a dull moment. The trio felt fortunate because they were usually on the spot when exciting events unfolded and of course they were fuelled by the adrenaline that they felt with each epic event that occurred.

On a scorching hot summer day in 1961, the young men were sitting around a small, makeshift table while sipping limeade and eating a meal of soft grits, Avocado pear and thick slices of Bologna sausage in tomato gravy. They were conversing about the current events of the day. Willard, who worked at the Bahamas Electric Company (BEC) happened to have a day off. His brother Anthony and Daniel were also off although Daniel was scheduled to work at 4 p.m. that afternoon. It was late morning, and they planned to make good use of the time they could spend together. Meanwhile, Willard's wife and baby son had gone to visit with her parents who lived several streets away.

Daniel initiated the discussion by asking, "So what you all think about women being able to vote in elections?"

Anthony rubbed his chin for a moment then expressed his views. "Well, you know, the women of today want their voices to be heard. They aint prepared to be in the background jus' minding babies and cleaning the house all day. Some of them workin' too. You all notice how every time there's a meeting or rally, plenty women come out and they always makin' plenty noise? They're working together as a team to make changes. They have a leader too, but I can't remember her name. Some carry placards and they don't seem to be scared either. You could imagine what 'll happen if they could vote, hey." He scratched his head and was thinking deeply.

"That's true you know. You all remember from couple years ago, that woman – The one who just came back home from studying somewhere. What's her name again?" asked Danny.

"You mean Ms. Johnson," chimed in Willard.

"Yeah Doris Johnson," said Danny. He continued. "She was speaking dead strong about the rights of women. She seems to be smart too. I swear I never hear a woman talk like that before. It seems like she was saying that all women who are twenty-one years or older must be able to vote in whatever election comes up next."

"Yeah man. She aint sound like she's backing down either," added Anthony. "To tell you the truth, I'll feel funny if I have to lock one of those women up for disturbing the peace or being a public nuisance as they say. You know those Bay Street Boys will do anything to stop poor colored Bahamians from getting ahead. Then another problem is we have so many police officers recruited from Trinidad and Barbados that you have to wonder whether they appreciate what we are going through," continued Anthony. "They might not understand."

Willard acknowledged the problem. "That's right. I even hear some people saying if women coulda vote, these Conchy Joes who been standin' on our necks for so long woulda been long gone. When you can't vote, you can't change anything and you sure can't improve anything."

Anthony added, "In January, Roy told me he was on duty outside the House of Assembly on another big day. He told me that there was some kind of a report

Chapter Seven

from a special committee, and it was passed in the House of Assembly that women will have the right to vote. I think they ruled that the women won't be able to vote until January 1963. Sure don't look like they have any intention of giving up though."

Danny interjected, "But remember now. It didn't quite go like that. Soon after that, the PLPs and the Independent members appealed against that to - I forgot what that place is called?" Danny paused for a few seconds to think, then he added, "O yes – The House of Commons in England. Then some time the following month a bill was passed for women to vote earlier than that in the general election coming up next year.

Willard mused, "Yeah man. It's plenty of them you know. You have some on the Out Islands too. The leaders of the females call themselves 'suffragettes'. I never even heard of that word 'til a couple months ago." Willard chuckled as he thought about these courageous women. "Yeah, and since they got the okay to vote, they just making even more noise. Then there's this woman named Ms. Johnson …"

"Who, you mean - Doris Johnson?" inquired Anthony. "She's a teacher.'

Danny was deep in thought with his fist under his chin as he pressed his elbow on the table. "Uh huh. You know she even been to London with Ms. Lockhart to complain that women here couldn't vote. She seems to be on a mission and aint scared at all. I hear talk that she even want run in the next election. Imagine a woman running! You think that could happen?"

Anthony was amazed at how much Danny knew about the political scene. He remarked jokingly, "Hey Danny, you must be does study this stuff for breakfast, lunch and dinner to know so much about it." Danny laughed in response.

"Don't forget now. There's another party that's looking to take down the UBP. They call themselves the Progressive Liberal Party with mostly black people. I had to work when they were having some of their meetings. You know our Chief wants to make sure nothing gets outta hand. I was close enough to see and hear what was goin' on. When I listened to one of them named Pindling who I believe is the PLP leader, I really wanted to join in but you know …" remarked Anthony as he threw his hands half way up in the air excitedly.

Danny pondered, "I remember that General Strike that they had couple years ago. When that was? Just after Christmas I think, eh Willard?"

Willard could remember that time like it had happened yesterday. He chided Danny. "Man, how could you forget that? That was three years ago. January 12, 1958 was when the ball got rollin'. I'll never forget those days. I had not too long started my job to BEC. Literally everything in Nassau was shut down by the next day. The hotels, government workers and other workers all went on strike. Remember, Danny, you had just come down here with your uncle looking for a job in the new year, right?"

Danny raised his hat and scratched the top of his closely cropped head for a few seconds. He thought about his own discouragement. "No man. Remember now, this thing started before that from around November 1957. I was looking for a job, but I was too young. I couldn't find anything worthwhile. Even though I had my School Leaving Certificate, I definitely couldn't get a government job because I wasn't twenty-one. On top uh that, when you black that makes it worse. Those white merchants on Bay Street wouldn't give you a chance unless you going to do hard labor." Danny kissed his teeth angrily.

Willard continued, "To tell you the truth Danny, I thought that was guh be like the Burma Road Riot in '42 that I always hear some of the older folks talk about, but this was a different kinda fight. Yeah. Trouble was brewing from 1957. Everything came to a head in January though. It was like a stand-off. The white Bay Street Boys owned the tour cabs and had an unfair advantage over the taxi drivers because the United Bahamian Party (UBP) supported them. When the tourists came from the airport at Windsorfield to the hotels and vice versa, the tour cab drivers took all the jobs. They had permission from the government."

"From what I heard, that was one for the history books according to how they described it," added Anthony.

Willard stood up as if he was giving a speech. He pounded his right fist into the palm of his left hand. He elaborated, "In January, everything came to a head. Man, I remember it started at the Emerald Beach Hotel out west. Then word got around town that nobody was to 'hit a lick' – They tell everybody to stop working. The taxi drivers took a stand and refused to let the tour cab operators take all the jobs when the tourists needed to get uptown from the airport. That man Lynden Pindling and some other men like Arthur Hanna from the new PLP party got involved and all work stopped in Nassau. Traffic was blocked for hours, and the unions joined in too to give them support."

Chapter Seven

Danny interjected, "Yeah. The General Strike was something else. Then to make things worse, the colored folks refused to buy anything on Bay Street and there was no work going on either. I was surprised to see the women join in the demonstrations too and march up and down with their placards. The Strike lasted for more than two weeks. Bay Street was practically a ghost town. That was a time, eh!"

All agreed and nodded to confirm these latest comments.

Anthony checked his watch right then and was amazed at how much time had passed. "Any way fellers, that's enough storytelling for one day. I gotta pick up my uniform from the Do Drop In Laundry on Ross Corner before they close for the day."

"Yeah Willard. I'm heading out too. Thanks for the lunch, man. Soon time for work." Danny excused himself also and the two friends left simultaneously.

1961 would prove to be a banner year. Randol Fawkes who was a lawyer, trade unionist and leader of the Labor Party had spearheaded the quest to make Labor Day an official public holiday and so it came to pass that Labor Day would be celebrated on the first Friday in June each year.

On July 31, 1961, the governor gave women the right to vote. The waves of excitement and optimism swept through the entire Over-the-Hill community. There were women crying, screaming, and shouting while some were running to and fro in disbelief as they hugged each other. Women could finally make a difference and when word reached to the other islands all the way up to Grand Bahama and down south to Inagua, the joy was indescribable. Women would be able to vote. Understandably, this event had led to a spirit of hopefulness, dissent in some quarters, and even heated arguments. Some residents held stereotypical views that did not enable them to conceptualize that women could make rational decisions about candidates because they felt that the fairer sex were mostly housewives and did not understand politics. In contrast, there were many people of all hues who felt that women could make a difference in the next election. This was a major topic of debate and a source of discussion among whites, some colored folks, the regular bar room patrons, between neighbors, friends and even some clergymen. It certainly was a new and frightening phenomenon for some people.

It was a Friday evening. As usual, with their week's earnings in their pockets, the regulars had gathered at various social establishments and most people were talking about local politics and women being allowed to vote. The sun had not gone down yet, but some men were already inebriated while others were well on their way to complete intoxication. The smell of greasy conch fritters, chicken-in-the-bag, old fat, and fried fish pervaded the air. It was a time that the locals attempted to de-stress, unwind, and socialize with friends.

The police had been called to deal with a scuffle that was taking place outside one of the prominent bars on East Street known as The Last Stop Bar. The raucous laughter greeted all who approached the area. There was quite a rambunctious assortment of males and a few females inside. Their voices echoed and ricocheted off the walls. It was a humid evening and, just as dusk set in, some people's nerves were getting on edge. The sounds of dominoes could be heard as they were slammed on the tables while agitated voices heralded the onset of some additional disturbance as the evening progressed. The quieter group who sat closer to the back of the room were absorbed in a serious gambling game of Poker. Two tipsy men were engaged in a heated argument in which one man was accusing the other of cheating in an earlier gambling game. At first the other patrons ignored these two rowdy customers. Then, some of the regulars like Maurice and TK attempted to intervene but eventually changed their minds. When the patrons heard the sharp clashing of a bottle being broken, the women screamed and scattered to the periphery of the room. Some men bent low or tried to head for the door to avoid being hit by missiles, but they stopped in their tracks when they saw the officers. PC Nairn, PC Wright, and PC Coleby in their immaculate white, black, and red uniforms had been dispatched to quell the melee. Officers Wright and Coleby lead the way followed by Officer Nairn who had been standing on guard at the door to ensure that no one left the scene. The two men were so engaged in their assault on each other that when PC Nairn shouted for them to stop and they were told that they were under arrest, they continued to fight. The smaller of the two men named Kermit had a big gash on the right side of his forehead and an injured shoulder, while the other man known as Whylly had sustained a 'busted' lip and (based on the blood on his face and on his shirt) had lost at least one tooth in the fight. There were overturned tables, spilled drinks, and several pieces of broken furniture lying around along with broken glass. After it finally dawned on them that they were making matters worse by resisting arrest, the two men capitulated. PC Nairn grabbed Whylly and PC Coleby ushered the other one out while he was still protesting that he had been cheated out of his money. PC Wright stayed behind to question some of the patrons about the incident. After taking a statement from Ross the bartender who was also the owner of the establishment, PC Wright left the scene and headed to the Southern Station to write the report.

Chapter Seven

As the population began to grow and the other islands began to develop, policemen were often transferred without notice for at least six months or more depending on the need. Anthony prayed that he would not be reassigned. He had not grown up on New Providence but there was something about this little island that especially appealed to him. The longer he stayed and worked, it began to feel like his home. He enjoyed the politically charged atmosphere particularly when he could see history unfolding before his eyes.

In September when PC Nairn was summoned to a meeting with one of his superior officers, he instinctively knew what to expect. After an exchange of just a few words, he found that he had been unceremoniously transferred to Grand Bahama commencing from the following week. The population was growing exponentially as more jobs began to develop in Freeport, Grand Bahama. There was a definite need for more law enforcement as a smorgasbord of individuals were drawn to the northernmost island to carve out a niche for themselves. Constable Nairn quickly prepared to depart Nassau and strived to put his best foot forward despite his reluctance to leave the city life. He made a mental note that he had to contact his parents before he left New Providence.

A few days before, Anthony went to see Willard to inform him of his impending departure. His brother was shocked at the news but offered him some words of encouragement. Willard put his hand on his shoulder and tried to reassure him, "Anthony, you might really like it up there. Who knows? You might even end up finding a girlfriend and staying there. Someone who meets your high standards, of course." Willard knew the nature of the beast and like a big brother should, he also warned him to be careful.

Anthony looked down and smiled because his brother knew him better than most people. In truth, he did prefer young ladies who were good-looking, well-educated and had a good family background.

Anthony responded jokingly, "Willard, you really troublesome, you know. Anyone hear you talking like that would think that I'm not a nice person, but the truth is if a girl is not of a certain class… You know I don't want my wife to be just barefoot and pregnant and can't hold a sensible conversation like so many women 'round here."

"You have a point there," agreed Willard.

"A family can't get ahead like that. I believe a husband and wife should be equally yoked. That may sound bad, but that's how I feel," said Anthony resolutely.

"Anthony, I get your point, but you need to be careful that you don't keep pickin' until you pick needle without eye, if you know what I mean." Anthony was becoming tired of Willard's brotherly jabs because his brother could never fully accept his point of view. As a matter of fact, Anthony acknowledged that his sister-in-law was a housewife, yet Willard and his wife appeared to be very happily married. He simply shrugged his shoulders to prevent an argument. Willard wished him well and Anthony was appreciative. Anthony shifted his attention to briefly converse with Willard's wife Marion, then kissed their baby and left. Willard walked with his sibling as far as the street, gave him a hug, patted him on the back and they exchanged goodbyes.

Grand Bahama was extremely large as compared to New Providence which immediately appealed to Anthony. He felt privileged to be working in a newly constructed police station that had some modern amenities. The exponential development of the deep-water harbor and the vast pine forest was a source of fascination to a fellow like Anthony who had lived his entire life in underdeveloped islands. He was impressed with the aura of sophistication that exuded from some of the locals there along with the opportunities that many people were receiving. Freeport had a lot of potential to become a booming, state-of-the-art industrial town and an affluent community that would attract immigrants from all over the world. By the new year, PC Anthony Nairn had settled comfortably into living in Grand Bahama, working with his fellow officers, and cultivating friendships. Apart from mostly work-related visits to Nassau or trips to see Willard and his fast-growing family, Anthony hardly visited New Providence.

Stephanie Swann came into Anthony's life quite by chance at a social gathering being held in Freeport. Kirkwood Swann, a Turks Islander who was employed at The Bahamas Cement Company, had been invited to a party hosted by one of his supervisors. It was there that he introduced Anthony to his sister who worked at Barclays Bank as a teller. Anthony guessed that Stephanie could not be more than twenty years old, but she was totally captivating from head to toe. Kirkwood saw the look on Anthony's face when they were introduced and he said sternly but with a slight smile, "Hey man, don't get no ideas. That's my baby sister so take it easy. She off limits to you."

There were a lot of people at the party and there was an assortment of charming ladies to choose from. Nevertheless, Anthony found himself following

Chapter Seven

Stephanie around the room with his eyes. She was a lithe creature who floated around the room like an experienced social butterfly. She spoke softly but her voice was deliberate and demanding. Anthony decided to sample some hors d'oeuvres and have another drink to calm his nerves and relax himself. He tried to convince himself that he should not let his feelings get ahead of his common sense, so he chatted with a few other young ladies then went to the bar again to get yet another drink just to fit in. Kirkwood noticed Anthony and called him over again to chat with his group of friends and Anthony reciprocated. Despite his efforts, he still found that he was distracted by Stephanie. At one point, he tried to fight the attraction by turning his back as he launched himself into exchanging pleasantries with another attendee whom he had met earlier.

Suddenly, Anthony felt a light tap on his left shoulder blade and knew it was her. Stephanie's eyes were glittering as she spoke.

"So how do you like the party? You don't look like you're having much fun." Stephanie smiled again mischievously while looking up at him through her eyelashes. She was wearing an updo that complemented her heart-shaped face.

"It's a nice party. Everybody seems friendly. What about you?" Anthony inquired.

"I'm having a pretty good time. You see my brother there. Don't take him seriously. I'm grown. He can't tell me what to do." Stephanie threw her head back and laughed. She had already drunk several cocktails and appeared to be enjoying herself.

"Would you like something to eat or drink? I could get you something," suggested Anthony hopefully.

Stephanie responded softly, "No no. I'm leaving soon 'cause I have church tomorrow. I don't want to stay out too late. You know – gotta get my beauty sleep." She chuckled at her own sense of humor.

"Kirk taking you home or you driving?" asked Anthony casually.

"Actually, me and two of my friends are riding together. They're outside waiting for me. I don't have a car yet but soon …" she explained. With that last comment, Stephanie glided towards the door swinging her hips knowing quite well that she had the attention of several males in the room including Anthony. Then she was gone.

Anthony saw Stephanie again while he was doing some banking the following week and they spoke for just a few minutes. PC Nairn was working in the area and used this as an opportunity to see his love interest. Stephanie was at her station. She saw him first and subtly waved to him. She was serving a customer, but she recognized him immediately although he was fully uniformed, and his high white helmet covered a lot of his face. Another teller had served him, and he was happy. It would have been embarrassing for him because he did not want her to know his financial status; that could have been awkward. He assumed that someone working in a bank probably made more money than he did. After her customer had completed his transaction, Stephanie spoke to her supervisor, then walked around to the front area and conversed with Anthony briefly.

"Hello Anthony. You ducked me, eh? You could've come and let me serve you."

"How you doing?" Anthony inquired.

Stephanie replied, "Alright. Through the week, things are a bit hectic in the bank you know and there are a lot of things I'm still learning plus I can't afford to make any mistakes. You know, when you dealing with money, sometimes it's a lot of pressure. Otherwise, everything's okay."

Anthony thought to himself that she looked different without her pinned up hairstyle, but she was just as beautiful. On this occasion, she wore her hair in a bob that followed the contours of her face to just below her chin. Stephanie was a dark-skinned girl with moderately full lips and a smooth complexion that made her look like a doll. She wore a neat uniform which comprised of a dark blue skirt, a floral blouse, and dark stockings.

"Your outfit is quite nice," he remarked.

"So is yours." Then she laughed lightly. "Sorry. I mean, you look smart too in your uniform."

She was funny too and he liked that. "So Stephanie, are you doing anything on the weekend like Friday evening maybe? If you're not busy maybe, we could go out somewhere. You know, wherever you want to go."

Stephanie responded, "That sounds good. I don't really have anything planned. We could do that." Then she looked over at her station and added, "I have to get

Chapter Seven

back to work now, but if you come back here when I get off from work today, we could talk about it some more." They agreed on the time.

"Actually, I'll be off by then too, so that'll be a good time. See you later Stephanie."

Anthony left the bank feeling as light as a feather. His heart was warm and fuzzy, and he felt happy.

Over the next couple of months, Anthony and Stephanie became almost inseparable. They had a whirlwind romance. Apart from a few minor entanglements with Stephanie's brother Kirkwood concerning their developing relationship, this seemed to be a match made in heaven.

One morning while the two men were at the park jogging, Kirkwood initiated the topic. "Anthony, I did tell you my sister was off limits."

"Man, what's your problem? I thought you were my friend," Anthony stopped abruptly and threw up his arms in exasperation. "What happen? I'm not good enough to date your sister? Really man!" He had a short fuse and Kirkwood was beginning to ignite it.

"See Anthony, you don't understand. One thing I know about my sister is she has an appetite for money and the finer things in life. She likes to move around in high society and if you can't give her what she wants, you aint gonna last long. She was like that ever since she left high school. You're my friend. I don't want see you get hurt and I don't want my sister to get in no problems either. I love her, but I know how she is." He shrugged his shoulders and threw up his hands then asked, "You think I would make that up?"

"Man, I don't know what you talkin' about." Anthony had no intention of accepting this illogical explanation. He regarded the warning as a feeble attempt to discourage him from pursuing a relationship with Stephanie.

"Kirk, I really don't want to talk about this anymore. If me and Stephanie are supposed to be together, it's going to happen whether you like it or not. I don't get it man. You supposed to be my friend, but I can't go out with your sister?"

"Alright man. We don't have to fight over this, you know. Don't say I didn't warn you though. I only trying to talk to you man to man. That's all. You still my friend." The two then parted company. From that point, their relationship remained cordial but slightly strained.

To say that Anthony was enamored with Stephanie is an understatement. He endured her antics and dug his heels in for the long haul. There were occasions when Stephanie promised Anthony that they would attend an event together or they planned a date together, but, at the last minute, she would disappoint him without warning or a reasonable explanation. Of course, this behavior angered him. It sometimes subjected him to the ridicule of his colleagues and friends. Stephanie's narcissistic behavior further exacerbated the situation.

Nevertheless, another Christmas season had just passed, and the couple seemed to have ironed out many of their differences. Anthony and Stephanie had never been happier. The holiday season had brought them closer together although it was not a perfect scenario. The rumor mill was still working overtime, but Anthony refused to believe what was being said. Stephanie sometimes enjoyed teasing him because she enraptured him. Anthony thought to himself, "Maybe she's just doing this because she wants to make me jealous." One evening in early February, Anthony was particularly peeved because his girlfriend cancelled their date unexpectedly. He discovered this when he went to pick her up at home and found that she was getting dressed to attend a work-related social function. She explained that she had forgotten about it, but she had to attend the event. She also explained that only employees were invited.

"I don't know why you're making such a big deal about it Tony. It's only for a couple of hours," complained Stephanie indignantly.

"Well can I come and pick you up at a certain time then Steph? Just let me know when and I'll be there," asked Anthony with a hint of desperation in his voice.

"No, that's okay," replied Stephanie smoothly. "I don't really know when the party's going to end, and I don't want to keep you waiting when you could be doing something else. She drew closer to him and began playing with the hair under his chin. You know we'll see each other tomorrow anyhow. You off tomorrow right, so we could have lunch and I'll see you after work, okay honey?" She smiled at Anthony and embraced him affectionately to reassure him.

"Stephanie, is something going on that I don't know about?" Anthony inquired while trying to maintain his composure."

Chapter Seven

At first Stephanie had a quizzical look on her face then she asked, "What do you mean? Don't be silly." She had returned to the mirror but was watching Anthony carefully. She began laughing lightly as she put on her glossy-red lipstick and applied some fragrance. "I don't know why you so jealous. It's only a company party!"

"I'm supposed to be your boyfriend but sometimes you treat me like a casual acquaintance. I have feelings too. I do love you." Anthony was sitting in the armchair now looking down at the floor at this point feeling humiliated. He needed some kind of reassurance.

"I feel the same way too, honey. You just don't understand office culture. It's different from your kind of work. You're in the military; I'm not. If we gonna be together, you have to learn to trust me," insisted Stephanie with a hint of annoyance in her voice.

Her roommate heard the elevated voices and peeped in the room curiously. She looked at both, waved and interjected, "Hello. Everything all right? I was just checking. OK then. Y'all have fun."

Anthony was cautious with his words, "This must be some kind of fancy party 'cause you're really dressed up Steph." Indeed, she looked stunning in the red off-the-shoulder cocktail dress.

Stephanie's words were calculated as she responded, "Look Tony. I'm due to get a promotion soon. You know my career is important to me and I do want to make a good impression. That's why I'm going to this event. Some of our top people from out of town will be there so (she threw up her hands) I need to look good. Is that a problem?"

"So this is about your looks then," suggested Anthony subtly.

"You know, I can't deal with you and your jealous attitude Tony. You need to lighten up a bit." Stephanie revealed her irritation as she slammed the bottle of perfume onto the bureau.

Outside, the loud honk of a car horn punctuated the quiet evening. Although it was February, it was uncharacteristically warm outside. Stephanie checked her hair and face one more time then quipped, "Tony, I have to go. My boss sent a car for me, and I don't want to be late. You understand, right."

"Your boss sent a car for you ..." Anthony's voice trailed off as he processed her last comment. He was puzzled and concerned, but he did his best to maintain his composure. Obviously, Stephanie was on a mission that did not include him.

Anthony relented although he was irritated by her flippant attitude. He was trying hard to digest the fact that his girlfriend's boss had sent a car to pick her up. Why? Despite his misgiving, Anthony decided that this was not the time or place to continue the conversation although he was unsettled about the situation. "Of course. I'll see you tomorrow." They walked outside together in silence. Anthony then headed towards his refurbished brown jalopy that he had recently purchased from one of his coworkers and got in without looking back at Stephanie.

Although there was intermittent turbulence, Anthony and Stephanie were able to patch things up. She promised to be more considerate of his feelings and he strived to suppress his jealousy. He took her out on more elaborate dates, and they even planned to take a trip together to the States when Stephanie had vacation time in April.

Nevertheless, Anthony had several friends and coworkers who were still concerned about him. After deliberating about what course of action they should take, two of his fellow officers sat him down one afternoon while they were in the mess hall and shared some troubling information with Anthony who was about to leave the station.

"Nairn, I have something to tell you and I'm taking a chance telling you this 'cause I don't know how you'll react. And I guess you could say it aint none of our business." Sarge explained nervously.

"Say what you have to say man." Anthony looked his colleague straight in the eyes as he spoke.

"Nairn, I really don't like telling you this, but I hear your girl sleeping with her boss. They're sweet hearting each other."

"Yeah man. You know the white Canadian feller with the bald plate. He married too." PC Roy Simmons finally got the words out and braced himself for the explosion.

Chapter Seven

Anthony got up suddenly, threw the table over and banged his fists on the solid cement wall. Seconds later, there was broken skin and blood on the wall. His friends held onto him as they struggled to calm the tempest that was raging. The words did not come but the tears of frustration rushed to escape as he gritted his teeth and groaned. His colleagues had only confirmed his underlying suspicions.

"Let me go man! I haven't done anything." The two officers wrestled with Anthony to restrain him as he shouted to be free.

"No Anthony. We can't do that. You're a good man and one of our finest. That girl aint worth it." Other officers had arrived by then and assisted in placating the situation. They did not like doing it, but eventually they placed Anthony in a cell overnight for his own good until he calmed down.

For the first couple of hours, Anthony was not in the mood to accept what others were trying to impress upon him and he was not ready to succumb to what seemed to be inevitable. He paced back and forth in the confined space and sometimes called out to be released. They had no right to detain him anyway because he had done nothing wrong. He desperately needed to see Stephanie and talk to her. If only they could just talk things over and clear everything up. Anthony wanted to turn back the clock to the happier times that they had shared together. He remembered the walks, the jokes, the expressions of love and all the good times that they had enjoyed. There were many things that they had in common. They both enjoyed cooking, and Stephanie shared his love for music and dancing. He relived those times when they would get on the dance floor as the DJ played their signature songs "Stand By Me" or "Spanish Harlem" by Ben E. King. He smiled when he remembered the good times when they had even talked about getting engaged and how many children they wanted to have. He refused to believe that Stephanie could be in love with another man. There must be some kind of mistake. Sam Cooke's song "Stand by Me" kept playing in his head as he waited and hoped that she would search for him until she found him at the station. As the night wore on, he began to brood and speculate. His battered heart yearned for comfort but there was none. Mercifully, he finally fell asleep during the early morning hours.

Next morning, Anthony awoke to a feeling of emptiness in the pit of his stomach, but he was not feeling hungry. His fists were still bandaged and feeling sore. He reflected on what had transpired the day before. Several officers of varying ranks had been observing him periodically. Anthony appeared to be subdued but resolute concerning the situation. His coworkers did not intend to take any chances with him. Roy came by to check on Anthony around 7:30 a.m. and offered him some breakfast before reporting for duty. He had also brought Anthony a change of clothing.

"Hey man. You okay? You had a rough day yesterday. How you feeling?" Roy inquired as he volunteered a smile to comfort his comrade. He pulled up a chair and they chatted for a while. Anthony appeared to be levelheaded and more like his usual self. After they had conversed, Roy was satisfied that Anthony had calmed down significantly. He breathed a sigh of relief as he left the cell.

"Anthony, the chief wants to see you. Time for you to get outta here. I gotta head out now. Take care of yourself now buddy and stay in touch." With that said, Roy was gone.

After walking along the short corridor, Anthony knocked on the office door of the officer in charge and was instructed to enter. Inspector Lewis was sitting at his desk with a stern look on his face. "Nairn, I am not going to waste any time talking to you about what happened yesterday, but I hope you learned something from that. Just make sure it never happens again. You gotta take control of your life. Understand me?"

"Yes sir. I'll do my best to make sure it never happens again," PC Nairn responded resolutely.

Inspector Lewis explained, "I got the news a little while ago that your father isn't doing too good. They brought him down to Nassau on an emergency flight by seaplane from Andros. He's in the hospital right now. You have vacation time so you can go to deal with that. Take two weeks and I hope everything goes well."

He saluted his superior officer, left the station, and arranged to travel to Nassau that same afternoon. Many thoughts were whirling around in Anthony's head. He had two more things he had to do before he left the island; he had to go to the bank for money and he needed to talk to Stephanie. He got there in five minutes, parked his car across the street and headed over to the bank. He couldn't figure out why his heart was beating so fast. The circumstances would not allow them to talk right then but at least he wanted to tell Stephanie why he had to leave. He was calm and resolute. Anthony intended to comply with the promise he had just made.

Chapter Seven

Anthony was so deep in thought that he inadvertently yanked the door open which startled a woman who was exiting the bank at the same time. He apologized and stepped aside for her to pass. He was surprised to find that Stephanie was not at her station. When he saw one of her coworkers who was also her close friend, he made inquiries.

"Oh, Stephanie didn't come to work today. She told me she had to travel to the States. I think she took a trip maybe to Miami. Sounded like it was sudden. I thought maybe …" Her friend Janice looked a bit confused and did not know what to say. She shrugged her shoulders, looked curiously at Anthony, and mumbled, "I have to get back to work. Excuse me."

"Tell her I have to go to Nassau to attend to something. I have to check on my old man. He isn't feeling well."

"I'll let Stephanie know you came to see her, okay?" With that said, she turned and walked away with a puzzled expression on her face.

At that moment, Anthony did not know what to think. As he drove to his home, he thought to himself, "I gotta get this girl outta my head for my own good." To say he was baffled by the whole situation was an understatement, but time was not on his side. He had to focus on other more pressing matters.

By late afternoon, Anthony was in Nassau and for some strange reason he felt self-confident. He had not felt that way for a long time. His major concern was his father, and he was looking forward to seeing his mother. Anthony arrived at his brother's home around 5 p.m. His mother spotted him long before he got to the yard and stood up waiting for him with open arms. It was an emotional time for mother and son.

"Tony, I didn't know you woulda get here so quick. You heard about your papa?" Blossom Nairn inquired.

"Yes ma'am. How's he doing?"

"Well the doctors saying it looks like he had a stroke and right now they just don't know …"

"If he'll make it?" asked Anthony cautiously.

Mrs. Nairn broke down and the tears began to flow as she spoke. "You know how your Daddy is. Although he's retired, he still does work hard. He's a deacon in our church now too plus he still likes working the farm. I keep tellin' him if he try to do all these things, he gonna get sick but you know how stubborn he is."

Before she could continue, Willard got in from work and was concerned about the fact that his mother was crying. She tried to hide her tears from Willard because she knew he hated to see her crying. "Now Mother, you know Papa guh make it. Stop crying like that." He walked behind her and rubbed her shoulders gently as she sat in a chair on the porch.

He turned his attention to his younger brother whom he had not seen in more than a year. They were overjoyed to see each other and greeted each other accordingly. Willard explained that visiting hours at the hospital was over for the day so Anthony would have to see his father the following day. As a matter of fact, he and his mother would be able to go there together and take the senior Nairn a change of clothing and other items while Willard would try to get into the hospital earlier that Wednesday because he was working the evening shift. Willard's wife had cooked a sumptuous meal of stew conch, white rice and plantains for the family. Anthony was relaxed. It felt good to be with family.

Anthony did not leave until around 8:30 p.m. to return to Marshall's Guest House on Market Street north where he planned to stay while he was in Nassau. Earlier, there had been a slight drizzle for at least an hour. There was a gentle breeze. The evening air was cool and refreshing, and the walk was invigorating.

Next morning, Anthony headed out early to look for some breakfast down by the waterfront on Bay Street. There was a clear blue sky with one or two scattered clouds. He walked under the arch on Market Street and, shortly after, he crossed to the other side of Bay Street. He welcomed the warmer air as he was wearing a short-sleeved cotton shirt and a pair of plaid Bermuda shorts with white tennis shoes. Several people hailed him and welcomed him as if he was an acquaintance. He walked past a couple of people outside a liquor store who were engrossed in an intense discourse about the unfair boundaries set up by the UBP party. He tipped his hat to them and kept walking. The familiar cacophony of sounds and smells competed for supremacy, and he smiled. The seagulls were in their element as they hovered, squawked, and dove into the sea with precision to retrieve the tasty scraps of fish and conch. Anthony reflected on the fact that he had not enjoyed a good meal of sheep tongue souse since he had been transferred to Grand Bahama; he felt a strong desire to eat some souse with

Chapter Seven

a big piece of johnny cake. As he walked past one or two vendors, he smelled the lemony pepper souse. After selecting a vendor from whom he purchased a bowl, he acknowledged that he had hit the jackpot.

After he had consumed his savory breakfast, Anthony headed to the Princess Margaret Hospital to see if he could get an update on his father. He also planned to return with his mother during visiting hours that afternoon. Willard had mentioned that Mr. Nairn Sr. was on the Male Medical Ward so Anthony decided to check that area first. PMH had never been one of his favorite places to go but this was an important exception. The walk was pleasant. He took a short cut through a side street near Royal Bank that lead him back onto Bay Street. Then, he walked past more than a dozen straw vendors and other artisans who had already set up their stalls with beautifully hand-made straw hats and bags along with other types of handicrafts. Many tourists were strolling around the market area curiously trying on or examining the displays while the locals were heading to work or other activities on Bay Street. Numerous stalls lined the sidewalk, particularly in the Rawson Square area. Hoping for a sale, vendors hustled and bargained with the tourists because if the price was right, they could get a sale. It was a reciprocal situation because the tourists were looking for bargains and the locals were heavily dependent on those "Yankee dollars". The scene was lively and dynamic. Surrey drivers entertained tourists in their horse-drawn carriages. It was amazing to see motorists, surrey drivers, pedestrians along with a few jitney drivers all endeavoring to coexist as they navigated the area going in both directions on Bay Street and traversed to the side streets that lead to the over-the-hill areas. At 10:00 a.m. in the morning, this major thoroughfare of New Providence was quite busy. Anthony spotted a fellow officer directing traffic in the middle of the street near Shirley and East Street. The constable, whose white helmet seemed to glow as the sun beamed mercilessly, briefly nodded at his coworker before focusing his attention again on the traffic. Anthony was familiar with that routine and felt fortunate that he was on vacation. He crossed the street at that point and walked past the City Market food store (making a mental note that he needed to purchase some groceries later) and continued east on Shirley Street, then in about fifteen minutes he was on the hospital compound.

After asking for directions, Anthony located the ward that his father was on, He explained to the nurse at the desk that he was Mr. Nairn's son and wanted to find out how he was doing. The Sister in charge of the ward was white, spoke with a British accent and happened to be walking towards the nurse's desk at the same time as Anthony. She responded to Anthony's inquiry by advising him that visiting hour began at 3 p.m. She could not allow him on the ward before that time out of respect for other patients and to protect their privacy. She instructed him to wait a moment until she returned.

The Sister reassured him by explaining, "Mr. Nairn, your father is resting comfortably right now. The doctors are still running some tests on him and making sure that he is stabilized."

"Thank you for the update. I'll come back later today and see him," Anthony replied and walked away.

Blossom Nairn returned to the hospital with her son Anthony, and they went in to see Mr. Nairn at precisely 3:10 p.m. The latter was in good spirits and seemed prepared and eager to greet his visitors. In recent years, the senior Nairn, who always had a commanding stature, had shed several pounds but he was still sturdy for his age. Anthony, who had not seen his father in almost two years, noted that even his hair had become completely gray, and his head was mostly bald at the top. Nevertheless, the older Nairn confidently confirmed that apart from being hooked up to a drip and being on a strict diet, he felt fine.

Blossom was just sitting on the edge of the bed near her husband struggling to hold back the tears and rubbing his free hand. Anthony did most of the talking. "Paps, how you feeling? You aint no youngster anymore. Seriously, you have to slow down," warned Anthony.

"Son, they say I had a passing stroke. I was talking and doing everything I always do then all of a sudden, I couldn't figure out what was going on. It's a good thing I was in the front room sittin' down just waitin' for Blossie to finish breakfast. Then my head start swingin'- everything was fuzzy and all I could do was slump back on the couch. My legs felt weak, you know like I woulda fall. Then the worst part (he paused and shook his head vigorously) – I have to do that cause sometimes the words don't come. I couldn't call Blossie when it happen."

Blossom chimed in, "Yeah, I even tried to give him some fever grass I had in the kitchen. The nurse to the clinic tell me it's a good thing I didn't give him that tea because it mighta made things worse. I didn't know what happen to your Papa and he couldn't tell me what happened. Lord knows, I almost fall out myself where I was so scared."

Chapter Seven

"I ready to come outta here now and go home, but they seem to think I need to stay longer. I could walk you know, but I have to take my time especially on this side (he pointed to his left side). You all … (his speech halted again) don't worry … I soon come outta here." The elderly gentleman smiled mischievously as he spoke.

"You need anything Winston 'cause I'll bring it tomorrow when I come back to see you?" asked his wife. She continued, "Looks like you have enough fruits and drinks at least until tomorrow but I'll bring some more clothes and stuff."

"No, except you know the food in here ain't that hot. They have me on this special diet too. The food don't have any taste. My pressure was very high when they first brought me in…" Mr. Nairn continued.

Blossom used this opportunity to rebuke her husband, "That's part uh your problem too Winston. You like too much salt in yer food. I always tell you about that, but you don't listen."

Right then, Willard walked in the room. The visiting hour was almost over. At that point Anthony decided to leave his family and head back downtown. He knew that his mother would be fine because Willard would take her home in his car. He was especially pleased that he had seen his father and it seemed that he was well on his way to getting better.

After spending a week in Nassau and connecting with family members, comrades and fellow officers, Anthony was basking in the feelings of peace and normalcy. He had already engaged in a serious conversation with his commanding officer in which he explained his personal situation in Freeport. He asked to be transferred back to Nassau. He still had strong feelings for Stephanie, but he also knew that staying in a relationship with her could have disastrous consequences. Anthony figured that even if they did decide to 'iron things out', some issues needed to be discussed and resolved before they could possibly reunite as a couple. With one more week left, he was thankful that he had enough time to collect his belongings and return to Nassau. Nevertheless, he was trying to avoid a big bust up with Stephanie who would probably succeed in provoking and belittling him. On the other hand, he did not know how he would react if he saw her with another man.

His brother Willard devised a plan that sounded quite feasible. He admonished, "Tony, you need to get one of your officer friends to contact your landlord and arrange to pack up your important stuff and send them on the plane to you. Just leave the rest. Don't even worry about the car. You don't need to be dealing with that girl who you get mix up with. You better stay away from her if you know what's good fer you."

Anthony agreed. "I guess you right, Will. Like our old man always say, "A fool once, second time a jackass."

Willard threw his head back and laughed with gusto as he reflected on the times when he had heard his father use that expression.

Another election cycle had rolled around. It was always an exciting time for everyone throughout the length and breadth of the Bahamian island chain. The young policeman was quite excited about the upcoming elections that were soon to take place on November 26th ,1962.

Anthony had become distracted by all the possibilities. This year was particularly significant because the Labor movement was gaining more traction. He was looking forward to the Labor Day holiday, especially since his vacation had already been approved to include that day. It was a rare occasion that he would be off from work on a holiday, so he was delirious with excitement. On June 1st after the Labor Day march, it seemed as if everyone on New Providence had gathered on the Southern Recreation Grounds for the Labor Day rally at which Randol Fawkes delivered a powerful, unforgettable speech to workers. It was a jubilant crowd. Anthony attended the event along with his brother Willard. This was a momentous occasion because it was the first official Labor Day holiday in The Bahamas, and it was taking place exactly twenty years after the Burma Road Riot of 1942.

Another major accomplishment for the people was that women were given the right to vote with effect from June 30th of the same year. Anthony had been on duty at the registration site on July 2, 1962, when Miss Ruby Ann Cooper became the first woman to register to vote in The Bahamas. It caused Anthony to think about his sister Sarah, his mother, his former girlfriend Stephanie and all the other women who would be able to vote and make a difference. Universal suffrage had been attained and so it was that on November 26th, 1962, women and men of The Bahamas who were eligible to vote cast their votes on election day. There was a need for change. Anthony was happy to be in Nassau to see history being made once again.

Chapter Seven

Oddly enough, over the past six months, Stephanie had left several telephone messages at the station for Anthony to call her. He found it quite odd that she wanted to speak with him so urgently when she had previously demonstrated disdain and apathy about their relationship. Occasionally, a colleague would say to him, "Nairn, that girl call again fer you, you know. She must be realize what a good thing she had. Why you don't call her and see what she want?"

Anthony smiled as he thought to himself, "You sure don't miss your water 'til your well runs dry." She had made a fool of him once, and he did not intend for it to happen again. Anthony had managed to rent a room in a two and a half room wooden abode located just off Market Street which he shared with a fellow named Riley whose uncle owned the property. Riley was a taxi driver whose addiction to foreign women and 'sweet hearting' had caused him to desecrate his marital vows and to finally lose his family. The living arrangement suited the two men just fine because they were both single and it was affordable. Many months had passed and life for Anthony was comfortable. He had begun attending church again and his daily routine had become almost predictable.

One morning in early December when he reported for duty after a day off, the officer in charge handed him a note which read, "Anthony, I need to see you urgently. I have to talk to you about something. Meet me at 3:00 p.m. on Tuesday by The Tiny Shop." It was signed by Stephanie Swann. They had not seen each other in about ten months, but Anthony was still conflicted concerning Stephanie who was his first love.

That afternoon, Anthony walked, still in full uniform, to the Tiny Shop. Bay Street was moderately busy with the usual assortment of individuals walking by. He spotted Stephanie right away although her back was facing him. Her hair was pulled back in one simple ponytail, and she wore a blue A-line dress. Then he was overcome with shock and confusion when she turned around to face him. She was holding a brown-skinned baby partially covered in a light-blue blanket in her arms. Her expression was a mixture of desperation and hope.

"Stephanie what is this? When …?" He was stuttering and lost for words. The baby was asleep in her arms.

"Anthony, I didn't mean to surprise you like this," pleaded Stephanie. "I did try to call you and left messages a couple of times, but you never called me back so that's why I came to see you." The infant squirmed just a little bit then settled back into sleep.

"You aint tryin' to say this my baby though! Can't be, Stephanie! You know how long we been apart? Almost a year. That's impossible." Anthony was adamant and had no intention of being fooled.

Her eyes began to fill up with tears as she tried to explain.

"Tony, it isn't a year. I found out I was pregnant just after you went back to Nassau. I started getting morning sickness and the doctor told me I was pregnant."

Anthony struggled to control his voice because he was conscious of people who were passing by and looking at them curiously. He started to regret that he was still wearing his uniform. He was talking between his teeth, "You think I don't know you were foolin' with that white man? I aint stupid you know! I came looking for you and you were nowhere to be found."

"Tony, look at him. He aint no white man's baby. This is our baby. Stephanie removed the blanket to reveal the baby's legs. She smiled, "See, he even has the same funny birthmark you have in the same spot below your left knee. Look."

"When was he born?" Anthony was stunned to the point of being breathless but anxious to confirm certain things. Undeniably, he and the baby bore the same birth mark.

"He's gonna be a month old in a couple days. His birthday is November 4th. Same as your birthday month." Stephanie looked downward in embarrassment. "I know I have hurt you and you have every reason to hate me, but I'm sorry for what I have done. At least for the sake of the baby, can we try again? I promise I will never hurt you again, Tony. You know I love you." Her piercing eyes now seemed to penetrate his soul as she looked hopefully into his.

Stephanie moved toward Anthony, and he reached out for the infant simultaneously. "Let me hold him for a moment. What's his name?" inquired Anthony.

"I call him Anthony. Little Anthony because he is so much like you even down to his color." Anthony and Stephanie had walked to a shaded area where there were benches in an arcade that led to some other stores.

For the first time since they reconnected, there was a hint of a smile on Anthony's face, and he began to beam with pride.

Chapter Seven

"So this is what it means to be a father," he thought to himself. Little Anthony awakened, squirmed just a little and looked directly into his Daddy's face.

As he held little Anthony securely in his arms, he asked "Where are you staying Steph?"

"I am staying with my Grand Aunt Libby for a couple of days until I get things sorted out."

"What you mean 'sorted out'?" asked Anthony.

'Well, you already know about my boss Mr. Weinburger who is the bank manager. Anyway, his wife found out about our affair. She didn't stop 'til she caused me to get fired. She told Mr. Weinburger if he didn't fire me, she was gonna leave him and go back to Canada with their children. So, of course, he chose his family over me. I know what I did was stupid. Things been really rough especially with me being pregnant and I didn't have a job for six months. My family, especially Kirkwood, aint been nice to me either. I do love you …" Stephanie was emphatic at this point. For a moment, Anthony wondered if she was telling the truth.

Stephanie held onto Anthony's right arm and appealed to him once again. "Honey, I know I was wrong. Please forgive me and give me a second chance."

"Stephanie, I'm gonna have to think about this. Yes, we do have a baby together. I will give you some money that I have now to take care of you and the baby until tomorrow 'cause banks already closed. I am working tomorrow. Give me directions to where you live, and I will come and talk with you tomorrow evening. I need some time to consider all of this." Anthony was navigating through a maze of thoughts, and he did not like any of his options.

"O.K. Anthony. I understand." She responded dejectedly. She reached out for the baby and was preparing to walk away when Anthony asked her how she was getting home. She indicated that her aunt worked nearby. He was prepared to stop a taxi to secure a ride home for Stephanie and the baby. Stephanie responded that she had arranged to catch a ride with her aunt and her husband when he came to pick her aunt up. Anthony handed the baby to his mother, smiled, and waved to him then walked away.

Anthony walked home at a moderate pace. He admitted to himself that after about ten months he had just about worked his feelings for Stephanie out of his system.

His dilemma was that although he was willing to accept that they had a child together, his feelings for her had greatly diminished. He considered going to have a talk with his brother but decided against it. Could it be that he had fallen out of love with Stephanie? He had to make decisions about this situation on his own. After changing his clothes, he bought a Chicken in the Bag and a sweet drink from a chicken shack on East Street. It was early evening as he sat alone on Long Wharf and indulged in deep introspection. The sea was calm with just a few boats anchored near to shore. He dangled his feet in the water. The cool December air provided welcomed relief from the sweltering summer heat that had lingered deep into the fall. Over the past couple of months, he had only taken a few young ladies out on casual dates. Experience had taught him to be cautious and vigilant. He sensed that Stephanie expected that they should get married. Unfortunately, the thought of her infidelity and her callous disregard for his feelings over the time that he had known her made him cringe. After about two hours, he had made up his mind.

The two star-crossed lovers met as planned by the Southern Recreation Grounds on Market Street at 4:00 p.m. on the following day. Unexpectedly, Anthony found that he had to work the late-night shift for an officer who had fallen ill. The upside was that he had been able to rest for a few hours in the morning then withdraw some funds from his account to give to Stephanie for their son. Anthony arrived first and secured a spot on the southern side of the park under a large, flamboyant poinciana tree that was full of red flowers. There was a makeshift wooden bench under the tree and a clump of high bushes nearby. Both individuals seemed mentally prepared as if about to go into a battle. Stephanie had left the baby with her grand aunt so that they could talk without any distraction.

The atmosphere was tense at first and they were both apprehensive. Stephanie sat a few feet away from Anthony on the bench. He decided to break the ice.

He looked directly into her eyes. "Stephanie, you are the first woman I fell in love with, and I will never forget you, but nothing can change what happened in our relationship. I don't blame you entirely for what happened between us. I should have been more responsible. Now we have a baby."

"But we love each other," Stephanie interjected.

"Do we really, Stephanie? Or is it because of the baby and you aint working that you want things to work between us?" asked Anthony with a hint of sarcasm. He could not help wondering how she felt now that the boot was on the other foot.

Chapter Seven

"Anthony, how could you be so mean? Why you talkin' like that? Yes, I made a mistake, but we could fix this. Let's make it right."

Anthony got up, grabbed her up by the shoulders and all of his hurt came gushing out. "What is the mistake, Stephanie? Going with the white man? Trampling all over my heart or getting pregnant? Which one is it?" Have you ever stopped to think about how I feel?" Anthony's voice was elevated, and he was trembling. He could no longer hold back his feelings. He walked away from her and stood facing the bushes to grieve. She started to follow him but changed her mind. She returned to where she was sitting. She began shuffling her feet up and down nervously. The situation seemed hopeless.

"I think the best thing for me to do is to leave you alone, Stephanie. Being with you is going to cause me to do something that I will live to regret." He threw up his arms hopelessly.

"Surely, you can't mean that. What about our baby?"

"I will take care of him. I am his father, and I will sign for him and give him my name. He deserves that. You don't have to worry about that, but you – I don't want anything to do with you."

"I know you aint serious Tony." Stephanie was weeping loudly and uncontrollably at this point.

"Stephanie, I loved you once, but you broke my heart, and I don't intend to let it happen again. I just can't get you and that man out of my mind…" Anthony was rubbing his forehead so vigorously that it appeared to be slightly bruised. "I was just about over you, and now this." He banged his fist wretchedly on the bench to release his frustration.

Stephanie got up and walked over to him cautiously. She turned him around gently and caressed the soft hairs on his chest. She spoke so tenderly that her voice seemed to sooth and comfort his wounded heart like a therapeutic balm. She got closer. Anthony was fighting with all his might, but he could not resist. He could not believe how much he desired her. The sun had almost completely slid down behind the trees in the west. They kissed for what seemed to be an eternity. Could it be that they were being blessed with a second chance? Only time would tell.

Chapter Eight

It was 1967. The mood in the country was tense, excited, and hopeful. Politics dominated the atmosphere. The curtain was closing on another election season. Over the last six years, there was an increasing appetite for equity and fair play that people, particularly in the 'over-the-hill' areas, were not prepared to wait any longer for. The populace had certainly come a long way from the days when a man could vote four times in the general election because he had four pieces of property.

The dominant United Bahamian Party had called the election prematurely (according to some), and it appeared that Mr. Pindling, his party members, and supporters were taken by surprise. Nevertheless, many public rallies were held, and election fever gained momentum. There was a proliferation of political posturing, paraphernalia, and propaganda. So much had transpired in the last few years, but one thing was apparent – There was a calculated movement afoot to create change and it was clear that the Bahamian people of color wanted it.

It happened on Tuesday, January 10th, 1967. People left their homes with a quiet, calm resolve to exercise their right to vote. The people had spoken with the casting of their ballots. In New Providence, as in many of the Out Islands of the Bahamas, the news soon spread far and wide that the UBP was out and the PLP was in. All Bahamians would have representation in Parliament. The full significance of this moment may not have resonated with everyone at first, but from this point on, there would be one vote per person. Most of the people did not concern themselves with how it happened, but they knew that the average, colored Bahamians would now have a voice and oversee their own destiny. There was no violence or turmoil, but the people had spoken.

Chapter Eight

The government truly reflected and represented them. Majority rule had been attained. No longer would Bahamians have to endure the oppression and suffer from the deprivation that they had faced under the calculated rule of their white counterparts. The people from Grand Bahama to Inagua were in a celebratory mood. Finally real democracy had been achieved.

It was a new era. January 10th proved to be equally as important as Black Tuesday which had unfolded on April 15, 1965. That was the day when the leader of the PLP, Lynden Pindling threw the Speaker's mace out of an upper window of the House of Assembly followed by Milo Butler who threw out the Speaker's hourglass. These symbols of power fell to the ground at the people's feet as both men were expressing their indignation over the unjust gerrymandering of constituency boundaries by the governing UBP. This time, in 1967, things would be different. Both the UBP and the PLP had each won eighteen seats in the general election. Independent member Alvin Braynen and Labor Party member Randol Fawkes broke the tie by supporting the PLP which led to the Progressive Liberal Party becoming the first black-led government. Thus, Majority Rule was born. For the average Bahamian of color and even some of the poorer whites, there would be opportunities that would improve many facets of their lives.

The Nairns had settled into Laird Street quite easily. Their neighbors naturally assumed that they were a married couple before they eventually got married after they had been cohabitating for almost two years. Anthony's father being a deeply religious man and his mother being the doting grandmother cajoled and pleaded with their son to marry the young woman despite her short comings. His mother never gave up. As she held his two hands between hers, Mrs. Nairn pleaded with Anthony one more time.

"You are going to kill your father if you don't fix this situation. You know he isn't doing too well. Now I know he aint perfect – in fact none of us are. Nothing more he would like than for you and Stephanie to get married. The two of you need to do the right thing. Aint Stephanie holding down a pretty good job to the bank? You all could make it you know. She just a lil immature, that's all. You gotta be patient with her. And the lil boy growin' so good. You all don't want him come live with me for a while eh? I love him so much." She chuckled hopefully.

"So Mama I guess you tellin' me because I make my bed a certain way, I gotta lie down in it, right?" asked Anthony.

Blossom was relentless. "No son what I mean is, sometimes you have to do what is right. It just aint right for you an' Stephanie to be living together out of wedlock, especially how you all have little Anthony. How you think he'll feel when he's old enough to understand how you all living?"

Anthony, who was always fascinated by politics and the ever-changing political landscape of his country was quite preoccupied with the events of this time. Of course, as a civil servant, he had to keep a low profile in the public arena, but he was a true champion of the cause for democracy and equality. Now that the election was over, people once again began focusing on their personal goals and ideals. He was being pressured by his family members to take Stephanie down the aisle, but he did not think this was the right time because there were so many uncertainties. He had virtually gotten past his fiancée's previous infidelity, but he preferred for them to get married after they had done some planning.

Undeniably, it took many prayers and promises to get the couple to the ultimate stage. Pastor Clarke had conducted several counselling sessions with Anthony and Stephanie before they took this major step. Just before Easter, Anthony and Stephanie were joined together in holy matrimony by Pastor Clarke in a simple ceremony at Sword of the Spirit Baptist Church which was located near where they currently lived in the Kemp Rd. area. They had decided to move from Laird Street into a four-room house off Kemp Rd. so that little Anthony could have more space. The accommodation was more pleasing to Stephanie who never adapted to their cramped abode in Laird Street. It so happened that Pastor Clarke who was the senior pastor of the church was originally from Mt. Thompson, Exuma and several members of his congregation were also Exumians. The Nairns were welcomed by their neighbors. They were welcomed by the Kemp Rd. community and the couple settled in quicky. They were even fortunate enough that several of the ladies in the neighborhood offered to babysit their son when they were both working. As the months and years passed the couple continued to cement their union. In fact, Stephanie had recently landed a job at Bank of London and Montreal (BOLAM) as a teller and was elated because there were prospects of promotions if she performed her duties well. On the other hand, Anthony was focused on the possibility of being promoted to a higher rank soon. Their dream was to purchase property in the eastern area and start building their home.

He was not prepared for the telephone call that informed him of his father being air-lifted to Nassau from Andros. Anthony had a bad feeling in his gut and braced himself for what could possibly be a negative outcome. It tore him

Chapter Eight

up inside to hear his mother weeping as she spoke to him, but he knew he had to be strong for her.

"Mama, everything is gonna be alright. You just need to be strong for Papa and I'll see you when you get here, O.K.?" promised Anthony as he tried to reassure her.

As usual, Willard and Anthony teamed up to ensure that their father's stay in hospital would be closely monitored and their mother would receive as much assistance and support as possible. They regularly updated their sister Sarah on their father's health; she was unable to travel because she had three young children and was expecting another in just a few months. Worst of all, she was having a difficult pregnancy, so the prospect of travel for her was out of the question. Their father had never introduced the younger Nairn children to their two older sisters, and it seemed as if the eldest son (who had spent most of his high school years in the United States with an uncle) had no desire to communicate with or connect with his Bahamian family including his father.

Blossom chose to stay with Anthony and his family on this occasion. Willard and his wife had been blessed with two more daughters. Since their family had grown, Willard was fortunate enough to rent one of two modest wooden houses that stood side by side in a yard on Windsor Lane. The Culmers, who owned the property, did not want to rent the house to anyone with small children but their son who was Willard's coworker was able to vouch for the Nairns and the deal was sealed.

Winston Nairn had spent a week at The Princess Margaret Hospital. This time, the senior Nairn was not recovering so well. He had suffered a second stroke which severely incapacitated him. At first, Mr. Nairn was conscious most of the time, but he was weak and looked like the shell of the man he used to be. Willard and Anthony did their best to console their mother, but she was sinking fast into the depths of despair. Winston was her whole world, and she was watching him fade away right before her eyes. Although the doctors and nurses worked feverishly to save him, he appeared to have given up. Finally, two days later, he died peacefully in his sleep.

Mrs. Nairn had agreed to have her husband buried in Nassau. She was at least in her mid-sixties and could not come to terms with being alone on their property in Andros. Just the thought of the loneliness she would feel made her panic-stricken. She decided to put off any long-range planning until after the funeral.

Arrangements were made for Mr. Nairn's funeral to be held at Sword of the Spirit Baptist Church on the following Saturday. Pastor Clarke, the senior pastor was officiating assisted by Pastor Miller from Mt. Olive Baptist Church in Andros (where the Nairns were members) along with clergymen of other neighboring churches in nearby settlements in Andros. As expected, numerous people from the Nairn's church and their community travelled from Andros to Nassau to pay their last respects to the revered Deacon Nairn. It was really a grand reunion day. People in the Kemp Rd. community had never seen such a large funeral. It was a hot day. By 12:00 p.m. the church was already full, and people were spilling out onto the church yard. Ladies were fanning in their seats while their male counterparts stood in any spot that they could find as the two and a half hours funeral service unfolded. There was standing room only by the time that the service started at 1:00 p.m. People who had not seen friends and relatives for years hugged and shed tears of sorrow and joy.

As the Nairn family filed in, Blossom had barely reached the casket to view her husband for the last time when she was so overcome by grief that she suddenly grabbed the casket, shook it, and began screaming. Her sons held her tightly and prevented her from falling. Willard and Anthony guided their sobbing mother to her seat and took turns supporting her on their shoulders. She was so overwhelmed by the whole situation that later she could not recall what transpired during most of the service.

After the funeral, the attendees arranged themselves to march in a procession to the graveyard which was also located on Kemp Rd. There was a solid sea of mourners dressed mostly in black and white who marched and sang as the band played funeral hymns and songs. Eight pallbearers lead the way closely followed by two cars which carried the immediate family. A beautiful royal blue, velvet covering was draped over the coffin which was being transported on an elegantly decorated gurney. The trumpets sounded along with the melodious playing of drums and other musical instruments while people sang "…Oh when the saints go marching in …". They sang several hymns until they got to the Out Island Cemetery which was located on a side road off Kemp Rd. Most of the bystanders did not know the deceased, but curious onlookers lined the streets on both sides to watch the homegoing procession to the graveyard. It had all the trappings of a triumphant march. This was an awesome sight.

By 5:00 p.m. many of the mourners and well-wishers had converged on the church grounds for the repast. There was food galore including peas and rice, baked ham, macaroni, fried fish, baked chicken, coleslaw and potato salad.

Chapter Eight

Someone from the Androsian entourage had even cooked a huge pot of crab soup, but this was reserved for the immediate family. Their neighbors and friends had donated generously. There was also an assortment of bush teas, fruit-flavored drinks as well as some 'hard liquor' that had been sneaked in surreptitiously by those who preferred the taste of alcohol.

Anthony, his wife, Blossom as well as most of their family members had changed into more relaxing clothing. Anthony was wearing a pair of dark grey plaid shorts and a white short-sleeved polo shirt and tennis. He was sitting with Blossom who was preoccupied with supervising Anthony Jr. so that he would not make a mess of his clothes or get into mischief. Willard was assisting with serving the drinks in the backyard while his wife and Anthony's wife were supervising the food service process that was taking place in a room at the back of the church. There were at least four other people working in the makeshift kitchen to ensure that everything went smoothly.

The charismatic Pastor Clarke, who was in his mid-forties, was mingling and chatting with the funeral attendees when he spotted someone whom he had known from his days in Mount Thompson, Exuma. The pastor waved to his friend and walked swiftly towards the couple.

"Hezekiah Rolle, come over here man," said Clarke warmly. Hezekiah complied. The two friends exchanged greetings. They had first connected after decades when Hezekiah had gone to discuss some business with his Exumian friend who was a builder. The man lived through one of the side corners off Kemp Rd. It happened that while Hezekiah was walking out to Kemp Rd., he spotted Pastor Clarke. They had a hearty talk and Hezekiah wrote down his friend's telephone number for future reference.

Pastor Clarke was overjoyed to see his former coworker and friend. "I am so glad to see you and your wife. How have you been Hezekiah?"

Hezekiah reminded Clarke that he had been teaching on several Out Islands for years, so he was again trying to get acclimatized to Nassau. He mentioned that he had met Winston Nairn when he was posted in Cat Island. Hezekiah explained that he was shocked to learn of Nairn's demise and decided to pay his last respects to the good gentleman who had been an exemplary police officer. Hezekiah alluded to the fact that Nairn had assisted him as he and his family tried to settle into the community.

Then Hezekiah introduced Pastor Clarke and his wife to each other. "Pastor Phil, this is my wife, Jennifer. Jennifer, this is Pastor Phillip Clarke. We were teaching together in Mount Thompson for a short while before he got transferred, then went into the ministry full time."

"Hezekiah and Jennifer, let me take you over to Mrs. Nairn who just buried her husband today. She is right over there sitting down under the tent. She is taking his death very hard as expected, but for the moment she is doing okay." Hezekiah had never met Mrs. Nairn previously, so he welcomed the opportunity to meet her.

Pastor Clarke greeted Blossom and Anthony and began to introduce them to Hezekiah and his wife when a strange thing happened. Each woman looked at the other as if they had seen a ghost. The older of the two looked as if she was about to collapse with shock.

Before Pastor Clarke could say another word, Jennifer seemed incredulous as she spoke to Blossom, "Rachel?"

Blossom fumbled as she stated reluctantly, "This can't be… Jennifer!"

Anthony was trying to make sense of this moment. "Wait a minute. You all know each other? Mama, what's going on? Why is she calling you Rachel? There must be some kind of mistake."

Some people who were walking past or sitting near them began looking at the two women and Anthony inquisitively. Someone had gone to call Willard from the back to intervene because the scene was becoming contentious.

"Where is my brother, Rachel? You took him and disappeared. What happened to him? Where is Justin?" demanded Jennifer. Her voice was elevated now, and Hezekiah was doing his best to placate his wife. He had never seen her so outraged. Anthony stepped forward to comfort his mother. It was then that Jennifer spotted the bright birthmark on Anthony's left leg and her heart leaped in her chest.

"O my God! Justin, it's you!" exclaimed Jennifer as she reached out to her brother tearfully. Anthony was in a state of shock and stood there as if he was in a trance.

Chapter Eight

Willard walked hastily towards the group and asked anxiously, "What's going on? Mama, you alright?" He clutched his mother protectively. "Somebody troubling you?"

Pastor Clarke took control of the situation to the best of his ability. First, he asked one of his congregants to take Little Anthony to another area for a while because he did not need to hear what was being said. He then told the group, "I suggest that we go to a quiet spot over there away from these people so that you all could talk this out. Everybody does not have to know your business." He also assured the onlookers that everything was alright. "There was a little misunderstanding, my brothers and sisters so carry on. There is nothing to worry about. You all know how it is when people haven't seen each other for a long time." Some people nodded in acknowledgement while others walked away with questioning looks on their faces.

Hezekiah was baffled. He had always known that Jennifer had a brother who was missing, but this development was totally unexpected. He held his wife's hand and endeavored to calm her as he walked with her. Anthony needed to do something with his hands, so he immediately grabbed a couple of chairs and brought them over to where their meeting would convene. The older woman was looking deeply into her hands as she cried openly. Pastor Clarke looked pitifully at the woman whom he knew as Blossom Nairn and beckoned for her to speak when she regained her composure.

She remained seated and held Anthony's hand tightly. When she began to speak, she continued to wipe away her tears. "My name is Rachel Blossom Butler before I got married to Winston. Jennifer, I didn't mean any harm." She looked at her son sadly, "Anthony, your real name is Justin." She pointed to Jennifer as she continued, "Jennifer is your sister. When your mama died, Jennifer and her sister Leah were young, and your daddy wasn't looking after any of you all. I took you when you were a young baby and raised you as my own child." Blossom was sobbing at this point as Anthony released her hand.

Jennifer retorted, "But why didn't you try to help all of us? We had a very hard time growing up and not knowing what happened to our baby brother made the whole situation worse." Jennifer was reluctant to accept the woman's story.

Anthony interjected, "I feel as if my whole life is a lie. I just don't know who or what to believe." He threw up his hands in an expression of outrage. This could not be true.

Jennifer stood up and pointed her right index finger directly at Rachel as she spoke, "What you did was selfish. I can't forgive you for that!" Hezekiah tried to comfort his wife who could not come to terms with Rachel's story. By this time, Stephanie had arrived on the scene, and she held her husband across his shoulder blades to placate him.

Blossom was regaining her composure at this point. She continued to explain, "That is what it looks like but it aint exactly like that. Yes, I really wanted a child of my own and at my age it wasn't much hope of me having one." She paused for a moment then continued her explanation. "But I knew that I could take care of him and give him a good life.

The woman turned toward Anthony and endeavored to explain, "Anthony I am so sorry. I was only trying to save your life. That's all. You didn't have anyone to take care of you, so I did what I thought was right. You are my son, and I have always loved you even if I didn't born you. Please try to understand that."

The tears began to flow from Anthony as he reached out to hug his mother. After a few seconds, he stepped away from her. He was still confused about something. Anthony had an important question to ask. "So Sarah and Willard are not actually my brother and sister then?"

"Yes, they are. Remember, y'all grow up together all your life." Blossom responded hopefully.

"So Mama, Papa knew about this?" asked Anthony.

"No. I was afraid that if I told him, I thought he might not let me keep you. He always thought that you were my child, so he accepted you just like he loved me. You never notice no difference, right? Even Sarah and Willard didn't know that. I thought it was the best thing to do. What else could I do? Your Papa (Theophilus Thompson) didn't seem to care. He turned against all of you all. Your mama died having you. She was my cousin. Two sisters' children. If I didn't take you, someone else woulda take you and your life could've been very different son. Who knows what mighta happen to you?" At this point, no one spoke as they all tried to come to terms with what had just been revealed.

Jennifer and Anthony looked at each other intently as they attempted to assess the situation. The siblings knew instinctively what they had to do. They bore a strong resemblance to each other even in the way that they smiled. Both

Chapter Eight

reached out to the other almost simultaneously and hugged. Jennifer broke the ice and looked up at her brother smiling as she said, "I have to call you Justin, because I woke up with your name in my head every morning from you were gone, but I will get used to calling you Anthony eventually. Believe me, I never stopped looking for you. Leah is our sister, and she will be so happy to see you Justin, I mean Anthony. I have always hoped that this day would come."

Willard was standing on the sidelines watching the reunion. Anthony called to him. "Come here Willard. Let me introduce you to my sister Jennifer who likes family and friends to call her Jenny. Jenny, this is my big brother Willard." The trio laughed together jovially.

Jennifer then introduced her husband to Anthony, and Anthony reciprocated by introducing his wife Stephanie to Jennifer and Hezekiah.

Pastor Clarke was pleased with the outcome. There was an abundance of love and hurt in this gathering. He acknowledged that healing would take place over time. He advised the family that it would not be easy to make the adjustments or to forgive and forget. He then encouraged everyone in the group to bow their heads in prayer. He prayed for love and unity in this family and that in moving forward they would protect and care for each other unconditionally. Pastor Clarke also made a commitment to provide counselling if any of them needed it. He reassured them, "My doors are always open, and you all have my number. So even if you just need to talk, I will always be here for you." Everyone thanked Pastor Clarke and they parted company amicably with the promise that they would stay in touch with each other.

Jennifer and Blossom rarely met or spoke to each other after that fateful day. The beleaguered woman was never able to overcome her guilt although Anthony and the other siblings did their best to support her. Blossom became paranoid to the extent that she believed that everyone in Nassau knew her story. Jennifer also struggled to come to terms with the situation. Since her childhood days, Jennifer remembered her father saying that "Marriage covers a multitude of sins." and she finally understood its true import. Jennifer visited Blossom one day at Anthony's home to tell her that she had forgiven her. The two women wept together, and this gave both a release. Shortly after their meeting, the middle-aged Blossom surprised her family when sheced that she could no longer live in New Providence. Her children were opposed to this move because they sensed that their mother would wither away and die there, and that is what she did.

Anthony, Willard and Sarah telephoned her daily to check on her, and she always expressed that she was "fine". A year later, Rachel Blossom Nairn fell asleep at home and never woke up.

Losing their mother was difficult for the three siblings, but Anthony's struggle was a unique one. Fortunately, he had his wife who became a pillar of strength for him along with his sister Jennifer. Jennifer was able to bridge the gap for him and after a while they became inseparable. At last, there was solace.

Chapter Nine

Roland Gibson was a one-man army. He certainly did not look his age. The fact that he never allowed his muscular physique to go to waste could not be denied. He did not seem to have an ounce of fat on his body. Whether it was 11 p.m. or 6 a.m., Mr. Gibson could be seen and heard chopping wood, using a hammer or pickaxe, and mumbling to himself. Most people figured that he had to be about 55 years old, but he looked at least ten years younger and was not bad looking either.

In later years, Mr. Gibson lived like a hermit. He had married his former wife Sharon Sears some thirty years before. The relationship was tumultuous and strained at its best. Their union resulted in two children (a girl and a boy). After enduring years of abuse and failed attempts to leave her tormentor, the woman and her two children surreptitiously fled to the United States to escape Gibson's brutality and psychological oppression. It was apparent that his wife's departure completely unraveled Gibson. This was an ignominious defeat for the man who had previously been the king of his castle.

Mr. Gibson always seemed to be peeved about something. He was well-known in Fox Hill. As the years passed, his eccentric behavior gained traction. Even newer residents of the area had grown accustomed to his bouts of outrage and righteous indignation. On those occasions, his heavy voice resounded in the area. Some of the residents even secretly called him Noddy because of a chronic habit he had of constantly bobbing his head up and down when he spoke; this involuntary habit was exacerbated at times, because he stuttered uncontrollably when he was angry. His strange persona attracted the curiosity of the children who were fascinated by his rants and raving. Ms. Aggie Rahming used to say,

"I wonder how dem church people manage him down by the Jumper church and school. I guess he's good at what he does do." Then she would shrug her shoulders incredulously and retreat inside her house where she could safely observe her neighbor's rabid tirade.

Mr. Gibson was a Jack-of-all-trades who had single-handedly built his home in the middle of 100 X 50 feet of property. His house had originally been the first house on Tyler Street in Fox Hill but gradually a cluster of houses grew up around his property. The area on both sides of the road became more developed and over time the population in the area grew rapidly. Mr. Gibson's neighbors had fenced him in on two sides of his yard, but he was too frugal to fence in the front and eastern sides of his yard although he could have done it himself.

The mischievous children in the neighborhood could not resist the temptation of teasing their eccentric neighbor by picking mangoes and sapodillas from his trees. When they were at their worst, the little urchins used to tease Mr. Gibson or overturn his pot sometimes because he often preferred to cook on an outside stove. During those moments, the irate man used to grab a stick, a dry coconut or any item that he could put his hand on and hurl it at the children, but he never managed to catch any of them.

The adults were not much better. Miss Aggie, who was Mr. Gibson's next-door neighbor was always proud to retell the story of his confrontation during the Battle of the Mango Tree. On a particular 'hot-sun' day, it happened that Mr. Gibson had peeped out of his kitchen window and spied a young man high in his mango tree while zealously trying to pick all of the ripe Haden mangoes. Mr. Gibson grabbed his recently sharpened cutlass with quiet determination and participated in a vigil to catch the rascal. The boldness of the fellow made him oblivious to Mr. Gibson's approach. The sun had just come up and it was still quite cool. The culprit had already hooked a large crocus sack of mangoes onto a branch of the tree and had paused momentarily to eat one of the succulent fruits. Gibson eased his screen door open slowly and stealthily crept up on the scoundrel. He aimed at the legs and swung the cutlass. Simultaneously, the agile fellow turned around just in time. He spotted Mr. Gibson, moved his right leg upward and leapt to another limb of the huge tree just as his enraged attacker swung at him again and again. He danced on those branches as if his life depended on it. By this time, a small crowd of passersby had gathered to view the spectacle after they heard the commotion. Fortunately, the thief was slim and agile. Mr. Gibson hurled vile epithets at the villain as he wielded the weapon. One aim caught the shirt of the terrified fellow which motivated him

Chapter Nine

to wiggle out of his shirt and jump for his life. As he landed, he groaned in pain but somehow managed to run and vaulted over the fence at the back of Mr. Gibson's yard. His blood-stained shirt still hung like a flag in the tree along with the sack of luscious mangoes. The passersby opted to move away and pretend that they saw nothing. Mr. Gibson was still brandishing his cutlass as he glared at the timid witnesses.

His neighbors, The Rolles, whose property was adjacent to his, were always civil to Mr. Gibson and he behaved in like manner to them. Hezekiah had gotten a good deal on a piece of property in Fox Hill and he and his wife Jennifer had been very diligent so that they could pay for the property in the shortest time possible. Mr. Gibson had expressed that his spirit "took to" Hezekiah and his wife Jennifer so it was not surprising that he eagerly offered them most of the mangoes that he had retrieved from the crocus sack. Although he was the strange neighbor that most of the residents handled with "kid gloves", over the last two years or so, a pleasant rapport had developed between Gibson and the Rolle family that promoted cordiality. Oddly enough, Mr. Gibson had become so enamored by the refined ways of the couple that he kindly allowed them to use water from his well as they needed it when the workmen were building their home.

As time passed, the Rolles were relieved to finally see the fruits of their labor taking shape. On a weekly basis, they used to order cement blocks and other building materials for their house. Hezekiah had hired one Mr. James Roker who used to bring a helper to work on the structure periodically. Hezekiah even assisted on his days off. They had managed to build the structure up to belt course and the Rolles were grateful. Their desire was to raise their children away from the hustle, bustle and congestion of the "Over-the-Hill" area. On New Providence, in particular, there had been significant developments in terms of infrastructure and communications in recent years, so the Rolles felt privileged to be building their home in the eastern end of the island.

When Hezekiah obtained an in-service training award, the couple had to put their building plans on hold temporarily until they returned to The Bahamas. Like their beloved country, they were beginning to experience their own independence. They had lived in England for three years while Hezekiah completed his formal teacher training and earned a degree in Education at the University of Reading in Berkshire. Indeed, Hezekiah had made such a great impression during his training that he received several teaching job offers in neighboring counties as well as an opportunity to pursue advanced studies but he declined those offers. While there, his wife Jennifer had done some upgrading courses by mail, and also accomplished her dream of completing a secretarial course. Their daughters (Angie and Gina) were in elementary and grammar school respectively while their son Lester had just completed grammar school and wanted to pursue a career in aviation.

The Rolles returned home by British Airways to an independent Bahamas. It was the summer of 1973 and Bahamian flags were being flown everywhere. The government owned Bahamasair had begun inter-island flights with a hope of expanding services elsewhere, the National Insurance Board had been created to provide social security for the people and plans were afoot to improve educational opportunities particularly at the tertiary level. The future looked promising, and Hezekiah felt that his decision to return home with his family was a wise one. He was keen and felt prepared to make his contribution to his country. Development was taking place, changes were being made to improve the lives of every Bahamian and the government was striving to promote national development. Hezekiah and Jennifer had always supported the Progressive Liberal Party and were elated that the party, lead by Prime Minister Lynden Pindling, had won a second term to continue their transformative and enlightening campaign for advancement. For the first time, The Bahamas had a Bahamian Governor General named Sir Milo Butler who lived in Government House. There was jubilation and a spirit of triumph that pervaded the air. The new nation was undergoing a metamorphosis that was unparalleled.

The Rolles and their three children were desperately in need of a temporary home. Miraculously, Jennifer's brother Anthony had made inquiries and assisted his brother-in-law in finding a small stone house for rent in the Palmdale area near to Wulff Rd. The cost of renting this house was phenomenal. Hezekiah assured his wife that they would have to get into their own house as soon as the roof and windows were secured.

They were anxious to see what was happening with their property. While in England, Hezekiah had been able to save enough money to buy a good used car so the first thing he did was to purchase one. Their next effort was to check on their property. For a short time, as they drove down Tyler Street, their attention was diverted to their neighbor's house that had previously not even been plastered with cement on the outside. They were pleasantly surprised to see that Mr. Gibson's house was beautifully painted and a car was parked in the front of the house but there was no indication that anyone was at home even after Hezekiah blew the car horn. That was also strange because Mr. Gibson had never attempted to drive a car but preferred to ride a bicycle. Nevertheless, they

Chapter Nine

decided to stop in front of the yard to greet him or to speak to anyone who was inside. Hezekiah walked up to the front door while Jennifer remained in the car. They sensed that someone was in the house, but no one came to the door when they knocked. It was all quite unusual.

Nevertheless, they looked in disbelief at what they found upon their return to their property. They were horrified to discover that a makeshift wooden structure had been built on their property in Fox Hill. There were at least two dozen chickens wandering around the yard and a portion of the yard was being used to grow bananas, peas and corn. The situation was compounded by the fact that they met a Haitian woman scrubbing some clothes in a tin tub on a makeshift table while several children of various ages were playing in the yard or sitting on the doorstep. They had to stop in their tracks when a medium-sized black mutt dashed from inside their incomplete concrete structure and expressed his fury aggressively.

For a second or two, Hezekiah was taken aback, then he shifted into a defensive mode to protect his family. He grabbed a limb that had fallen from a nearby tree and aimed at his target. The dog retreated after receiving the first lash. The woman stood up beside the tub. She seemed to speak a little English but understood most of what Hezekiah was telling her. She explained in broken English that her husband Sammie had built the wooden structure there because no one was living there. She suggested that they only wanted to stay a little while until they could find some other place to live. The woman returned to her washing and the children continued to run around the yard. She shouted at the children in Creole, and the dog began barking again from a distance. She added as she looked down at the clothes she was scrubbing, "My husband just get job far far out west. He don't come home 'til late. When he come, I tell him what you say, then he decide what to do. We don't have no place else." The woman threw her arms up in the air to indicate that she had no more to say about the matter.

Hezekiah was becoming a little irritated because the woman did not appear to appreciate the urgency of the situation. Jennifer was just as annoyed and said to her, "This is our property. You just can't build on someone's property, and you know it's not yours." She pointed at the unfinished structure and continued, "See, this is our house that we want to finish. You have to move!"

Hezekiah added, "When we come back, by Saturday, you all have to be gone from here. I don't want to meet you all or your belongings here when we come back or there's going to be trouble. You can't just squat on our land and expect to get away with it. Do you understand?" The woman did not look up, but he knew she understood what he had told her.

Additionally, they were still surprised when they did not see Mr. Roland Gibson anywhere. In their last interaction with Mr. Gibson before they travelled, he had assured Hezekiah and Jennifer that he would "keep an eye on the yard to make sure that nobody is trespassing" while they were gone. They were even more perplexed when they heard the rumor about what had happened to him. Word had spread around the Fox Hill community that Mr. Gibson appeared to have had a confrontation with some Haitian people who were planting crops in the Rolle's yard across the street. He had admonished the bold squatters several times to cease their activities when he saw them planting their crops. One day, he became so irate with these individuals that he began cursing in his usual manner and threatened to harm them if they did not stop what they were doing. Several passersby watched in disbelief. Suddenly, Mr. Gibson stopped shouting, began clutching his chest and within seconds he was on the ground lifeless. Only a few of his family members attended Gibson's funeral along with some neighbors including the Rolle family. Hezekiah gave a tribute on behalf of his family. Mr. Gibson was laid to rest in St. Anselm's graveyard.

So much had changed in the three years that Hezekiah and his family had been living abroad. He was surprised to find that Highbury High School on Robinson Rd. where he had recently been assigned to teach had been renamed R. M. Bailey High School in the previous year. He knew that he had to make many adjustments because prior to this posting, he had only taught mostly at all-age schools on several of the Family Islands including Exuma, Cat Island, Andros and Eleuthera. Each island brought a new brand of experiences for the Rolles. As he became more adept as a teaching professional, he served as vice-principal and was later appointed to the post of principal. Nevertheless, he reassured himself that the transition to teaching in the city should not be too challenging because he had extensive experience. More recently, he had endured the grueling rigors of successfully completing teaching practice in a predominantly white community where he had sometimes experienced racial prejudice and disdain because he belonged to the African diaspora.

Hezekiah was overjoyed to be home. This was the one place in the world where he was not an immigrant but was a citizen of the Commonwealth of The Bahamas. He had returned to New Providence and was on a mission to claim what was rightfully his. By the following week, the situation was resolved with

Chapter Nine

the Haitian woman and her family. It became a police matter and subsequently an immigration matter. He and Jennifer were eager to continue the building process. One of Hezekiah's coworkers at the school had a brother who was a renowned builder, so Hezekiah engaged his services to work on their house in stages as they were financially able to spare the money. Meanwhile, the Rolles resided in temporary accommodations in the Soldier Rd. area. His sister-in-law Stephanie Nairn had also assisted Hezekiah and Jennifer in getting an appointment to see the Loans Manager at Bank of London and Montreal (BOLAM) Bank. As Hezekiah was a government employee with a good credit history, he had no problem obtaining the loan. This enabled him to borrow enough money to work on their home to the point where it was habitable. Jennifer, on the other hand had managed to secure a job in customer service at a well-established insurance company and this was a boost to the family's income. Although the house was not completed, the Rolles were able to move in and spend Christmas in their own home.

The three Rolle children had been born while their parents were on the out islands. Although Hezekiah was an educator with a comparatively decent salary, he and his family lived frugally. The goal had always been to save as much money as possible to minimize their debt when they built their home in Nassau. It had not been easy; there were numerous temptations and obstacles, but the couple were able to overcome them. Jennifer had honed her skills as a seamstress, so she earned money sewing for some of the residents in the settlements where they had resided. She also did some office work when the opportunity arose which assisted in providing extra income to take care of the family's household needs. Even their trips to New Providence had been carefully orchestrated.

Hezekiah and his family planned to celebrate this Christmas like they had never done before. Their house was not fully plastered and needed to be painted but the family was not daunted by that. They had cut a shapely Christmas tree from the Pine Barren out west and installed it in a central location in their living room. Jennifer took pride in decorating the tree almost as if it was her personal project. She and her daughters had baked three fruit cakes and soaked two of them in rum in preparation for Christmas. They bought the biggest ham and turkey that they could find, and the family feasted on a typically Bahamian spread on Christmas Day. Anthony and Stephanie had joined them for dinner along with Anthony Jr. and their daughter Siobhan. It was truly a jovial family gathering.

The Rolle clan had unanimously agreed to attend Junkanoo on Boxing Day. They wanted to experience the pulsation of the goatskin drums once again, the clank of multiple cowbells and the melodious sounds of the horns as Bay Street rocked to the rhythmic musical celebration that was uniquely Bahamian. Around 2:00 a.m. on the day after Christmas Day, the Rolles headed out to Bay Street to enjoy the Junkanoo rush out that would last until daylight that morning. The colors and costumes were fantastic. It was standing room only on Bay Street as police officers of all ranks patrolled the area and the junkanoo groups performed on Bay Street and Shirley Street. The crowds rocked, swayed, and danced as they shouted, "Saxons!", "Valley Boys!", "Music Makers!" in support of their favorite groups. It was a cool night so many people were dressed in their best outfits, fashionable sweaters, jackets, boots, and hats. Among the crowd, you could see dignitaries and the 'who's who' of Bahamian society along with international guests and tourists. People travelled from all over the world to see Junkanoo. The crowds cheered for their favorite groups and anticipated which group would emerge as the winner of the parade. Some believed that the Music Makers had come to take it all that year, but the Saxons and the Valley Boys were not giving up without a fight. There was, as usual, a lot of trash talking and exuberance. Junkanoo was the epitome of the holiday season in Nassau.

Chapter Ten

Throughout the years, Leah Thompson-Holt never relented in her quest to find her sister Jennifer despite all the challenges that she had faced after they lost contact with each other. She had worked for a white American family in Fairfax, Virginia as a live-in maid and nanny for more than ten years until the children grew up. She had met the Gallagher family quite by chance in New Providence when she had been babysitting for another American family on the Eastern Rd. The Gallaghers were house guests and were so impressed by the way she cared for the baby and other children that they immediately gave her an offer of full-time employment in the States. Her work was arduous and sometimes enervating but she was quite young then, and she had no comparative work experience, so she never complained. Sometimes the husband and wife had left her to care for their son and daughter for days while they travelled on skiing trips or went on boat cruises. Despite the long work hours, modest wages, and virtually non-existent social life, she never complained. As the years went by, she had received several pay increases from the Gallaghers which enabled her to save quite a bit of money. The family had been kind to her and always treated her with respect. There were also enjoyable times when she was invited to travel with the Gallagher family on their annual vacations to various parts of the U.S.A., Canada and a few times to Europe which left her with indelible memories. It was through the efforts of this family that she received her work permit so that she could work in the United States legally and she was grateful. Leah stayed with this family until the children grew up and went off to college.

Leah had obtained her U.S. citizenship and continued to work in the D.C./Tri-State area for a while. Eventually, she began working in Georgia. Leah was using her savings to complete a practical nurse training program at a nearby college and working at the same time. While there, she met a smooth-talking, jerry-curl wearing, African American named Gerrard Holt who worked two jobs for two popular retail stores in Atlanta along with an occasional playing gig with a band that sometimes required him to travel. He was the first man with whom she had fallen in love, and he referred to her as his "island girl" because she had been born in "the islands" as he called it. Leah's naiveté about relationships propelled her headfirst into this recipe for disaster. She was flattered by his attentiveness and his romantic disposition. Soon after their nuptials, Leah discovered that he had lied about his past and his future potential. During their marriage, they had to move several times because they were delinquent in paying the landlords. In fact, on one occasion they had been evicted and had to leave most of their possessions in their cold basement apartment. Although Leah and Gerrard had two children together, he never seemed to assume responsibility for the wellbeing of his family. As the demands of providing for them began to overwhelm him, Gerrard began to drink excessively, gamble and stay away from home for weeks at a time. Leah even suspected that he had a sweetheart or perhaps another family. Of course, he denied it whenever the subject came up. They had many altercations that sometimes became violent.

He complained, "Leah, we need to use some of that money you have saved up in the bank to pay off some of these bills. You know I got laid off from one of my jobs and the money aint coming in like it used to. You could go to school when we have more money to spare. We can't afford all of that now."

Leah retorted, "No, I am almost finished my training. I'm not stopping now. I can't depend on you. The kids have outgrown most of their clothes, they need shoes, and we hardly have any food in the house."

Gerrard became enraged. He shouted, "You don't have any confidence in me Leah! You never did. I don't know why I bother. You aint nothing but a selfish nag! I am tired of you!" She could smell that he had been drinking. Leah knew what was coming next. This time, he grabbed her roughly and threw her across the room where she fell against the clothes closet and banged her forehead. Leah fell to the floor crying and curled up in a fetal position to minimize her injuries if he continued to attack her. She could never forget the time when she had miscarried their middle child because he had abused her. She was relieved that the children were at school this time and did not witness another violent scene. His behavior had become predictable. He would then disappear for days or even weeks on a routine basis. Benevolent neighbors sometimes called the police, but Leah always downplayed each episode to avoid her husband being arrested. She was a serial optimist.

One day her oldest daughter asked her, "Mummy, why do you let Daddy do that to you? Suppose he kills you. What will happen to us? We don't want you to leave us, Mummy." There was fear and anguish in the child's voice.

Leah knew what it was like to lose your mother at a young age. She would cringe when she heard the haunting sounds of screams, cursing and contentious voices that echoed throughout the building as she climbed the stairs to their apartment. She was fortunate to have a few good neighbors who sometimes kept her girls after school until she got home. She had never seen her own parents fighting but she was reminded of how her mother had suffered and died at a young age because their father had failed to provide for his family. Eventually, Leah swallowed her pride and began collecting welfare assistance by pretending to be a single parent. Nevertheless, once she had finished her training course, she found a way to take her children with her and escape her abuser.

To say that Leah had struggled to provide a decent life for her girls and herself was an understatement. Despite her hardships, she was still quite attractive and caught the attention of several suitors. Like so many women, she yearned to meet someone whom she could settle down with and 'live happily ever after'. On one occasion, the man whom she had trusted after they had been dating for several months left her when he discovered that she was pregnant. She had choices but she chose the only one she could live with; she decided to keep her baby. She had no regrets. Candace Thompson was the most beautiful baby that she had ever seen.

By God's grace and her own determination, Leah raised her three daughters while working two jobs as a Licensed Practical Nurse (LPN). She was still slim and trim and for the first time was beginning to recognize her own self-worth. She worked in New Jersey for a while, then found a more promising job opportunity working as an LPN at Mt. Sinai Hospital in Miami Beach, Florida. Leah was thrilled. She had negotiated a favorable pay package and was just about 45 minutes away from The Bahamas. She had only visited Nassau twice since she went to the United States. On each visit, she had gone into Bain Town where most black Bahamians lived and inquired about her sister Jennifer as well as her brother Justin but to no avail.

Leah met many people including several Bahamians and people of Bahamian descent because of her job at Mt. Sinai. Each time she met any Bahamian, she always asked if the person knew Jennifer or Justin Thompson. On one occasion when Leah was doing her rounds and checking on her patients, it was by what she called 'amazing good fortune' that she met Pamela who was the daughter of her childhood neighbor Mrs. Allen from East Street. Pam was recovering from surgery at the hospital and was expected to stay in hospital for at least a week. Her husband Wyatt had accompanied her to Miami but was staying at a nearby hotel. She recognized Leah right away and called her by name. As they reminisced about old times, Pam explained that Jennifer had visited her mother (Mrs. Allen) several times before she passed away two years before. After Pam had paused to reminisce, she added that Jennifer revealed to her that she was married to a teacher named Hezekiah Rolle. Pam explained that Jennifer had been living on the Family Islands for many years and only came to Nassau on short visits. Leah had many questions, but she was grateful for the tips that she had received from Pam.

Pam was happy to tell Leah, "Jennifer has a couple of children too. They are big now. You know, someone even told me that Jennifer and her family are living in Fox Hill, but I don't know where. You know where Fox Hill is Leah?"

Leah was smiling and threw her hands up in the air as she gave thanks to God for her good fortune. She assured Pam, "Not really, but I'll find it. Thank you so much Pam. Let me give you my telephone number and you give me yours please so we could stay in touch. I'll come back to see you later."

In 1974, when she had vacation leave, Leah made another trip to New Providence. She was even more determined to find her sister. This time she had travelled with her oldest daughter Carla and her husband Byron Gaskin along with their daughter Ronique who decided to join her on their vacation. Based on Pam's advice, Leah decided to search for her sister in Fox Hill. She had never been to Fox Hill and had no idea how big it was, but she planned to conduct a comprehensive search and ask the residents any questions that could lead to success.

Fox Hill had sprawled all the way from the western end of Bernard Rd. to the Fox Hill parade and side streets, as well as over to Prince Charles Drive in the east and spread out to the Fox Hill Prison area in the southeast. It also spilled into the Johnson rd. area and extended as far as East Bay Street to the north. It was quite a large area, but the population was still rather sparse. Despite its size, Fox Hill was a close-knit village. The original residents who had settled in the village were descendants of African slaves and everyone knew each other. Just like a typical family island village, the indigenous people were clannish and protective of their own. In the last two decades, a few families had decided to

Chapter Ten

settle in Fox Hill because it was quiet, peaceful, and spacious. There were many secrets and intriguing tales that were only partially told or would never be shared with outsiders. Some of the older folks still proudly maintained many of the traditions that they had learned from their parents like piercing their ears with a needle and inserting a short cactus needle into the hole until it healed, bathing in Sauve Bush to cure chicken pox, or drinking the boiled Cerasee plant to alleviate the flu and several other ailments.

Nevertheless, the residents were friendly and hospitable to non-native Fox Hillians so if you searched long enough and gained people's trust, you could find even the most elusive information. Leah had a good feeling that this time her efforts would be fruitful.

Leah had arrived at the Nassau International Airport on Sunday afternoon and about two hours later, she and her family checked into the historic Sheraton British Colonial Hotel which was located on the western end of downtown Bay Street. It was the peak of summer, and many visitors were taking advantage of the "sun, sand and sea" that the island was renowned for.

On the following day, Leah's family members went on surrey rides and caught a taxi over the Paradise Island Bridge to go swimming on the island. She instead was committed to continuing her quest to find her sister. She was going into unfamiliar territory and did not know what to expect but she was not afraid. She drove the rental car onto Wulff Rd. As she drove past the Three Queens Restaurant, Leah made a mental note that she would stop there on her way back to get some lunch when she left Fox Hill. She had not eaten conch salad for so long and hoped that she could find her favorite food even if she had to drive to the Potters Cay Dock on her way back to the hotel. It was a sweltering hot August day and Leah was happy that she was wearing a wide-brimmed straw hat which she had purchased in the Straw Market, a cool outfit and comfortable tennis. Leah was grateful to feel the breeze blowing gently as it touched her face. She drove into the Johnson Rd. area and spent time talking with some of the residents and making inquiries. Beads of perspiration drained down her face at times and her smooth brown skin glistened in the sunlight, but she was relentless. She had ventured as far as the area near St. Anne's School on Fox Hill Rd. and even chatted with men and women who lived on Bernard Rd. Since she could not give an accurate physical description except for what her friend Pam had told her, Leah did not have much luck in getting any information about Jennifer. By mid-afternoon, she was exhausted and felt that she had done enough exploring and searching for one day. The upside was that she had made some new friends, collected some juicy sapodillas, an assortment of mangoes, sugar apples and plums in her travels that day. Fox Hill was abuzz with excitement. Several people had told her about the major celebration that was always held in Fox Hill each year on the second Tuesday in August. She vaguely remembered hearing about it as a child, but she had totally forgotten about it over time. Her heart began to beat fast. Leah could not believe her good fortune. Something in her gut told her that this time she would not be disappointed. Despite her enervating day, she headed back to Three Queens to buy some conch salad wearing a smile on her face.

Leah had heard that Fox Hill Day was a huge festival that was held to celebrate the emancipation of their African forefathers in 1838. It was a signature event that was held annually in which native Fox Hillians gathered on the Fox Hill Parade and Freedom Park to sell locally grown fruits and vegetables along with a wide variety of native food and drinks. Apparently, Fox Hill was well-known for its proliferation of fruit trees such as sapodilla, mango, guinep and tamarind. Fox Hill Day was so significant that some people even took the day off from work to ensure that they did not miss any part of the celebrations. Carla, Byron and Ronique eagerly anticipated attending the event and they hoped that they could assist Leah in finding Jennifer.

It was Tuesday. This time Byron was driving. Although he and his wife Carla had honeymooned in Nassau more than fifteen years ago, the couple had not travelled to the eastern side of the small island. He was being extra careful because he was still trying to get used to driving on the left-hand side of the road. Nevertheless, Fox Hill was easy to find once you got onto Bernard Rd. It was just a matter of following the road heading east past St. Augustine's College on the right until you reached Sandilands School. They could see some stalls and tables in the distance that were manned by vendors who were already prepared for Fox Hill Day. When the group arrived at the destination around 12:30 p.m., the police officers were just putting up the barriers to control the crowd that they anticipated would descend upon this location later that afternoon. The family were able to drive up as far as the compound that housed the Fox Hill Post Office and library along with Sandilands School. It was still early so they easily found parking near the entrance of Foxdale which was directly opposite.

The residents welcomed the influx of visitors to the village. There were vendors, stalls, tables, and tents everywhere. Leah and her family strolled eastward towards the Fox Hill Parade while absorbing the assortment of smells that greeted them. The vendors were especially generous to them when they realized that their

Chapter Ten

customers were American tourists. There was just so much to choose from, and like most visitors, they wanted to sample everything. The vendors were selling an assortment of items such as mouth-watering conch fritters, crab and rice, peas and rice, peas and grits with steamed conch, fried snappers, baked macaroni and cheese, crab fat and dough, lots of baked items and many delicious fruits.

Leah had spotted a stall on the southern side of Freedom Park that was adorned with a poster which read "Andros Crabs" and her new friend spotted her at the same time in the crowd. Hermese Johnson was waving anxiously to her and beckoning for her to come to her stall. They had chatted for a while during her visit to the Johnson Rd. area on the previous day. Hermese had spent all her life in the Johnson Rd. area and bragged that she knew everybody in Fox Hill.

"Girl, I'm so glad to see you. How you doing today?" asked Hermese. She continued, "I have something to tell you but first let me show you what I have on my stall."

Leah was excited by what she saw. "Miss Hermese, your stall looks so good. O my! Tell me what's all this please. Everything smells sooo good."

"Call me Hermese chile. You makin' me sound old when you start callin' me Miss. I's a young woman you know. Age aint nuttin' but a number." Then she bent over and laughed jovially.

Leah smiled broadly and responded, "O.K. Hermese."

Hermes specialized in crab dishes. She stated confidently, "You just wait 'til you taste it, then you'll really know how good it is. Try this Leah and tell me what you think." Hermese was a middle-aged lady who had the energy of someone half her age. Several of her children were helping her at the stall, so she was able to divert her attention to Leah. Hermese had offered her some crab soup, then she sampled a stuffed baked crab, and Leah thought she was in heaven. By this time, Leah's granddaughter, whom everyone affectionately called CeCe had walked up and became excited about what she saw. She also wanted to try everything.

Leah cautioned her granddaughter as she inquired, "CeCe, where your Mommy and Daddy at? Do you have any money 'cause I can't pay for all these things you're trying." CeCe chuckled mischievously and showed off her five dollars that she had in her pocket.

"That's O.K. Leah. Let the chile taste the food. It's alright. Come. You all try the crab and rice. I cook that myself too." Hermese was beaming with pride as she spoke.

Leah admonished CeCe, "Say 'Thank you' CeCe. Don't forget your manners especially when someone is kind to you." CeCe obeyed her grandmother.

"Thanks, Hermese. We are going to buy a couple of dinners from you before we leave. Your food really tastes good. I love it," said Leah encouragingly. She was hoping that Carla and Byron could get a taste of this down-home food although she knew that they were probably sampling some other good stuff wherever they were on the parks.

Then Hermese got down to serious business. "Guess what Leah? Not long after you left yesterday, I went down the road to hail a lady name Miss Faye Bridgewater who live through Mucumba Lane which is a lil ways down from Tyler Street. I wanted to pick up some seasoning and other stuff from her shop to put in my pots today plus I wanted some oil for the lil stove. You know how that is."

"Uh huh?" responded Leah curiously.

Hermes stepped to the left side of her stall for privacy to explain. "Well, I was talking to Miss Faye about your sister Jennifer. Just inquiring, you know. Then I mentioned the fact that her husband was a teacher. My dear, you aint guh believe this. Miss Faye say jus' like this, 'That sound like some people who does come to my shop sometimes.' Then Hermes asked Leah, "What you say the lady name is? Yeah, she say she's Jennifer Rolle. Then she say to me, 'Ms. Rolle and her husband live right down the road from here on Tyler Street'."

"What?!" Leah could not believe her good fortune. She clutched Hermes by the shoulders hopefully.

CeCe politely interrupted the two women, "Excuse me Grammy. I'm going back to Mommy and Daddy. I see them over there. See you later." Then she ran off to find her parents. They were standing under the gigantic Silk Cotton tree that stood majestically on the eastern end of the parade grounds.

"I swear on a stack of bibles she tell me it just like how I'm telling it to you." Hermes tried to reassure her friend Leah. "Yeah, Miss Faye said the lady is a brown-skinned lady with shoulder length brown hair. She told me

Chapter Ten

the husband has a funny name that she couldn't pronounce too well. When I said the name, she roll her eyes at me and she said, 'That's right! Hez – Hez – Hezekiah. That's his name. He's a schoolteacher somewhere in town. She say he's a tall, nice-lookin' man too.' Hermes continued, "Well chile you know you coulda knock me down wid a feather how shock I was." She said emphatically as she hit the table, "As God is my witness, that's jus' what the woman tell me."

Leah's eyes sparkled as she implored, "Hermes, can you take me to the house, please? If you show me where the house is, I will appreciate it."

Hermes agreed to take her there a little later as she did not want to leave her stall in the children's care during that busy time. She also suggested to Leah that it also might be better to try a little later when the couple might be home. The crowd had thickened on the parade grounds as people watched the plaiting of the maypole by the children from the area. Then, as the afternoon progressed, several men from the neighborhood courageously exhibited their sportsmanship one-by-one by climbing the greasy pole hoping to collect the prize money at the top. This was also a crowd pleaser.

Leah linked up with her daughter and son-in-law as they watched in fascination while some men tried unsuccessfully to get to the top of the greasy pole. After trial and error, eventually, one of the men would win but this could take hours. Leah met the couple devouring some cracked conch and washing it down with some ice-cold limeade when she found them. The music was loud. People were dancing and enjoying themselves as they wished. Carla and Byron were excited about what Leah had learned and they promised to accompany her when she was going to the street where her sister and family might be living.

At 5:45 p.m. all five of them got into the small, rented sedan and drove through Fox Dale so that they could cross over Fox Hill Rd. and get to their destination because vehicular traffic had been diverted from the Fox Hill Parade and Freedom Park area. Hermes sat in the front passenger seat and gave Leah directions. Seven minutes later, Leah had parked the car directly in front of the unpainted house on Tyler Street. A silver-colored car was parked in front of the yard, but they did not see anyone at first. Leah tooted the car horn and waited. A woman emerged from the house and started walking toward the visitors. Suddenly, Leah practically flew out of the car and dashed to greet the woman. They both halted midway and stared at each other for about two seconds then the screaming and crying began as they called each other by name. Leah had found her long lost sister. A man came to the door trying to figure out what the commotion was about. He saw the people standing up and he watched his wife hugging the woman. Instinctively, he knew that Jennifer's wish had come true.

Jennifer could not stop hugging her sister as she cried openly. Leah clung to Jennifer and kept crying out, "Thank you Lord! Father, I thank you for letting me see this day. Thank you, Lord!"

Hermes Johnson slipped away quietly to return to her stall because her job was done. Nobody noticed that she had walked away. She felt satisfied because she had provided closure for this family. Hermese was elated that she was able to reunite the sisters, and this was heartwarming. Some people greeted the family as they walked by the Rolle's yard seemingly unaware of the significance of this momentous occasion. Hezekiah welcomed Leah and her family inside and they all introduced themselves. They had so much 'catching up' to do. Of course, Jennifer and Leah sat beside each other holding hands like they did when they were growing up. CeCe complained that she was feeling tired due to the exciting events of the day. Jennifer allowed her niece to take a nap in the back bedroom while she and Leah chatted incessantly. Hezekiah invited Leah's daughter and husband to relax in the TV room while the sisters reconnected.

Firstly, Leah wanted to find out about Anthony. Leah was incredulous when she found out about Anthony whom she had always known as Justin. The tears of joy flowed without ceasing.

"Jenny, I want to talk to him. I need to see him. I will not believe it until I see him. Jen are you sure?" Leah asked doubtfully.

Jennifer tried to reassure her sister, "Leah, I assure you. Anthony is our brother Justin. Remember – Rachel took him when he was a baby and we never saw him again. Well, more importantly, he still has that same walnut-shaped birthmark. And guess what Leah. His son has the same birthmark in the same place. You know that can't be a coincidence, right?"

Leah paused and acknowledged that to be a fact. "Yes, I remember that birthmark. Jen, I want to talk to him. It's been so long. Where is he?"

"I have his telephone number. He may be at work. He's a policeman. I'll call his house and ask his wife to give him a message if he's not home."

Chapter Ten

All the emotions that she had kept in over the decades were being released as if the flood gates had been opened. Leah could not stop crying but they were tears of joy. Jennifer contacted Stephanie at home, and she stated that Anthony was working his shift at the Fox Hill parade. Leah started laughing in disbelief. Then she got up from the sofa and responded hopefully, "Jen, God can't be this kind. Let's go out there to look for him. He'll be in uniform, right?"

Jennifer smiled and tried to appease Leah's anxiety. "Leah, there's so many people out there. Trust me, whenever Anthony gets home tonight from work, Stephanie will let him know and he will call. Leah reluctantly accepted the advice and they continued to talk. As they sat in the dining room, Leah offered Jennifer some of the food that she had bought, and they ate together from the same plate like in the good old days that were sometimes not so good. Jennifer had arranged for her children to buy some food for them and bring it home for Hezekiah and her whenever they returned home that evening. The sisters were so caught up in celebrating their reunion that they did not hear the police siren in the front yard. Jennifer was startled by the brisk knock on the door then she smiled when she saw the flashing lights as she glanced out of the window.

"Anthony, is that you?" Jennifer inquired confidently. She looked back at Leah and beckoned her to come to the door.

Leah got up nervously and walked with measured steps to the door. Her knees felt weak. Anthony stepped inside simultaneously and hugged Jennifer. Instinctively, Leah knew that for the first time since his infancy, she was gazing upon her long-lost little brother.

"Steph said you called for me. How you doing, Jen?" asked Anthony who was attired in full uniform.

Leah was standing right next to Jennifer as she tried to hold back her emotions. She didn't know whether to touch him, hug him or weep with joy. Jennifer turned to Leah and held her hand then said to Anthony, "Anthony, this is our sister Leah. She has been looking for you just like I've been looking for you, but she moved away to live in the States when she was very young. She has been looking for both of us and now we are all together."

Jennifer then turned to Leah and said, Leah, this is Anthony. You remember him as Justin."

Anthony stepped toward Leah and said, "Leah, pleased to meet you. I sometimes wonder why things happened the way they did but it sure is good to have you in my life. It's going to take us some time, but I hope we'll all get to know each other better." Anthony reached out to hug his sister.

Leah could not contain her emotions. "My dear brother. O how I have missed you. Both of you. Didn't know if you were alive or dead." The tears were flowing freely at this point. "My God is awesome. He has been kind to all of us. Just look at you Justin, I mean Anthony – You have grown into a handsome young man. You sure look dashing in your uniform." Leah laughed joyfully and wiped her eyes. I want to hug you, but all my makeup will be on your uniform. Hope you don't mind."

Anthony reached out and hugged his big sister. "Don't worry about that Leah. I'm getting off from work in a little while and the fellers will drop me home anyway." He reached out to her, and they embraced each other warmly. Then he said jokingly, "I want the two of you to promise me that there'll be no more surprises please."

Jennifer and Leah responded in unison, "No more surprises."

Anthony added apologetically, "Jenny and Leah, I'm still on the clock so I gotta get back …"

Before he could finish his sentence, two teenage girls ran through the door and shouted simultaneously, "Uncle Tony!" and rushed up to him seemingly oblivious to the others who were there.

"Mind your manners girls. I know you all can see a couple of adults in the room, right?" Jennifer scolded them for interrupting adult conversation.

"O sorry Mommy. Excuse me," said Angie and Gina added her apology.

Hezekiah came in followed by Carla and Byron. "Hey man. How are you doing?" Hezekiah shook hands with Anthony, and they smiled at each other broadly. Leah quickly introduced Carla to her uncle then Anthony had to leave. They all promised to get together before Leah returned to Florida. The day had been productive after all, and they were overjoyed with the outcome.

Chapter Eleven

Since the days of 'the Contract' or 'Project', many Bahamians had settled in Florida and other American states. During the 1980s, Bahamians were travelling back and forth between Florida and The Bahamas, sometimes several times per month. Many of them had obtained in-store credit cards at several retail stores which was very beneficial especially to the fast-growing middle class. Plane tickets and hotel accommodations were relatively inexpensive. The high-rise McAllister Hotel, Flagler Street, The Flea Market on Le Jeune Road, Biscayne Boulevard and 103rd Street were popular stomping grounds of the average Bahamian. Most Grand Bahamians boasted that they did not travel to Nassau but were frequent visitors to Florida and other parts of the United States. Some had remained since the days of the 'Contract' and established families. Over the decades, many Bahamians had settled and made a life for themselves in places like Coconut Grove and Liberty City, Florida just to name a few. Some people joked that you sometimes saw more Bahamians on Flagler Street than on Bay Street. They looked forward to the shopping trips that were always rewarding. Disney World in Orlando and other major attractions were appealing to the island folks as well as people from all over the world. Likewise, tourism began to boom as many American tourists and others were travelling to the islands of the Bahamas for their vacations or just to get away from the 'hustle and bustle' of city life.

For numerous Bahamians, this was a period of self-actualization and empowerment. Anthony Nairn had already served for twenty years on the Royal Bahamas Police Force, had advanced through several ranks and had received specialized training. Stephanie, on the other hand was doing exceptionally well in the banking sector having received extensive training in her field and a promotion to a supervisory level. She, like so many women during this time, were embracing opportunities to excel in various professional fields and to stand side by side with their male counterparts. Stephanie had become a card-carrying member and avid supporter of the Free National Movement along with her husband who had secretly supported the cause of the dissident eight several years before when they had stepped away from the Progressive Liberal Party (PLP). Stephanie especially admired women like Mrs. Janet Bostwick of the FNM who fearlessly championed the cause of women and the disenfranchised and in 1982 became the first woman to serve in the Bahamian House of Assembly.

Together Anthony and Stephanie bought a previously owned home in Seabreeze, New Providence near the canal. The house had been repossessed by the bank, so Stephanie was able to secure a good deal for her husband and her to purchase the home at a reasonable price. It was truly a dream come true.

For the next five years, Hezekiah and Jennifer worked assiduously to complete their four-bedroom and two-and-a half bath house. They had made many sacrifices to build their house mostly 'out-of-pocket'. Because of life's uncertainties, they committed themselves to overcoming debt. Jennifer did her part by participating in asues (which is an old African tradition) to save money cooperatively within a group and have quick access to funds. She preferred this to getting bank loans because she always considered banks to be predatory whereas when she contributed to an asue, she could get her 'draw' within a short time without owing anyone money. On the other hand, her husband Hezekiah did not trust asues because he was aware of unscrupulous individuals who had received an early draw then reneged on their agreement to continue paying until each participant got his/her draw. The couple agreed to disagree on the matter of raising funds for their home. They were always able to pool their resources amicably and build their savings in their joint bank account. The couple was proud because they did not have to obtain a huge mortgage but occasionally sought small loans as the need arose.

Jennifer Rolle had defied the odds. She had become a refined lady who blended very well even into the upper middle-class stratum of society, yet she never lost her connection with the poor and marginalized persons in the community. She had worked hard to obtain her associate degree from the College of the Bahamas (COB). Additionally, she had received several certifications related to insurance and had been promoted to the position of supervisor of her department. She was active in several charitable organizations and taught sewing and handicraft at her church on alternate weekends. Recently, she had formed a girls club

Chapter Eleven

called P.R.I.D.E. (which was the acronym for Pride, Respect, Inspiration, Determination, Endeavor) for girls up to eighteen years old. Her goal was to steer young girls away from abuse, drug use, prostitution, domestic violence, single parenting, and to promote their sense of self-worth. Jennifer was acutely aware of the obstacles that many teen girls faced because of neglect, abuse, and unplanned pregnancies. She made a commitment to try to assist and encourage girls and young women to resist the temptations that could lead to their demise. She had returned to her roots in Bain Town where she managed to find an old building on Fleming Street owned by a pastor who agreed to allow her to use it on Saturday mornings free of charge from 9:00 a.m. to 12 p.m. to work with the girls. After meeting with parents and caregivers to obtain their permission, the program began with five girls, then quickly increased to fifteen. As the program expanded, two of her coworkers volunteered to work with her in her efforts to motivate the girls during this very vulnerable period in their lives. Pastor Edward Brown, who hailed from Eleuthera, also encouraged his wife to assist with the program and his church supported this venture by providing lunch and personal supplies for the young members of the club.

Like many Bahamian parents, the Rolles had always strived to create a comfortable home and to ensure that their children obtained the best possible education. They had been able to accomplish both. They felt that a great measure of a family's success is reflected in the achievements of their offspring. Hezekiah always had dreams of self-actualization despite his humble beginnings, and he instilled this principle in his children. There was no room for procrastination. In just a few short years, Hezekiah had been promoted to Head of the Mathematics Department, Senior Master and his last appointment was as Vice Principal of a senior high school. He felt that with determination and hard work, he would achieve his goal of becoming principal of a Grade 'A' high school before he retired.

Both Rolle daughters had been able to secure full academic scholarships for most of their studies. Their youngest daughter Angie was attending COB and was in her last year of completing a degree in banking and finance. On the other hand, her sister Gina, who had begun her studies at COB went on to the University of the West Indies (UWI) to complete her Law degree. Gina's aspiration was to ultimately complete advanced legal studies in England.

Lester seemed to be the most adventurous of the Rolle children when he pursued his dream of becoming a pilot after training at Embry-Riddle Aeronautical University in Daytona Beach, Florida. He had received a partial scholarship and his parents took care of the remaining fees. He was fascinated by Florida and had travelled to several neighboring states. The 1980s brought forth its own brand of appeal to young college graduates like Lester. To him, America was the land of freedom, opportunities, and endless, wide-open spaces. He did not entertain the thought of permanently returning to his tiny island home anymore. Instead, he sought and obtained a job as a pilot in Daytona.

During Thanksgiving, while his parents came over to spend the holiday with him, Lester Rolle surprised his parents with the news. He formally informed them that he was engaged and planned to marry the young African American stewardess that he had been dating named Heather Bennett. He had met her while he was still in training. Jennifer was in shock and Hezekiah did not know what to make of this decision that to him seemed rather hasty. Lester had invited his parents over to Tampa where his fiancé was living, and they were introduced to Heather's parents. The meeting was amicable and plans advanced in preparation for the wedding that was scheduled for June of the following year.

Jennifer and Hezekiah laughed as they reminded each other about the reasons why they had to suddenly get married. "Let's not be too hard on them. They probably have their reasons," suggested Jennifer.

Hezekiah chimed in, "I hope she's not pregnant. These young people need to learn to wait."

"And what if she is? He loves her and wants to marry her. I think that if they have planned things out properly and they are committed to each other, they should be fine," stated Jennifer.

Hezekiah was still pondering about the situation. Jennifer joked, "If she is pregnant now, she sure wouldn't be able to fit decently into any wedding dress seven months from now, would she?"

"You're so right my smart wife. I didn't think about that," chuckled Hezekiah as he capitulated.

She continued, "Kiah, I know you don't want them shacking up together, do you?"

Hezekiah replied, "No. That wouldn't be right. Plus, they have known each other for a while now so this is probably a good time."

Chapter Eleven

"I like her. She seems to be serious and in love with our son," said Jennifer.

"Anyway, it would be nice to have a grandchild, wouldn't it Jen? I'm looking forward to that," suggested Hezekiah hopefully.

As the sun set, they walked down the garden path of the hotel holding hands and contemplating the thought of their first grandchild.

Chapter Twelve

One afternoon in late June, while he was sitting on the patio at home, Hezekiah found himself deep in thought as he reflected on his life. He was thankful that school was already closed, and he had taken two weeks of vacation from his administrative post. He could just put his feet up, relax and let his mind wander wherever it wanted to go. He acknowledged that God had been good and merciful to him. He was fortunate to have a lovely home and a wonderful family. After all this time, he and his wife still loved each other like they were newlyweds. He really had nothing to complain about, but he could not help where his mind was wandering.

Hezekiah was outstretched on a lounge chair in his backyard and found himself drifting into a pensive mood. He began thinking about Exuma. He was nostalgic and reminiscent of those wonderful boyhood days that he had enjoyed in Steventon. Life had been quite simple and predictable then. So much had changed since those days. He had only returned to his island home three or four times since his marriage. He tried to justify why his visits to Exuma had been so few and far between. He found himself reflecting on his life to determine why this happened. He could not think of any specific reason except his excuse that he had been so busy building his family life and career that he just did not find the time to go back to Steventon. He felt guilty. He had lost three of his brothers (Malachi, Livingston, and little Josh) which saddened him. His mother never quite forgave him for getting married without the full consent of his parents. Additionally, she had maintained a tepid relationship with Jennifer despite Jennifer's efforts to make her mother-in-law feel welcome when she visited them which hurt him profoundly. It was also lamentable that his father had passed away and he was unable to attend the funeral because he was in England. He knew his Mama was slow on forgiveness and wondered what the atmosphere would be like when she came to Lester's wedding. He loved his mother and worried about her failing health too. She was alone at home most of the time since most of her children had moved away to live their lives independently. Even Eulease (whom everyone assumed would have stayed with her Mama) defied the odds by getting married in her late twenties; she became the second wife of a middle-aged pastor from Moss Town who had lost his first wife after a long illness. Altogether, the couple had five children. Hezekiah smiled and mused as he thought about his sisters who were as tough as nails just like their Mama.

Despite her mother's anguish and her father's disapproval, Willie had also gotten married soon after her eighteenth birthday to a fellow from Deadman's Cay, Long Island named Wilber Knowles. He was a curly-haired, light-skinned man with a charismatic personality. The two were introduced to each other at a church Rushin' through a mutual friend. Willie had always been bold and vivacious so when her parents displayed angst concerning the developing relationship, she became more resistant while the young man was very persistent. When Wilber presented his petition to Mr. Hezekiah Rolle Sr., his soon-to-be father-in-law frowned and grunted then took six months to agree to it. Of course, by then Willie was already eighteen, and after indicating that she would 'run away' to be with Wilber anyway if she did not get her father's consent, Mr. Rolle relented. They had settled down nicely, had several children and were operating a successful business on Long Island.

One of Hezekiah's brothers, Alpheus, was living with his fiancé in Grand Bahama and was planning to get married soon. They had one child, and Hezekiah had admonished Alpheus to settle down and get married. He made a mental note of the fact that he would soon have another wedding to attend. The two brothers often communicated by phone and the last time Hezekiah had spoken to Alphaeus, he was still working at the Bahamas Oil Refining Company (BORCO) and was doing quite well.

Hezekiah reassured himself that his mother was not totally alone. Tommy and Leviticus, who remained extremely close even in adulthood were builders and fishermen who still lived on the Rolle property in Steventon. Each of them had built impressive concrete houses on the land and were married with children. They had done some renovations to the original family home which pleased their mother. They also watched her and had other family members check on her daily to ensure that all was well with their elderly loved one. Hezekiah was grateful to God that his brothers had matured to become responsible, productive men.

Hezekiah began thinking of his little brothers' antics. In particular, he sadly remembered Livingston. Livingston had always been a fun-loving boy and he had not changed much in adulthood. He apparently died in a boating accident during a holiday outing. This tragedy happened while Hezekiah was teaching on Eleuthera, but Hezekiah did not receive the news until his brother had been buried several days before. It disturbed him because he had heard so many versions of what had happened. There was even a rumor that it was a drug deal that went wrong out to sea. None of the stories sounded logical, and those who knew the facts about the incident seemed determined that the truth would not be told.

He wondered what his youngest brother Zach was doing. He always grew worried if he did not hear any news about him for a while. Zach, who was a musician, always wore his hair in shoulder length dreadlocks and enjoyed wearing Afrocentric attire. Hezekiah regarded him as whimsical because he sang and played in a band called Zodiacs. When Zach was in his twenties, the band (Zach and the Zodiacs) used to play in various hotels on Paradise Island. More recently, he and his band had begun travelling a lot, sometimes playing with popular entertainers overseas. It seemed that he had made quite a bit of money and had acquired some property in the United States. Zach admitted that he had fathered several children along the way, and he did his best to support them all. More recently he had married an older American woman from New Orleans. During their last talk, Zach had explained to Hezekiah that he was still working as a musician there and had finally settled down with the Creole lady from New Orleans who had also enjoyed a successful career in show business.

Then there was Ruthie – dearest Ruthie. Hezekiah smiled to himself as he thought about his 'baby sister' Ruth who seemed to have more courage than all his siblings combined. She was currently living in Philadelphia, Pennsylvania where she settled after serving in the U.S. army and becoming a highly decorated soldier. Ruth and Zach communicated with each other on occasions which comforted her other siblings to some extent. His youngest sister Ruth had always been an independent spirit, and her story was one that Hezekiah reflected on with admiration.

It happened that on one of Hezekiah Sr. and Zilpha's trips to Florida, Ruth was born unexpectedly while they were there. She was intelligent, athletic, and outgoing. For many years, Ruthie (as she was nicknamed) was unaware that she had been born in 'The States'. She had been on several trips to New Providence but did not recall travelling to U.S.A. When she completed school in Exuma,

Chapter Twelve

she was resolute in her quest to further her education or secure a decent job for herself, depending on which came first. Of course, she received very little encouragement from her family members (especially her parents) who tried to instill in her that she must wait humbly until a gentleman came along to take her hand in marriage. Ruth was diametrically opposed to becoming what she called 'some man's chattel'. She had no intention of following that path. Ruth was an avid reader who treasured and read any book that she could put her hands on. At the age of seventeen, she told her parents that she needed her birth certificate because she planned on seeking a job or was going to do some studies in Nassau. Her father refused to comment on the matter and her mother continued to ignore her despite her pleas. It so happened that as the subject came up in a conversation that Ruth was having with a neighbor who was a close friend of her mother, the truth was unfolded about her birthplace. Without revealing the source of her information, Ruth boldly approached her mother about the matter. Of course, Mrs. Rolle threatened her and even slapped her for being 'fresh' and ill-mannered. She told her angrily, "Girl, I'll take your head right off your body if you ask me that again."

Nevertheless, her persistence paid off. After several years, Zilpha Rolle eventually capitulated and confirmed what Mrs. Zelrene Roach had revealed to Ruth. She was an American citizen. Mrs. Rolle reluctantly gave Ruth her American birth certificate, sensing that she would eventually obtain it anyway because of her age. Hezekiah Sr. was inconsolable and never forgave his wife for her actions. Much to her parents' chagrin, Ruth packed her things one day and went to seek her fortune in the United States. They were not sure where she got money to travel, but it was rumored that she had been talking to some American missionaries who periodically visited Exuma. It was quite possible that they had assisted her in emigrating. Hezekiah had not received any news about Ruth for years, and he prayed that all was well with her.

Hezekiah's thoughts were punctuated by Lester and his fiancé Heather who came into the house gleefully. They had been out sightseeing and doing some final checks to ensure that everything was prepared for their wedding which was taking place on Saturday. They walked to the back door of the house searching for him until they found him on the patio.

Hezekiah responded to their greeting, "What have you two lovebirds been up to?"

"Dad, we've been all over the island. Heather wanted to see the whole island in one day." Lester chuckled and continued, "She was fascinated by the statue of Christopher Columbus in front of Government House, so we took some pictures there as well as at the Queen's Staircase, then we went by the caves for more pictures and went swimming at Saunders Beach." Lester pretended to wipe some perspiration from his forehead symbolizing the sweltering June heat.

Heather was smiling as she boasted, "Papa Rolle, look at all this stuff that I bought at the Straw market. Heather had somehow forced her big afro into a wide-brimmed floppy hat. She touched the hat that she was wearing and posed. "I got this lovely straw hat and bag on Bay Street. I found a cute sundress, some gorgeous earrings, and necklaces and lots of souvenirs. I bought something for Mrs. Rolle as well. I hope she likes it."

Hezekiah replied cheerfully, "Jen's still at work. I'm sure she'll like it. She should be home soon if you all don't have any plans." He smiled to himself because he knew that his wife Jennifer was an accomplished artisan when it came to sewing and handicraft and could probably make fancier trinkets than the ones that Heather had bought for her. He also knew that Jennifer was so gracious that she would show appreciation for the gift anyway.

Jennifer drove up about two hours later struggling with two large soursops in her hands and her handbag on her left shoulder. She called as she entered the house, "Where is everybody? My hands are full. Kiah, where are you?"

Lester greeted his mother, "Hey Mum. How you doin'? Dad's sitting outside catching the cool. Let me help you with those." Lester reached out to assist his mother and placed the ripe fruits in the kitchen. "I guess we'll have soursop for dessert tonight. Wow! I can't remember when last I tasted that. Yum!" He rubbed his hands together and licked his lips in anticipation. The succulent, green-skinned fruit was a definite crowd pleaser. He was checking the cupboards at this point. "Do you have condensed milk, Mum? If not, Heather and I could go to the store and get a couple of cans."

"O gosh. I forgot the sweet milk!" Jennifer tapped her forehead with her fingers and confirmed that they needed some.

Heather had been outside chatting with her soon-to-be sisters-in-law (Angie and Gina) for a while when she heard the voices inside. She trotted over to Jennifer and hugged her. "Hi Momma Jen. How are you doing? Did you have a good day?"

Chapter Twelve

"I had a good day hun. What about you?" asked Jennifer.

"We had a fabulous day. Les and I were all over the place doing lots of cool stuff. I'm going to show you what I got later. I got something for you too. Hope you like it." Heather was excited and happy. Lester held her around her waist.

"Heather, let's run to the store real quick to pick up something for Mum," suggested Lester.

"Sure. Let's do that," replied Heather and the couple departed. Angie and Gina headed back into the kitchen to complete the preparation of some steamed crawfish, white rice, fried plantains, and coleslaw for the family dinner.

Jennifer kicked off her high heeled shoes and parked them in a corner then headed to the kitchen in her stockinged feet. The intoxicating smell was consuming her. She poked her head into the kitchen and inquired as she sniffed the air. "Uhmm uhmm. Something smells real good. Girls, I could smell the food from outside. Where you all got crawfish from?"

"Daddy brought some big old crawfish home from the dock. I think he said some Abaco fishermen had some. And we already had a couple plantains in the fridge, so Angie came up with the menu," said Gina proudly. The sisters had always been close and enjoyed this opportunity to cook together since they were apart for most of the year.

Hezekiah must have heard his wife's voice and came inside to greet her. "Hello beautiful. How was your day?"

"Hectic but everything went okay. What about you?" Jennifer replied. He responded positively then Jennifer excused herself so that she could change into more comfortable clothes for dinner.

Dinnertime was a lively and fun-filled time. Mr. and Mrs. Rolle had recently purchased a large dining room set to accommodate their immediate family and a few guests. Like the rest of the house, this room was tastefully furnished. The contents of the China closet were already impressive although (as Jennifer suggested) it was a work in progress. Suspended over this attractive setting was a dazzling crystal chandelier that seemed to have a hundred sparkling lights illuminating the room. Jennifer was always enchanted by chandeliers; this room in their home filled her with pride and joy. Since the wedding was only a few days away, the main topic of conversation at the table centered around the guests and the soon-to-be-married couple.

Heather informed the group that her mom and dad would be arriving on Wednesday, and they would be staying at the Ambassador Beach Hotel for a week. She planned to stay with her parents until the wedding on Saturday while Lester would continue to reside with his parents until their nuptials.

Lester inquired, "Dad, when's Grandma coming in? She still coming to our wedding, right?"

"Now son, you know your grandma wouldn't miss your big day for all the money in the world. You know she loves you to death," stated Hezekiah. He continued, "She doesn't like flying though. Mama's coming in on the mailboat tomorrow. She'll be here by tomorrow evening."

"I can't wait to see Grandma. I haven't seen her in a couple of years," added Lester.

Hezekiah chuckled, "Well, you know, she doesn't travel to Nassau that much. Most of the time, she comes here for her doctor's visits. Mama always says there are too many people on this little island and there is too much crime. She really prefers to stay in Exuma where everybody knows everybody, and people treat each other like family."

Lester acknowledged, "Yeah. Nassau sure has changed. The crime rate has increased. There are some people using drugs hard and where there is drugs, you have drug trafficking and prostitution. They go hand-in-hand.

Mind you, the same type of thing is going on in Florida." Heather nodded her head in agreement.

Hezekiah mused, "Yes indeed. The whole world is changing. Life is no longer simple like it used to be. I like the comforts of modernity, but there is a part of me that misses the simplicity of life that we used to have. I can remember when Bahamians used to be content with whatever they had and made the best of it. Now, so many people are willing to steal, kill and destroy just to acquire material things."

Angie, the audacious one tried to redirect her father, "Daddy, stop being so serious. Things aren't that bad."

Chapter Twelve

Jennifer smiled and remarked jokingly, "Well you all young folks wouldn't know because you all just reach."

"That's true you know Mummy," added Lester.

Hezekiah relented and returned to the original topic, "Lester, your Uncle Ishmael is picking your grandma up tomorrow. She'll be staying with him. I believe he's still free, single, and disengaged. He told me that when he gets off from the hotel tomorrow morning, he'll cook and pick up Mama in the afternoon. He's trying to finish the other half of his duplex in Carmichael Rd. He's living in one part."

Angie inquired quizzically, "Dad, is he still with Debbie or did he go back to Yvonne?"

"I don't think he is with either of them now. You know your uncle is not so gifted in the relationship department. He's like a rolling stone. Anyway, he'll find the right lady one day." Hezekiah suggested hopefully." I know Mama will talk to him about that when she gets here.

Gina chimed in, "I hope he's cooking some good old native food for Grandma 'cause she does not like processed food. Just saying …" She shrugged her shoulders and continued eating. The grandchildren had only spent time with their grandmother on a few occasions, but they knew that she could be dictatorial and opinionated although she had a soft spot for her grandchildren.

Lester responded optimistically, "Knowing Grandma, she's probably bringing a lot of homegrown stuff from Exuma anyway, so she'll be alright."

Gina added, "She might even bring some crabs for us. I haven't had any crabs for the year. I don't mind if they're black or white just as long as they have plenty fat in them."

The conversation was easy, and everyone was relaxed as they savored this opportunity to converse in familial intimacy. Jennifer briefly went into the kitchen to retrieve the soursop desert. She checked it and stirred it to make sure that it was just right, came to the dining table and asked, "Everybody ready for soursop?" The general response was in the affirmative. They were not disappointed.

Jennifer was delighted that she had the rest of the week off. She had two days. This would give her time to render any last-minute assistance to her son and his future wife, prepare herself for the wedding as well as socialize with her sister, in-laws, and other family members. She knew that her husband was proud and excited also. Hezekiah had engaged in that father-son conversation several times; he was assured that Lester was ready for this new stage in his life and he hoped that Heather felt the same way. As Hezekiah and Jennifer settled in for the night, he kept chattering and inquiring about aspects of the wedding like a child awaiting Christmas Day. It all seemed surreal to him.

Thursday seemed to pass by in a blur. The parents on both sides had conversed as they had done daily since Heather's parents arrived in Nassau. The atmosphere was light and breezy as family and friends engaged in necessary activities to ensure that all preparations were being made for the great event.

Jennifer picked up Leah and her three daughters from the Nassau International Airport around 11:00 a.m. that morning. This was another joyous day for the two sisters who were appreciative that God had allowed them to reunite once again. Leah checked in at their hotel on Paradise Island then they all took the scenic route on East Bay Street, driving past Montague Beach and continuing to the eastern end of the island. Nothing much had changed. The group then enjoyed lunch together at the Poinciana Inn on Bernard rd. After their meal, Jennifer and Leah moved to a nearby table to speak privately. Two of Leah's daughters, Chauncie and Candace selected songs on a jukebox while the eldest remained at the table contemplating her mother's concerns. Meanwhile, Leah and Jennifer tried as much as possible to provide each other with updates since their last reunion. Leah had confided in Jennifer advising her that she had a 'friend' who was gradually becoming a love interest. He was a divorcé with one daughter who was married and living in the mid-west with her husband and two children. Leah assured her sister that she had no plans to get married again anytime soon although her 'friend', who was eight years her senior, seemed enthusiastic about 'getting hitched' as Leah called it. She explained, "He's employed as a sanitation supervisor at a food processing plant, but he wants to retire soon and start a small business of his own." Leah was anxiously awaiting her sister's reaction.

Jennifer asked calmly, "How long have you all been seeing each other, Leah?"

Leah responded, "We have been dating for more than a year now, but after all that has happened in my life, I'm scared…really scared. Howard is a very nice

Chapter Twelve

man. He's kind and sensitive, but I still feel like I need more time. You know what I mean Jennifer?"

"Sis, don't do anything you're not comfortable with. You're quite right to take your time. Has he proposed to you?" asked Jennifer.

"Well, a couple of times actually. He's talked about us getting married, but I always tell him that I need more time, or I change the subject. I have told Howard that I would prefer for us to be friends for a while longer until we get to know each other better."

Jennifer confirmed, "Leah, we'll continue this conversation later – definitely before you go back to the States. You're staying until Sunday, right?"

"Actually, I got an extra day off. I'm flying out on Monday at 1 p.m. I have to go back to work on Tuesday afternoon for the late shift at the hospital," Leah replied triumphantly.

"O we have time to get together then," suggested Jennifer.

Leah agreed, "Sounds like a plan Jen."

"Remember our girls planned to go out later to see a movie at the Shirley Street Theatre. I'm gonna let Carla drop me home, pick up Gina and Angie and the five of them can go and catch a movie. I can't spare the time. You should join them, Leah. I have too many things to do. My husband will cook sometimes, but I don't think today is one of those days." Jennifer laughed lightheartedly and headed back to their original table.

Leah mused, "I think I'm going to hang out and relax by the pool this evening. No harm in that right? Probably sip on a couple of Pina Coladas, Kalua and cream or something like that. You know – Just to relax my nerves. I might even decide to go into the water. The weather is really nice."

Jennifer warned jokingly, "You better don't drink too much and let none of these fellers run off with you. Plenty of them hang around the hotels trying to pick up unsuspecting ladies if they appear to be vulnerable. Especially if they buy you a drink 'cause they sometimes believe they can 'build a hotel on you' if you know what I mean. She smiled as she bent two fingers on both hands to emphasize what she was saying.

"Jennie, I know what you mean and to tell you the truth, I have enough on my plate right now dealing with Howard. I'm not ready for commitment right now, and I sure didn't come over here to get myself in any trouble." Leah was determined to eliminate stress from her life and being in The Bahamas for a couple of days would help her to achieve that.

Jennifer reassured her, "I don't blame you girl." She also knew that Leah was planning to purchase a house with her savings to provide security for herself and her daughters. She was proud of Leah, and the feeling was mutual.

Jennifer was in the kitchen when the phone rang that evening. She could hear Hezekiah conversing with someone on the phone.

"Mama, how you doing? You O.K.? I know. I really wish you used to travel on the plane because that boat ride is rough .... Yes. I want you to get some rest so you wouldn't be so painful. I will come to see you later this evening after dinner.... Ishmael, you need me to bring anything for Mama? .... O.K. then. I'll see you all later. Alright. Bye."

Hezekiah went to the kitchen door and revealed, "Jen, Mama's in Nassau."

Jennifer inquired, "Is she doing okay? I hope the boat ride wasn't too rough for her."

"She's down by Ishmael getting something to eat, then she'll rest for a while. She told me she felt tired and wanted to sleep for a bit," explained Hezekiah.

"Are you going to check on her tonight?" inquired Jennifer as she laid the table and prepared to serve dinner.

Hezekiah answered, "I'm going down there to see Mama after dinner."

"Would you like me to go with you Kiah?"

"Sure Jen. I could use the company. It's a good little drive to Carmichael Rd."

"Alright Hun. Soon as we are finished eating. I'll throw on something and we could be on our way." Jennifer was getting dressed in a hurry, but she still took an additional moment to pay attention to the details of her attire and hair. In more recent years, Jennifer had gained a few pounds but was

Chapter Twelve

still shapely. She had also acquired several streaks of silver-grey hair that especially highlighted her face; she was proud of it and kept her dark brown, permed hair carefully coiffed because, as some of her coworkers stated, it gave her a majestic look. Even after all these years and despite the reassurances of others, she was still mindful of her appearance when she presented herself before Mama Rolle.

Ishmael had cooked his Mama a pot of mutton stew which included potatoes, cabbage, carrots, and eddoes (one of her favorite vegetables), and she had thoroughly enjoyed her meal. By the time that Hezekiah and Jennifer had arrived there, Zilpha Rolle was relaxing and dozing in a reclining chair which was positioned on the left side of the sitting room. In a relatively short period of time, Ishmael had become an accomplished chef at his workplace. As a matter of fact, he loved to cook, and he paid attention to every detail especially when cooking for himself or his family members. Although his building was only partially completed, he used every opportunity to furnish his home stylishly. Fortunately, the hotel where he worked occasionally changed the furniture in the rooms and he, like other employees of the hotel, had the opportunity to purchase whole rooms full of furniture for a nominal cost. Ishmael always took advantage of this.

Hezekiah threw a compliment at Ishmael as he entered the home. "Hey, Ishmael, I smell the food from the door. I know one thing - you sure don't take any short cuts when it comes to cooking your pot." He laughed and hugged his brother fondly. "Where's Mama? She sleepin' eh?"

"She might be dozing. Go right in there, Kiah. Hi Jennifer." The two in-laws greeted each other warmly.

"Come here boy. Give your Mama a big hug. I aint see you in so long." Hezekiah and his mother were locked in a tight embrace for about a minute.

"Mama, I thought you were sleeping," said Hezekiah in surprise.

Jennifer gave mother and son a moment then she entered the room. Zilpha spotted her immediately.

"Jenny. How you doin', darlin'?"

"I'm fine thank you, Mama Rolle. How are you ma'am?"

"I'm alright. The boat ride was kinda rough and you know I does have these lil aches and pains but otherwise I thank God for life." She beckoned to Hezekiah and Jennifer to sit with her for a while. Jennifer was particularly relieved that Mama Rolle was in a happy mood.

"Kiah and Jenny, let me get something for you all to eat and drink while you chat with Mama," interjected Ishmael hopefully.

Hezekiah held his stomach and shook his head vigorously as he explained, "Ish, I can't eat another morsel. Jen and I just finished dinner, thanks."

Ishmael was a gracious host. He suggested, "Well, let me get you all something to drink then. I have coconut water, Fever Grass tea, sodas, fruit punch or limeade. Of course, if you want something stronger, I have that too." Ishmael knew his brother didn't drink casually, but he joked about it anyway.

Hezekiah laughed and answered, "Now, Ish you know I don't really bother with the strong stuff. I tell you what. Let me try some of your Fever Grass Tea. Haven't tasted that in a long time."

"Jen, what would you like?" Ishmael inquired as he closed the curtains in the living room.

Jennifer answered, "I'll try some coconut water please, Ishmael."

"Sure Jenny. I'll have you guys sorted out in a few minutes. Be right back." Ishmael headed to the kitchen, quickly returned with the drinks then quietly left them to talk.

"So, my grandson say he ready to get married." Zilpha smiled and threw up her arms. "I hope the two of them sure 'bout what they doin'. You know, these young people today sometimes don't know what they getting' into 'til its too late."

"Mama, he seems to be ready, and his wife-to-be is equally as eager to settle down."

Zilpha continued, "What she name again? I have trouble remembering all these names nowadays."

Chapter Twelve

Hezekiah held his mother's hand and explained calmly, "Her name is Heather, Mama. She's American and they are going back over to live in Daytona Beach (for a while) after a few days of honeymooning in Las Vegas."

Zilpha continued to quiz her son. "What you mean by 'for a while'?"

Jennifer knew from experience that at times like these, it was best for her to sit quietly because any comment that she made could be misconstrued by her mother-in-law and held against her for a very long time. On the other hand, Mama Rolle would be more inclined to accept what Hezekiah said even if she disliked the rationale. Jennifer sat looking at the television and sipped on her coconut water while the conversation went on.

Hezekiah explained, "Well Mama, you know how these young people are. Plus, they both have jobs that involve travelling, so who knows where they may end up?"

"Oh, I see. Well, I hope they settle down soon. I have couple dollars to give them – just a lil something from my savings," said Zilpha exuberantly.

"No Mama, you don't have to do that. They don't need it …" suggested Hezekiah.

"It don't matter if they need it or not. I want them to have it. That's why." Zilpha was not accepting "No" for the answer and she was becoming slightly peeved. Hezekiah knew that it was not a good idea to pursue that subject anymore because his mother had already made her decision.

Then Zilpha directed her attention to Jennifer. The latter was slightly apprehensive because she really didn't know what to expect from her mother-in-law particularly when she was in an argumentative mood.

"Jenny, let me and you talk now." Before she continued, she leaned over to Hezekiah and told him, "Hezekiah, go see what Ishmael doing while I talk with Jennifer for couple minutes. Oh, and let Ishmael give you the box I bring for you all. I even bring you all some Exuma crabs. You could start puttin' them in the car." Hezekiah looked at Jennifer, smiled encouragingly then left the room. Mama adjusted her red and black cotton headcloth that was tied at the nape of her neck to a more comfortable position.

"Yes ma'am?" inquired Jennifer.

Mama Rolle began, "Jennifer, you know that me an' you didn't always agree on everything, but you know teeth and tongue does fall out. That don't mean nothin' though. You are a good wife to my son and the best mother any children could ever have. You have made Hezekiah happy, and I appreciate you for that."

"Thank you, Mama Rolle. That means a lot to me." Deep inside, Jennifer knew that there was no love lost between them and at best they had managed to be cordial with each other since her marriage to Hezekiah. Nevertheless, she found herself receptive of these kind words although she still expected some scathing remark as if she awaited the punch line. She sensed that Mama Rolle had something to tell her, but she had no idea what it could be.

"Jennifer, I didn't want to upset you all with the wedding coming up and all but …."

"What is it, Mama Rolle?" asked Jennifer anxiously. Deep inside, she was saying to herself, "Whatever Mama Rolle is about to say, you better stay calm Jennifer."

Zilpha got straight to the point, "Well, I haven't been feeling too well these last couple months. The doctor to the clinic home say it's my heart. He say muh pressure does be lil up sometimes too. Then, I been having some pains in my stomach, but they don't seem to know what causin' it. Must be gas, I guess. Right now, I feelin' alright though. The doctor to the clinic give me a bunch uh pills to take but since I'm down here in Nassau, I'll see if I could see the hospital doctor and get a checkup, you know. They call it follow up."

"Sorry to hear that, Mama Rolle. You going to talk to Hezekiah about it, right?"

"No, no, no…." Mama Rolle glanced at the door and quickly interjected. "I don't want upset him. Now, you know how upset he does get when he hear anything happenin' to me. I don't want him to know 'til at least lil time after the wedding. This a happy time for everybody, and I sorry to burden you with this Jennifer." Mama Rolle was holding Jennifer's hands together in hers. Jennifer knew that her mother-in-law was being sincere.

"Mama Rolle, you can depend on me. I understand what you are saying, and I will do my best," she assured her mother-in-law.

The older lady exhaled as if she had been relieved of a heavy burden. She responded, "I been wantin' to talk to you for a while now, but with so many

Chapter Twelve

things happenin' and me being on the island most of the time, I said to myself I have to talk to you and tell you how I feel. I guess this ole pride got the better of me for all these years. I really sorry Jennifer. You didn't deserve some of the things I said. I hope you can forgive me." Mama Rolle was looking down and crying softly at this point.

Jennifer was happy with the discourse so far but concerned about her mother-in-law. She leaned towards Mama Rolle and hugged her. Mama Rolle reciprocated, and Jennifer felt the tears running down her own cheeks because she never envisioned that this moment would ever take place.

The women could hear the two brothers chatting and laughing as they returned from outside. Mama Rolle quickly dried her face with a handkerchief. As she looked hopefully into her daughter-in-law's eyes, Jennifer knew exactly what that meant. They automatically turned their attention towards Ishmael and Hezekiah.

Hezekiah kissed his mother on the cheek and said happily, "Mama, I don't know how you got all those things to hold in that box. I mean that box is jam-packed. Thank you for the crabs too. The children gonna go crazy when they see all those crabs." Before she had departed Steventon, Mama Rolle had secured the crabs in another box for Ishmael and asked him to share them with his brother once he got them home.

Jennifer chimed in, "Yes. Especially Gina. She was just talking about crabs this evening." She smiled as she anticipated cooking a big pot of crab and rice along with fried Grouper cutlets or Snappers for the family's Sunday dinner. Jennifer hoped that Leah and her girls would join them because Leah's daughters had probably never eaten this popular Bahamian dish before.

Friday whizzed by in a whirlwind of activities. The members of the bridal party were preoccupied with their final preparations for the wedding. The Rolle clan, other family members and friends also engaged in ensuring that they were prepared for the wedding. Jennifer surprised herself by successfully hosting a surprise bridal shower for Heather that Friday afternoon. Although the timeline had been short, the event was a success. Heather was overwhelmed by the unexpected event. Her family and friends had already held an elaborate one for her back home, but she was touched and overjoyed by the hospitality of her Bahamian family who treated her as if they had known her 'forever' as she so aptly put it.

"Mama Jenn, you have been so kind to me, and I really appreciate it."

"Heather, you are family, and you are my daughter. I want you to always feel at home here. I hope you like your gifts. Everything had to be done so quickly." Jennifer gave a sigh of relief that everything seemed to have worked out well and her daughter-in-law was glowing with happiness. Hezekiah and Lester had gone on a 'Men's Day' Outing which included a visit to the barber and enjoying a baseball game. The wedding was scheduled for 11:00 a.m. next morning so Heather had a lot to do and needed to be well-rested for the long day ahead. She and Jennifer hugged each other. Gina and Angie took Heather and her best friend Jackie (who was in the bridal party) back to their hotel. The bridal party was staying in a large suite, so the rest of the evening would be spent with hair stylists, beauticians, the seamstress and other assistants.

Saturday morning was welcomed with open arms by everyone. The young couple had been blessed with a beautiful, sun-kissed day. There was hardly a cloud in the sky as the couple completed their nuptials. Heather was a stunningly beautiful bride. Her white dress sparkled as if adorned with a thousand diamonds in contrast to her warm brown complexion and elegantly styled black hair. Lester, on the other hand, was elated as he stood tall beside the love of his life. He looked debonair and extremely handsome in his elegant blue suit. The church was tastefully decorated, and Lester and Heather looked perfect together. Their guests were enamored by them as they exchanged vows.

The reception was held in the scenic ambiance of the Botanical Gardens just south of Long Wharf on West Bay Street. This secluded tropical paradise was filled with a myriad of green, flowering trees and plants. The couple had just completed their photography session with Toogoods Studios (all arranged by Jennifer who was able to engage their services at short notice through her work connections). Some guests who had been waiting patiently for at least an hour were sipping on mixed drinks and an assortment of mouth-watering native and international hors d'oeuvres. The parents of the bride and groom were beaming with pride as they savored this special moment. They were second only to Mr. and Mrs. Lester Rolle who were quite naturally at center stage. Family members and friends were all comfortably seated in the spacious outdoor setting that consisted of numerous decorated tables that were strategically arranged under wide tents. With a combination of jokes, comments, remarks and tributes, the Master of Ceremonies skillfully managed the entertainment of the attendees. The menu was a delicious combination of various native Bahamian foods and beverages that delighted the palates of the guests.

Chapter Twelve

Fortunately, they had prepared for more people than they had invited. In typical Bahamian style, several people showed up unannounced, but that was not a problem; everyone was welcomed. Mama Rolle was wearing her 'Sunday go to meeting glasses' and a new hat which matched her lovely dress. She felt like the bell of the ball as she sat with her son Hezekiah, Jennifer, and their daughters along with Ishmael, Alpheus and his fiancé. Lester had graciously accepted his grandma's gift knowing how much it meant to her. Hezekiah was pleased to see his mother so contented. She was excited like a child on Christmas Eve. Mama Rolle loved being in the company of so many 'dressed up' people and she certainly was enjoying the pomp and the pageantry that this occasion cultivated.

Anthony and his family sat at a table with Leah and her daughters. He and Stephanie were expecting a baby again soon, and Stephanie was visibly uncomfortable. After all, they had a son who was in college and a teenage daughter. Obviously, their efforts not to have more children had failed and Stephanie had difficulty coming to terms with this turn of events. Anthony, on the other hand, was surprised but not overly concerned. The couple had discussed possible options, but they knew that they had to prepare for the new baby. Leah tried to provide her sister-in-law with some useful survival tips and Stephanie was appreciative.

The bride and groom took their first dance as husband and wife. They had requested that only Bahamian music be played at their reception and their wish was granted. The DJ (who was a friend of Ishmael) skillfully and tastefully played a mixture of local music and songs that brought smiles to the faces of the attendees. In short order, many of the guests had taken to the dance floor demonstrating their dance moves and having lots of fun.

The celebration ended that afternoon around 4:30 p.m. Lester and Heather said their goodbyes to their family, friends, and well-wishers, then headed off to begin their new life together. They planned to spend that night at Loews Harbour Cove hotel on Paradise Island, then depart on an early morning flight via Bahamasair to Florida where they would commence their honeymoon.

By the following week, life had gotten back to normal for the Rolles. Jennifer had returned to work, and Mama Rolle was sharing her time between her two sons Hezekiah and Ishmael. She spent her days at Ishmael's home in Carmichael rd. mostly watching television and resting as required by her doctor. Ishmael always left his mother's food, snacks and drinks organized and easily accessible to her. Then, in the afternoons, Hezekiah picked up his mother after he completed work and took her home in Fox Hill. Zilpha Rolle certainly was enjoying all the attention she was getting and the time that she was able to spend with her sons. She sometimes slept in the east with Hezekiah and Jennifer, and she especially looked forward to those times. Despite the years of suspicions and misunderstandings, Zilpha was fascinated by the congeniality that had developed between Jennifer and herself.

Chapter Thirteen

Life was changing and becoming more complex in the islands. The Bahamas was paying the price for modernization. By the 1990s, developments in media were occurring exponentially both locally and abroad. The populace had greater access to various radio and television stations, newspapers, and magazines. There were many advantages to being close to America, but it could not be denied that "When America blew its nose, The Bahamas caught the cold". Both at home and in Florida, the drug culture was extending its seedy tentacles and impacting the way people were living and dying. Travel was easy by boat and airplane. Somehow, all sorts of guns were entering the Bahama islands unabated. Many legal and illegal immigrants had decided to make The Bahamas their home which brought new cultures and lifestyles. Crime and nefariousness were on the rise globally. Jennifer and her husband always prayed for their children's safety. Despite their successes, Jennifer worried about her children. They had provided their children with everything they could, but they could not shield them from life. She secretly prayed that Lester would decide to live in Nassau again because she felt that she could somehow guide and protect him from all the negative influences and dangers. She knew that was unlikely because he had a family. Lester and Heather had welcomed their twin girls (Bianca and Brittany) two years after their marriage, and it was unlikely that they would give up their current lifestyle or the amenities that were available in the U.S. Many were seeking to partake of the American dream. Some were obtaining unparalleled wealth while others were falling victim to crack cocaine addiction and other vices in the land of 'milk and honey'. Nevertheless, life was exciting and there were opportunities to make an honest living despite the temptations, so the Rolles appreciated that Lester was committed to making a successful life for his family and himself overseas.

Jennifer had experienced a long, busy day at work. Her managerial post was demanding but she enjoyed it. She was feeling a little exhausted after attending a long afternoon meeting and arriving home from work after 6:00 p.m. This was a day when she was quite willing to eat leftovers from the previous day, but she knew that Mama Rolle hated leftovers. She wanted to sustain the good impression that Mama Rolle had of her. Her mother-in-law was staying with them for a few days while she was attending her doctor. Jennifer opted to cook a quick meal of steamed lamb chops with scalloped potatoes and fresh vegetables that all could enjoy.

Hezekiah and Jennifer had an empty nest now. Angie was a career banker who was engaged to be married, while Gina was still in England finishing her additional legal training. Her parents hoped and prayed that Gina would return home and be called to the Bahamas Bar.

Mama Rolle had been ailing for some time and had been in and out of the Princess Margaret Hospital almost like a revolving door over several years. In recent months, the senior Mrs. Rolle had spent quite a lot of time living with Hezekiah and Jennifer due to her medical issues. Nevertheless, her comfort zone was still her home in Exuma. She had been losing her sight progressively, particularly in her right eye, and she had previously been diagnosed with heart problems. Although her health issues had impacted on her independence, she remained opinionated and confident.

That evening over dinner, Hezekiah, Jennifer, and Mama Rolle were able to engage in a lively conversation about the past. Mama Rolle always spoke boldly about the 'good ole days' like it was a part of her religion that she did not plan to relinquish. She was quick to boast about the achievements of women. It was amazing how she knew so much about current affairs and life in Nassau although she spent most of her time on Exuma. Nevertheless, she was an avid reader, and always listened to the radio. Hezekiah got up and rubbed his Mama's shoulders supportively. He was so proud of her and sometimes called her an Exumian suffragette. During her life, she had been denied many opportunities, but she was a bold and typically resilient 'island woman'.

Mama Rolle was adamant, "Women was tough in those days. We used to hold de family together even if aint no man was around. A woman could have ten or twelve chirren and somehow, she used to take care of all dem chirren just like she only had one.

Chapter Thirteen

"That's true Mama. Everyone had a house. Some kind of house and they took pride in it," agreed Hezekiah. "Wives used to keep the family together and raise the children while the husbands went on 'the project' and sent the money back to her. Sometimes when he returned home, his wife may have built a better home with the money he sent.

"Das right Hezekiah. You coulda lease piece a land until you paid enough to buy it and knock up one clapboard house on the property and live and raise yer family. Right here in Nassau and on the out islands too. No excuses and nobody to help you. Sometimes der man gone but de woman never used to give up." Mama Rolle sounded like she was preaching.

"You're right Mama," replied Hezekiah supportively.

"Hezekiah, you know if it wasn't for us women, the government woulda never change. Them white people woulda still have der foot on our necks until now. I right or I wrong?" She lifted her two arms upward thankfully. Hezekiah nodded and smiled.

"Yes ma'am," Jennifer endorsed her mother-in-law's comments. She added, "Women have always worked hard whether on the family islands or here. They work in the hotels, in people's houses, in government and other places too. Some women still struggle but they do everything that they can to provide for their families. Hezekiah, you remember when a man could hardly get a loan from the bank even if he was working?"

Hezekiah responded in the affirmative to Jennifer's question. Indeed, he was proud of his mama. He acknowledged that Bahamian women like his mother and his wife understood their purpose and fulfilled their roles to the best of their abilities. He stated, "I see women getting loans from banks like Commonwealth Bank and furnishing their homes, taking care of their families, paying their children's school fees, and not looking back on anybody to help them. Plenty of them are single parents too."

Jennifer endorsed what was being said, "Bahamian women are hardworking and enterprising. Husbands and wives working together to raise their families makes the society strong and stable."

Mama Rolle continued to reminisce. "Yes, there was a time when people was more neighborly though and helped one another – watched over the children in the neighborhood. You didn't have to lock up your front door like nowadays." (She elevated her right arm in affirmation then continued.) "You all remember when you just had to put one lil light lock on your door and nobody woulda try come inside? Neighbors used to be helpful and look out for one another. The neighbour coulda talk to your children and correct them if they was doing something wrong but now, chile you can't say nothing to the people children. Nowadays, some people want fight ya or cuss you out if you say anything to their children. What a time eh!"

Hezekiah stated ruefully, "Well, it certainly doesn't help that we have adopted a new drug culture. I hear that it's getting pretty bad on some of the Family Islands too." Hezekiah scratched his head as he added, "It's affecting some of our young people. I see it in school sometimes. Some of the fellers are walking around on the streets all 'based out' like zombies. Hopefully, we can get rid of it before it gets worse. It's a fact that some people are becoming rich from drug trafficking. The eighties and nineties have brought on a different kind of revolution and I'm not so sure it's a good one."

Jennifer saw where the conversation was going. She had seen her mother-in-law become anxious and begin hyperventilating on one or two previous occasions and she tried to avert another episode. She made eye contact with her husband who perhaps had similar thoughts.

Hezekiah responded to the cue by clarifying his point of view on the matter. "Anyway mama, this kind of conversation can't lead to a positive outcome and will only make us feel more despondent."

He checked his watch automatically and remarked jokingly, "Mama, it's getting kinda late. I know this is way past your bedtime. Let's continue this conversation tomorrow." His mother smiled in agreement while admitting that she was feeling tired and could do with some rest.

Jennifer winked at Hezekiah to acknowledge his sentiments, then she asked Mama Rolle if she wanted a cup of tea. She knew that her mother-in-law liked pear leaf, fever grass and ginger tea, and she did have the latter. Mama Rolle agreed to having a cup of ginger tea before going to bed.

The Rolles had seen their dreams come true. They had been able to accomplish what some could only imagine. Their marriage had survived the test of time and, over the years, their love for each other had become more strongly cemented.

Chapter Thirteen

As fate would have it, Hezekiah would finally be able to come to terms with his past life in Steventon, and reconnect with his roots in Exuma.

Hezekiah woke up one morning with a strange feeling that something wasn't right. Jennifer leaned over him and gently massaged his shoulders as he sat at the dining table. She saw the perturbed look on her husband's face and began quizzing him.

"Kiah, what happened?"

"Oh, it's nothing. I just didn't sleep too well last night. That's all. I'm going outside to catch some air," he responded pensively. For some reason, his chest was heavy, and he couldn't understand why. He had just been to his doctor in December for his annual physical examination and had been given a clean bill of health. As a middle-aged man, he still went jogging occasionally and he had never been ill except for the occasional influenza attack and pink eye which he had contracted at school during a community outbreak about a decade before. He stepped outside. The chilly January air was refreshing to him, and a calm came over him.

For some reason, when the telephone rang late that morning, Hezekiah was not surprised. Jennifer had a bewildered look on her face as she handed the telephone to Hezekiah. She looked away sensing that something bad had happened. After about ten minutes, a disoriented Hezekiah hung up the telephone and walked toward the window momentarily to think. He regained his composure, then gave his wife the news. He wasn't sure but he believed his mother had suffered a fatal heart attack.

"Tommy said that he found Mama on the floor near her bed this morning. She was wearing her warm night clothes, socks, and a head cloth like she always did. She was probably trying to get her heart pills because they were all over the floor and the bottle was open. He said there was nothing he could do. She was already gone." Jennifer shook her head incredulously. Hezekiah continued sadly, "Apparently, it probably happened earlier, but Tommy discovered Mama early that morning when he went to check on her around about 8:30. Tommy was crying when he told me he had taken her some souse that his wife had cooked for breakfast." Tommy was especially distraught because he and his brother Levi along with their children usually arranged for one of the family members to spend the night with their Mama just in case she needed any assistance. On that evening, they did not find it odd that she decided to spend the night alone, because she cherished her independence and occasionally would say to Hayley, Jason, Gareth or one of the other grands that she would be okay, and they didn't have to bother.

"O Lord, Hezekiah, I'm so sorry. We just talked to your mama on the weekend, and she was talking brisk and strong. O no. This can't be." Jennifer was distressed but she clung to Hezekiah and tried to console him in this very difficult time. The next few days flew by in a blur of telephone calls, visits, scurrying around to ensure that all arrangements were made, and finally the travel to Exuma for the funeral.

Mrs. Zilpha Rolle's funeral was held in Steventon, Exuma almost two weeks after her passing. Initially, her body had been brought to Nassau, then it was released to the undertakers. Although her husband had been buried in Nassau, she had made it quite clear that she wished to be laid to rest in the graveyard in Steventon. It was no secret that she disliked the capital. Hezekiah and his siblings willingly granted their mother's wish.

On the day before the funeral, family members and neighbors were preparing for the 'setting up' that evening in Steventon. Hezekiah had just stepped onto the porch of his parents' house after working around the yard with several men, including his brothers, to ensure that the yard was clean, and furniture was arranged. The workers walked toward the kitchen to get some lunch and Hezekiah was about to follow them. For some reason, Hezekiah turned around. When Hezekiah first spotted his baby sister, he responded as if he had just seen an apparition. The siblings had not seen each other in decades but instinctively he knew it was her. A Caucasian gentleman with a slightly balding head was talking with Ruth as they both stood sideways near a silver vehicle that was parked in front of the Rolle family home. Without hesitation, Hezekiah rushed off the porch to greet his sister. Ruth was still slender and about five feet six inches tall. She was of medium brown complexion with thick, shoulder-length hair that was locked like her younger brother Zack's. She jumped upon Hezekiah with glee, held him around his neck and screamed with delight, "O my God Kiah! Look how long it's been." Then the tears began to flow. They clung to each other desperately.

"Hey Ruthie. What you been up to?" inquired Hezekiah with the same excitement.

"First let me introduce you to my husband." Ruth stood again and held her husband's hand. She smiled as she said, "Robert, I'd like you to meet my oldest brother Hezekiah Rolle. We haven't seen each other in so long that we have

Chapter Thirteen

plenty catching up to do. Hezekiah, this is my husband Robert Jacobs." Robert and Hezekiah shook hands. Robert didn't seem to mind. He and Ruth had met in college and overcame the many struggles associated with being an interracial couple. After twelve years of marriage and two lovely children, Robert and Ruth had established an equilibrium that surmounted the usual challenges of life. The man whom they had paid to drive them from Georgetown to Steventon had been waiting patiently in the car. Robert paid the driver who subsequently drove away. The weather was perfect. Robert was content to walk over to the beach on the other side of the road and explore the flora and fauna that adorned the area. He stood soaking up the sun and felt at peace. His job as a stockbroker in the New York Tri-State area was stressful and demanding, so he relished this opportunity to decompress and travel with his wife to The Bahamas where she could reunite with her family members. Hezekiah and Ruth chatted profusely for at least thirty minutes on the porch. By that time Zach and his wife had arrived there in a taxi, and they were all able to gather to catch up on old times.

The 'setting up' was an evening of singing, reflection and reminiscing about good and bad times. The attendees were eating various types of souse and boiled fish along with johnny cake and potato bread. The weather was so pleasant on this Friday evening that most people were sitting outside comfortably in the moonlit atmosphere. Jennifer along with Eulease, Wilhelmina and several of the older women were assisting with serving the food. Jennifer found that Eulease was her usual self. It seemed that she still had a bit of a 'chip on her shoulder' because Jennifer had won her favorite brother's heart and taken him away permanently. Jennifer tried to engage her eldest sister-in-law in small talk just to 'keep cold hominy from souring' as the old people used to say, but Eulease would respond mostly in monosyllabic or cryptic answers. Wilhelmina, on the other hand was congenial and cooperative. Otherwise, the time passed uneventfully.

As was customary, neighbors and friends had contributed food and drinks liberally to ensure that the event was an uplifting success and indeed it was. There was no shortage of non-alcoholic drinks and bush teas. Of course, a few individuals had come to the event slightly inebriated, while some had sneaked in liquor despite being instructed not to bring alcohol. (Most people knew that Mama Rolle was diametrically opposed to alcohol use.) Ruth was inclined to spend a lot of time with her husband because he was totally unfamiliar with Bahamian culture, and she wanted to ensure that he was comfortable. Some people were curious about him and maintained light conversations with him. Robert had experienced cordial interactions with most of Ruth's family members. He was quite adept at interacting with heterogeneous and incongruous personalities, but he occasionally could not understand the flection in word usage or accents of some of the people who conversed with him. Ruth lightheartedly whispered in his ear, "Robert, you're a trooper. Anyway, you know you've heard worse." She pecked him on the cheek playfully and he reciprocated with a smile.

The funeral was 10:00 a.m. the next morning. Demeritte's Funeral home had done a wonderful job with their mother and the children were pleased. Yellow was her favorite color, and she got her wish. The luscious floral arrangements at the front of the church complemented the scene as they stood on both ends of Mrs. Rolle's casket. It seemed as if everyone on Exuma had come to pay their last respects to the woman who was well known on the island as Miss Zilpha. There were so many people in attendance that it was standing room only. Mourners adorned mostly in black attire spilled out into the church yard where a large tent had been erected to shelter some of the excess people. Obituaries were being distributed. The steady procession of viewers wanting to say their last farewells walked up to take a final look at the lady who lay elegantly and peacefully as if she was sleeping. Hezekiah, his wife, and children, all of the siblings, the grandchildren, great grandchildren, and in-laws occupied the first five or six rows while other relatives, neighbors and friends had quickly filled up the other available rows of pews.

Although the weather was inclined to be warm, it was at least comfortable. The sea breeze was a godsend. For family members and close friends, the service was a blur of tributes, reminiscing and fervor. Reverend Thaddeus Davis (a distant relative of the Rolle family) did an awesome job of eulogizing Deaconess Zilpha Rolle. She had always been active in her church, particularly after her children grew up and moved away. The reverend declared that Mrs. Rolle had been devout in her faith, knew her bible inside out and 'She is truly deserving of all of the accolades that she is receiving." Mama Rolle had lived a good life and was viewed as a matriarch in her community. Heartwarming tributes in words and song that lasted an hour were rendered by numerous family members and friends. As he sat listening, Hezekiah was reminded of one occasion when he had travelled back home for a visit, and his mother confided in him with a special request that surprised him, "Son, when God call me home, I want you all to have a big party for me. Let all the people come. Make sure you all have plenty food." Then she pointed to her house. "Muh house aint big, but I gat plenty yard, so who can't fit in the house will fit under all these trees outside." Hezekiah was astonished. She chuckled and didn't discuss the matter anymore. He was comforted in knowing that his mother's wish was being fulfilled.

Chapter Thirteen

Despite the seriousness of the occasion, most attendees displayed a spirit of acceptance and were generally in a celebratory mood. There were no tears. For many, it was a glad reunion day also. Hezekiah was experiencing mixed emotions. He was not easily moved to tears, but he was equivocating between feelings of nostalgia, remorse, and gratitude. It was regrettable that it took their mother's demise to reunite the Rolle siblings. Five of them along with the relatives who accompanied them bunked between the original Rolle family homestead and Levi's and Tommy's homes. On the other hand, Zach and Ruth, who surprised everyone when they arrived, had opted to stay at Peace and Plenty hotel in Georgetown. The two youngest Rolle children had remained close, especially in recent years, and they occasionally had visited each other in the United States.

After the funeral, the bereaved family and well-wishers once again gathered at the Rolle's home to have some refreshments. The repast was well-attended as expected. Coretta and Shirley, who were the wives of Tommy and Levi respectively, had coordinated the planning for the menu and food preparation for the post funeral meal. Although most of the food was prepared by a family friend who had a restaurant, several neighbors had also donated additional food including some peas and rice, baked chicken, ham, pans of macaroni, potato salad and coleslaw.

Hezekiah appreciated this rare opportunity to chat with all of his siblings on one occasion. They decided to spend time together at the family home later that afternoon to talk about the old days and reestablish bonds that had become fragmented with the passing of time.

"Hezekiah, how are you man?" said the middle-aged gentleman who had just entered the room. He knew that voice instinctively, but he was sure that he was mistaken. Hezekiah almost did not recognize him. He turned around and responded, "Toby?"

"Yes. How have you been?" Toby inquired. He seemed hesitant and a bit uncertain at first.

Hezekiah studied his friend for a few seconds then inquired, "Man, what have you been doing with yourself? You just disappeared off the face of the earth. For years I was worried sick about you Toby, and nobody would tell me what happened to you. Why didn't you ever come back?" Hezekiah was a bit peeved and felt that he needed to get that off his chest. It was therapeutic.

"It's a long story Kiah, but I'll fill you in. I don't know where to start. It's great to see you though, good buddy." He patted his friend on the back. They both realized that nothing much had changed between them. In this moment, it felt like all was well in the world.

The two friends hugged. "Toby, you put on a pound or two and you have salt and pepper hair. I hardly recognized you," said Hezekiah jokingly. Indeed, Toby was almost unrecognizable because of the amount of weight he had gained.

"You're not doing so bad yourself Kiah. You have more grey than me, and you're wearing glasses too," replied Toby jokingly.

The two friends were keenly interested in what had transpired in the life of each other. Toby consoled Hezekiah, "Have my deepest sympathy on the passing of your mother. I remember Mrs. Rolle and your father very well. They were good people. Your Mama never used to play though. She was a serious woman. Tough as nails. You were scared of her and your papa."

"Man Toby, what choice did we have. You obey your parents and live to see another day, right?" He smiled as he reminisced on one of his mother's favorite sayings, "Boy I bring you in this world, and I could take you out too! Don't show off with me." That time, she's got something in her hand to hit you with or throw at you." Hezekiah was becoming emotional, "I miss her voice, her hard mouth. But she was loving too."

Toby knew exactly what his friend was talking about. He had recently lost his father also. Hezekiah reciprocated by expressing his sympathy to Toby. They were sitting in the living room talking. Jennifer had brought each of them a cool drink and Hezekiah introduced his wife to Toby.

"Kiah, your wife is a beautiful lady. You are a lucky man."

"I try my best to keep her happy. She is the wind beneath my wings. You know what I mean? And my children – They mean the world to me. I have three."

"Yes Kiah. I totally understand. I was living in New York for a while, then I moved to Maryland. For some reason, I never seemed to be able to find the right woman. I have tried but I can't seem to find the right one. I got married in my early twenties but that didn't last long. Both of us were probably immature. Eventually we got divorced. It's like an itch that you can't scratch. I have met

Chapter Thirteen

some nice women, but eventually something goes wrong, and I have to move on, or they get tired of me, I guess. Maybe I'm cursed."

"Don't say that Toby. You just haven't met the right person yet. That's all."

"I do have a couple of kids though. I have about five," mused Toby.

"What do you mean? You don't know how many kids you have?"

"Well yes and no. I have worked at a number of jobs, but in the last couple years I have been in the real estate business. I travel a lot. Anyway, I have two kids with my wife. When she left, she took my boys, but of course, I got hit hard for alimony and child support. Then, you know how it is – I had two more - girls. I take care of all my kids. I don't get to see them as much as I would like, but we get together when we can. Now the last one, to tell you the truth, I'm not too sure about her. Her Mama claimed that I am the one, but the timing seemed to be a bit off. But Kiah, I can't deny her. I really don't want to know. She doesn't look like my other children, but I have accepted her as my child. We have a great relationship and too much time has passed. You know what I mean?"

"Man, that's a serious situation. I understand though. You're doing the right thing," Hezekiah reassured his friend.

Hezekiah wanted to talk about something that was weighing heavily on his mind. "Man, I always think back to that night in Rolleville, Toby. I felt bad leaving you like that on the porch. Suppose you had died. I became sick with guilt and worry about you. For years I struggled with the thought that you may have died or was seriously impaired by that injury. I had lost my best friend who was like a brother to me. Also, my poor brother Malachi passed away around the same time which was devastating. I never forgave myself for not being there for him. He was a gentle person who simply needed help, and there was no one to help him – not even me."

Toby did his best to comfort his friend who had kept those thoughts and feelings bottled up inside for more than forty years. This was a serious moment for both and the only way to move past it was to discuss it openly.

"Hezekiah Rolle, you saved my life. I love you man for life." Hezekiah reciprocated by expressing the same sentiment. Fortunately, Toby still had the ability to find humor in most things. He chuckled as if he was proud of his accomplishment. "See." He got up from the sofa, removed his hat and pointed to his head. He continued, "Well, I still have the scar on the back of my head to remind me. Those fellas really did a number on me. It took me months in hospital and therapy. The incident really traumatized me. I got really good medical care in the States which accelerated my recovery. I used to dream about the incident over and over again. That's why I didn't come back home until recently. I returned home when Papa died."

Hezekiah and his friend Tobias had talked for what seemed like hours. They parted company with the reassurance that they would reconnect very soon. Toby planned to return to Exuma in June. He intended to renovate his family's home since his siblings no longer lived there and his stepmother had passed away about five years before his father. He was even considering setting up a small business on the property to bring some life to Steventon. He assured Hezekiah that he would contact him and let him know when he was coming to Nassau so that they could spend some time together. Hezekiah promised to show Toby around New Providence and Paradise Island whenever his friend came to the capital.

Chapter Fourteen

Sunset ....

It was August 1992, and another political season was coming to a climax. A fever and surge of intense energy was sweeping through The Bahamas that had not been experienced for decades. There was a hunger for change, yet an overwhelming fear of the unknown gripped some of the population. The events of that fateful month were almost musical in their orchestration. Hurricane Andrew and the political season were headed on a common trajectory that would result in a phenomenal crescendo.

Hurricane Andrew was a category 5 storm that came like a thief in the night on August 23. The islands of the Bahamas were under attack. Eleuthera and Cat Cay were the hardest hit, but Nassau was not totally spared. There was nowhere to run and no place to go. Hezekiah and Jennifer hit the floor in an inner room of their home as the storm raged throughout the night. Telephone lines were down, trees and other vegetation were strewn everywhere, and many roads were impassable. There was catastrophic damage. As a result of this merciless storm, several people lost their lives, and it destroyed almost two thousand homes along with several schools. This was unprecedented and horrifying to residents throughout the archipelago.

After the dust cleared, another leader emerged to propel the nation forward to unprecedented levels of free speech, achievements, and national pride. It was a clean sweep which heralded a new style of leadership and direction for the nation. The Honorable Hubert Ingraham and his Free National Movement (FNM) party emerged victoriously after a ferocious campaign.

There was a changing of the old guard as the PLP were sidelined and became the opposition.

Following the storm, people throughout the islands began to pick up the pieces of their lives and restore life as they knew it. The political landscape had changed. Hezekiah mused, "The people have spoken, Jen. Whether we like it or not, this is a different era, and we're going to have to accept the changes for better or for worse."

"Kiah, we survived many storms in our lives. The hurricane just passed, and God spared us. We have a bit of damage to the roof and the car got hit but praise the Lord we have our lives. God has been good to us." Jennifer felt a sense of calm. She was ambivalent about politics. Her personal belief was that you should not rely on any government for your success or survival. No matter who was governing the country, you had to make your own way and endeavor to fulfill your own dreams. Also, she had a strong conviction that no matter which party was in power, they were like the seasons that come and go but the people would always be there. Hezekiah was more politically grounded as a diehard PLP, but he appreciated what Jennifer was saying. This had never been a source of contention between them.

The years continued to roll by with even more intensity. "There have been so many changes. Look at how far we have come as a people, Jen. It's 2000. Things are not perfect, but we certainly have been blessed," mused Hezekiah. He continued, "We just have to take care of what we have individually and as a nation."

"You're right. We do have a lot to be thankful for although some of us don't realize or appreciate what we have," replied Jennifer.

Jennifer decided to go inside to refill their glasses with another refreshing drink and bring out some conch fritters that she had fried earlier. In five minutes, she returned with the tray. It was one of those days when they felt comfortable just sitting under the shade of the trees in their yard. As they reminisced, they could feel the easterly sea breeze blowing on them although they were not living near the beach. It was heavenly.

Hezekiah said in amazement, "Jen, it is so hard to believe how simple life was back in the old days. Nowadays, young people have so many opportunities to excel. They have everything at their fingertips. They can stay in school until they're almost twenty and get a full, basic education. That's something, eh."

Chapter Fourteen

Jennifer smiled and added, "That's right. Most of us had to leave school at fourteen or even earlier. We didn't have much to look forward to, but we sure never looked back."

Despite the challenges they had encountered, Hezekiah and Jennifer were contented with the sunset of their lives and were excited about the possibilities that lay ahead for their family and the country. Their daughters were successfully following their dreams. Lester and Heather had another baby on the way, and the couple were overjoyed. Jennifer was grateful for the bond she had with her siblings and their children. Hezekiah was humbled by the fact that he had reconnected with his brothers and sisters and rekindled his relationship with them. He visited Exuma at least once or twice a year and contributed to the upkeep of the family homestead in Steventon. Their family network was strong and secure. It could only be divine providence.

Jennifer was fond of saying, "Man is like a flower. You are born. You flower, you bloom, you begin to wither and then you are no more." The couple assured each other that the years to come would be their best years. They would have no regrets.

Hezekiah held Jennifer's hand reassuringly as they basked in the twilight of their lives. They felt the light breeze gently brushing their faces while the air cooled in anticipation of the night.

Made in the USA
Columbia, SC
26 September 2024